AN
INDEPENDENT
FOREIGN
POLICY
FOR
CANADA?

A CARLETON CONTEMPORARY

McCLELLAND AND STEWART LIMITED

AN
INDEPENDENT
FOREIGN
POLICY
FOR
CANADA?

Edited by Stephen Clarkson
for
the University League
for Social Reform

The Canadian Publishers
McClelland and Stewart Limited
25 Hollinger Road, Toronto

Printed and bound in Canada

CARLETON
CONTEMPORARIES

A series of books designed to stimulate
informed discussion of current and controversial issues in Canada and to improve the two-way flow of ideas between
people and governments

ISSUED UNDER
THE EDITORIAL SUPERVISION OF
THE INSTITUTE OF CANADIAN STUDIES,
CARLETON UNIVERSITY,
OTTAWA
PAULINE JEWETT, DIRECTOR

TABLE OF CONTENTS

PREFACE

This book is the product of a two-year collective effort. The chapters singly and the book as a whole reflect what has been a continuing effort by the many who participated in the meetings of the University League for Social Reform (ULSR) from September 1966 to April 1967, to reassess the objectives of Canada's foreign policy. Our first wish is to acknowledge the volume's general debt to those colleagues, diplomats and journalists who contributed to our general discussions.

Turning a series of off-the-cuff colloquia into a book for public consumption is a surprisingly tortuous process: and our second wish is to express our gratitude to the following people whose contributions helped to transform a project into a reality:

Abraham Rotstein, former editor, President of the ULSR and friend, for his continual inspiration and counsel on all editorial decisions great and small throughout the entire gestation period;

John Holmes, grand middle man of Canadian diplomatic research, for the original stimulus to turn the ULSR's collective attention to Canada's foreign policy, and for obtaining from the Canadian Institute of International Affairs the generous financial support – a model of aid without strings – which made it possible to bring experts to our discussions from campuses as far away as Dalhousie and Yale;

Cranford Pratt, Naomi Rosenbaum and Peter Silcox, for their astute editorial advice on individual manuscripts;

Abby Hoffman, for her efficient assistance throughout the summer, and the International Studies Programme, University of Toronto, for the enabling grant;

Secretarial support, organizationally from the Department of Political Economy, University of Toronto, which again supplied the ULSR with office facilities under the intrepid direction of Mrs. Margaret Tolnai, and individually from Mrs. Lorraine Kennedy, Mrs. Gloria Rowe, Miss Dianne Kislashko and Miss Elaine Pyatt, who managed to meet improbable typing deadlines as chapters progressed through their several drafts;

Murray Ross, President of York University, Escott Reid, Principal of Glendon College and Douglas Vervey, Chairman of York's Political Science department, for the most gracious hospitality offered at several ULSR seminars;

Fred Schindeler, Director of York's Institute for Behavioural Research, for his expertise in making the Reader's Questionnaire suitable for tabulation by his Institute's computer centre, and Tom Hockin, for kindly taking the responsibility for the administration of this experimental project;

Duncan Macpherson, for his generous permission to lighten our academic gravity with the penetrating creations of his cartoonist's pen;

Lloyd Axworthy (United College), Brian Crane (Ottawa lawyer), William Dobell (Western Ontario), Barry Farrell (Northwestern), Douglas Hill (Department of External Affairs), Bruce Macdonald (*Globe and Mail*), Roman March (Carleton), Paul Noble (McGill), Naomi Rosenbaum (York), Rufus Smith (US State Department) and Charles Taylor (McGill) for preparing and presenting papers to the ULSR during the year;

Finally the authors themselves, whose patience in the face of editorial pleas for cuts and alterations often went beyond the reasonable limits of human tolerance.

It would be only prudent to warn that, while the views that the contributors express are entirely their own, the overall editorial judgements – literary, aesthetic and political – are the responsibility of the editor.

STEPHEN CLARKSON
December 1967

INTRODUCTION

"Canadians often find it difficult to comprehend the role that their country can play in international affairs," wrote the London *Times* last year,* neatly summarizing the dual concern that inspires this book: Canada's unrealized potential for effective international action; and the misconception of this potential by the Canadian people – leaders, diplomats and public alike.

Though foreign policy has traditionally been reserved as the private domain of the Government and its diplomatic service, their exclusive competence can no longer be accepted without question in a policy area where rapid change requires continual reappraisals of the fundamental assumptions involved. For, as no less an authority than the Prime Minister recently acknowledged, what the men at the top lack is precisely the freedom to make the necessary re-evaluations. "At a time when the need for reflection and thought has never been greater," he confided, "the practising politician has less and less time to think before he must act."† The paradoxical impact of the communications revolution is to bombard the political leader with too much information, to involve him in too many urgent problems demanding instant decisions for him to afford the luxury of thinking carefully about general policy problems. A new phrase, "crisis management," has even been concocted to enshrine no-think as the legitimate condition of leadership.

* London *Times*, February 28th, 1967.
† Address to the Canadian Political Science Association, June 8th, 1967.

In our textbooks we take comfort in the presence of the permanent civil service. Does not the professional, bureaucratic voice behind the throne provide the Government with its intellectual rod and staff? Unfortunately in the real world of foreign policy, "crisis management" is equally apt as a description of the atmosphere in which our diplomats operate. They are understaffed for the heavy administrative demands put on them. Their daily whirl of memoranda drafting and international negotiation allows no peace of mind for raising fundamental questions about the rationale of the country's over-all external policy.

Yet, if the professionals are too busy to reflect, the amateurs are too ill-informed. The traditional élitism and secrecy of the diplomatic corps make foreign policy a monopoly where the public, apart from the academic specialists, fears to tread.

The purpose of this book is to break the vicious circles which have been paralyzing thinking on Canadian foreign policy.

Open Discussion . . .

In its polemical format, this volume is designed to provoke an open discussion of the basic issues of Canadian foreign policy that the professionals have no time or inclination to question. For these chapters do not attempt to give a history of Canadian diplomacy or pretend to be an exhaustive treatment of our relations with the world's 122 accredited nations. Rather they contain a debate, the product of a year's discussions that were held at the Universities of Toronto and York under the auspices of the University League for Social Reform (ULSR), an organization that provides a forum for younger professors from all faculties who share an interest in discussing public policy problems.* Though our base of operations was Toronto, colleagues came from fifteen other universities and research institutes, Canadian and American, to contribute papers. The subject for our symposia was the independence of Canadian foreign policy, but we were not all experts in international relations. Historians, philosophers, scientists and English scholars joined the economists and political scientists in our seminars. Nor were we exclusively academic: diplomats from the Department of External Affairs were regularly invited to join our discussions as were some

* The ULSR has published two books, the product of previous discussions: *Prospect of Change*, edited by Abraham Rotstein, Toronto, McGraw-Hill, 1965 and *Nationalism in Canada*, edited by Peter Russell, Toronto, McGraw-Hill, 1966.

former civil servants, a few journalists, one businessman and even a senior member of the US Department of State. If to this multi-disciplinary, inter-professional character of our group the dimension of ideological conflict is added – for our discussions included Conservatives, Liberals and New Democrats, not to mention the dogmatically uncommitted – it should come as no surprise for the reader to learn that we did not develop a complete consensus about Canadian foreign policy. In fact, the controversy of our seminars is deliberately reproduced in this volume so that it will be impossible for all but the intellectually schizophrenic to agree with every point of view expressed in the pages that follow. Lalande does not accept Painchaud's criticism of biculturalism as a fitting basis for our diplomacy; Peyton Lyon spiritedly rejects the attacks by Hanly and others on Quiet Diplomacy. It is our hope that the reader will be aroused by this disagreement among our authors to take sides and make up his own mind on the various problems at issue.

. . . for Public Response

If there were no controversy within these pages, it would have been necessary to invent it, since our aim is also to stimulate public involvement in this debate. Involvement requires the desire to take part; taking part in a debate implies being able to respond. Yet this is an age of repressed involvement when everyone can observe what is going on in the world by watching the screen in his living-room while feeling powerless to react. It is becoming increasingly important to provide means to convert the citizen's frustrated sense of being a spectator into active participation in policy-making. Letters to one's MP, phone calls to an open-line show and group demonstrations in front of the US consulate are erratic types of public "feed back" that are difficult to transform into policy. This is the reason for our questionnaire.

In response to the one-way communication of the printed page, there is usually only more one-way communication via the book-review columns. Exceptionally a book may strike a perticularly sensitive chord and be adopted by the media as an issue for indecent exposure on Sunday night television. Normally, however, there is no such popularization. All one can expect is that the reader will discuss the book's ideas in his immediate circle. He has no way to communicate his reactions except by writing to the author, an effort that has little political effect. As letter-writing is increasingly falling out of style, we have incorporated as an integral part of the book a questionnaire – an experiment to find out what the readers feel about the various issues debated in these chapters. To make it politically as well as intellectually worthwhile for the reader to respond, we will tabulate the answers and send the results to the Prime Minister and Minister of External Affairs, communicating them to the public through a national magazine. "An independent foreign policy for Canada?" is thus not a rhetorical question. It can be answered by you, the reader of these pages.

The Menu

The title, *An Independent Foreign Policy for Canada?* raises two distinct issues – the possibility of independence, and the purposes of an independent foreign policy. Whether Canada *can* be independent depends first of all on our external position, particularly on our relationship with the USA, the subject of section I. What do "independence," "dependence" and "interdependence" mean in Canadian-American relations? Is there a utilitarian justification for an independent approach to our foreign policy or does *raison d'état* argue for Quiet Diplomacy that gives cultivating American friendship higher priority than autonomy? Is there in fact a choice at all: or does the economic dominance of the USA mean that Washington can force Canada to toe the line by threatening retaliation or does the Cuban example show that Canada has in practice been able to carry out a distinct policy once it makes a firm decision? One cannot look at dependence in the American relationship without examining its most burning case: Canada's Vietnam policy.

If it can be established that Canada is not necessarily dependent on American policy, we then have to ask whether the reasons for our sorry international performance are not internal rather than external. Section II examines some possible internal restraints on our foreign policy. Canada, after all, has its own problems of independence in Quebec's drive for more autonomy even in external relations. Is this a cause of weakness or of strength for Canada's foreign policy? If the latter, the reasons for Canada's diplomatic anaemia must lie elsewhere. One candidate is the "closed circuit" of our foreign policy structure that denies itself the dynamism of public participation. Another is the transposition into international affairs of our "federalist" political style that is more concerned with setting up organizations than with solving problems.

If our Canadian-American relationship is compatible with greater independence and if our foreign policy's ineffectiveness can be traced to domestic conditions that are in our power to change, we can raise the next issue: Independence, for what purpose? The traditional area of Canadian middlepowermanship has been activity in the international organizations (section III). What are the implications of our armed service unification for our old military commitments and other roles? What options can Canada choose from in the effort to control proliferation? Can Canada's continued activity in Nato be defended or is the opposite position more valid: that Canada should break the shackles of its old alliance commitments in order to be independent for more important foreign policy initiatives?

What these initiatives can be is the subject of section IV that concentrates on Canada's role in the under-developed world. Is peace-keeping still a viable role for Canada? How should we relate to revolution in Latin America? More concretely, what should be our policies toward the white racist government of Southern Rhodesia? And aid, that cliché of foreign policy discussions: what future do we have in coping with the increasingly serious, continually widening gap between us, the rich nations, and the poor?

The thread running through these sections is that Canada does have a choice. We can choose the comfortable, safe path of a quiet, gentlemanly but less effectual foreign policy or we can choose the more dynamic, more demanding path of an effective, independent role. Such at least is the substance of the conclusion.

PART A:

THE
POSSIBILITIES
OF
INDEPENDENCE

Section I:
The American Relationship:
Liaison Dangereuse?

Section II:
The Domestic Environment:
Independence Begins
at Home

THE SITUATION IS WELL IN HAND

SECTION I:

THE AMERICAN RELATIONSHIP: LIAISON DANGEREUSE?

Independence, most Canadians seem to feel, begins in Washington. To raise the issue of independence is to conjure up the spectre of American domination, whether economic control, cultural penetration, military absorption or political hegemony. Does the disparity of power between our two countries necessitate international quiescence for Canada? Do the clichés concerning the undefended frontier, the north-south continental pull and inexorable economic integration really mean that the "pale carbon copy" theory of Canadian identity must extend to our foreign policy too?

The section begins with our one American contributor who questions the conventional wisdom concerning our "special" American relationship, in all its conflicting versions. David Baldwin does not come to a conclusion except to advise that sleeping dogs be left to lie. But sleeping dogs wake up and policy-makers have to make policy. For Charles Hanly there is a basic choice to be made between a foreign policy strategy of independence and one of affiliation, or loyal support for the world policy of our friendly neighbourhood super-power. For both ethical and pragmatic reasons he argues in chapter 2 for independence: we should decide our policies on their own merits, not on emotive or ideo-

3

logical grounds. Peyton Lyon denounces this talk as "moralistic" self-righteousness. Our policy, he says in chapter 3, should be Quiet Diplomacy whose declared objective is to achieve influence in Washington by supporting American international goals without question.

Do we really have the freedom to choose an "independent" over a "quiet" diplomacy, or does not the preponderance of American power deter Canadian leaders from adopting policies out of line with those of Washington? The round-table discussion in chapter 4 faces the problem of retaliation as a restriction on Canadian initiative. A. F. W. Plumptre, formerly a senior officer of the Department of Finance, rejects "retaliation" as an inappropriate term for describing the complex repercussions that Canadian and American actions have on each other. In A. E. Safarian's view, however, the reality of retaliation is underlined by the web of inter-relations that connect our two countries at all levels of policy-making. Pauline Jewett recalls from her own parliamentary experience that the fear, if not the fact, of retaliation is a major constraint on our legislators. It is therefore vital, in Abraham Rotstein's opinion, to tackle the problem of fear by working out in advance lines of response to possible acts of American retaliation for future Canadian intiatives.

For Denis Stairs the problem of retaliation is a red herring. In chapter 5 he examines two cases, Cuba and Korea, when Canada did in fact pursue a policy directly opposed to the American position. There was no retaliation despite strong public and private disapproval of our policy in the United States. If Stairs shows how Canada has on occasion practised an independent policy despite American opposition, James Steele looks at an opposite case, Canada's subservient support for American escalation in Vietnam. This sad record cannot, in his view, be blamed on constraints imposed by the USA; there is no one responsible but our government, and we who support it.

4

David Baldwin

THE
MYTHS
OF
THE
SPECIAL
RELATIONSHIP

David Baldwin is Assistant Professor of Government at Dartmouth College. He has written two books, Economic Development and American Foreign Policy *and* Foreign Aid and American Foreign Policy.

Most students of United States relations with Canada emphasize the unique aspects of the situation. Some, however, have suggested that the relationship is merely typical of international relations today. Douglas LePan, for example, advises policy-makers to study the relationship because it "contains within itself most of the problems of the whole planet."[1] A cursory review of major world problems, however, reveals none that figure prominently in American relations with Canada. The population explosion is certainly not one of Canada's problems. World poverty is not involved: Canada and America are the two richest nations in the world. Race relations do not significantly affect the relations of the two nations. The differences in language and culture are negligible compared to the clash between Western and non-Western cultures. Both nations draw their basic political orientation from the same Western tradition. And there is no threat of one using nuclear weapons on the other. In short, study of Canadian-American relations tells one almost nothing about the big problems facing the world. Emphasis on the unique aspects of relations between the two nations is fully justified.

Opinions vary not only on the kinds of problems that exist but on their seriousness as well. Although John Holmes thinks Canadian-American policies have been "good," he argues they are no longer "enough."[2] One is tempted to ask, "Enough for what?"

Bruce Hutchison has argued that Canada "has become more important to the United States than any other foreign nation."[3] Even if this were true, it would not necessarily follow that relations are bad. One might ask, "With what other nation in the world does the United States have more satisfactory relations?" In a world that daily threatens to fall apart, American foreign policy makers cannot afford a standard of perfection. If one rejects the contention that Canada is more important to the United States than any other nation, it becomes even more difficult to argue persuasively that relations are critically bad.

From the standpoint of world peace, Canadian-American relations are no problem at all. In fact the relationship of the two nations is often cited as a prototype of international cooperation. Some scholars have even argued that relations *between* these two nations are more tranquil than those *within* many nations of the world.[4]

From the Canadian viewpoint, of course, one would expect the problems of relations with the United States to loom much larger. No doubt such problems matter more to Canadians than to either Americans or nationals of third countries. But even many Canadians do not regard the state of relations with America as critical. Walter Gordon, one of the most outspoken critics of Canadian-American relations, advised his countrymen to keep things in perspective: "Canadians should stop harping about their problems. We have our problems, but they are as nothing compared with those that other nations have to face."[5]

With this healthy perspective in mind, let us consider the variety of ways to define the Canadian-American "problem."

Neighbours Taken for Granted

The title of this recent book on Canada and the United States, neatly sums up one common way of defining the problem. This needs to be qualified in order to show that although each nation takes the other for granted, it is the United States' attitude toward Canada which is generally considered as a problem.

One way Americans are accused of taking Canadians for

granted is by *incorrectly* believing that Canada is some kind of northern extension of their own country. This is a partial and misleading truth. If this were the problem, it could be solved merely by educating Americans. Unfortunately, the problem is more deep-seated. The real problem is that Americans are justified in believing that Canadians are very much like themselves.

Another way in which Americans are charged with taking Canada for granted is by failing to give Canada the attention she deserves in scholarly and other writings on foreign affairs. The implicit assumption underlying this charge is that Canada is really much more important to American foreign policy than is generally recognized. Once again, we have confused the symptom with the disease. Canada's problem is not that American scholars fail to give Canada the attention it deserves in discussing American foreign policy. Canada's problem is that American commentators do give Canada about as much relative attention as it deserves, and that is not very much. The painful truth is that the United States has worldwide responsibilities and that events in Vietnam, Europe, Russia, China, India, Latin America and the Middle East have higher priority in American foreign policy than do relations with its northern neighbour.

In a similar vein American foreign policy makers are often charged with neglecting Canada. One American refers to "the obvious fact" that our government is so "preoccupied with serious crises in other parts of the world that we tend to devote less time and attention to Canada than she deserves."[6] By what criteria are Americans to decide how much attention Canada deserves? In the best of all possible worlds, of course, all nations would receive much more attention. But what about a world rent with racial strife, filled with undernourished millions and threatened with nuclear annihilation?

Interdependence

A common theme running through most writing on Canadian-American relations is that "interdependence" is a useful word for describing the basic nature of the situation. This concept is highly misleading and probably confuses more than it clarifies: it implies a mutuality of dependence which simply does not exist.

This is not to say that the United States does not depend on Canada at all. It is merely to warn against overestimating the degree of such dependence. Canada does contribute to continental defence, but it is a gross exaggeration to argue that "without the closest cooperation of these two states it would be *impossible* to provide for the defense of North America."[7]

In the economic and cultural spheres the "interdependence" is also lopsided. Although Canada is America's best customer, the average American wallet would not be greatly flattened if all economic interchange between the two nations ceased. Canada, however, would feel a significant economic hardship.

The distortion of reality inherent in the concept of "interdependence" as applied to relations between Canada and the United States is epitomized in J. B. Brebner's unfortunate metaphor describing the two nations as "the Siamese Twins of North America." It is difficult to imagine an elephant and a mouse as Siamese twins.

There is an equally well accepted assumption that interdependence between the two nations will increase in the future. The Merchant-Heeney report, for example, refers to the "virtual certainty"[8] that interdependence will grow. In an era of revolutionary change such certainties are a rarity; therefore the projected growth in interdependence should not be uncritically accepted.

In the field of defense it is by no means clear that interdependence will increase. The recent Canadian *White Paper on Defense* predicts that the main responsibility for deterring nuclear war will continue to rest with the United States.[9] It also observes that revolutionary developments in military technology and political circumstances since 1945 have caused obsolescence of many strategic concepts.[10] There is no reason to expect the next twenty years to be less revolutionary than the last. Already the replacement of the Soviet threat by that of the Chinese and the advent of the missile-carrying submarine have altered the strategic significance of Canada.

In the diplomatic field there is a similar lack of evidence of growing interdependence. Although Canadians have distinguished themselves in United Nations peace-keeping operations in the past, there is no reason to believe that they are indispensable to the continuance of such operations in the future. Norwegians, Danes, Swedes, Africans, Asians and Latin Americans will be increasingly available for these activities. Although Canada has served as a useful mediator between the United States and others in the East-West conflict, there is no reason to believe that American dependence on Canada in this respect is growing. Canada's usefulness as a mediator in the increasingly important North-South split is likely to be limited. From the standpoint of the poor nations in the southern part of the globe, Canada is too rich and perhaps too light-skinned for this job. The United States may be tempted to lean on Mexico rather than Canada as a go-between in the North-South confrontation.

In the economic area the crystal ball is also cloudy. Jacob Viner has predicted that a growth of regional trading blocs to which neither Canada nor the United States belonged would increase the economic entanglement of the two nations, but he has also observed that increased relative economic importance of the poor countries or disappearance of the Iron Curtain as a trade barrier could have the opposite effect.[11] The Merchant-Heeney Report argues that the modern technological revolution will continue to "extend the interdependence of the two economies."[12] On the other hand, one could just as well argue that technological innovations might increase the advantages of trading with third countries or that lower transportation and communications costs would reduce the advantages of dealings with nearby nations. The least one can say is that future implications of technological change for Canadian-American economic interdependence are difficult to predict.

The assumption that the two nations will become increasingly interdependent does not deserve the status of an axiom, a status which the literature on Canadian-American relations too often accords it.

Some writers have argued that Canada's standing in the society of nations has been hurt by her close relations with America. Is this true? One should at least consider the possibility that increased Canadian dependence on the United States has resulted in increased independence vis-à-vis other nations. Proponents of the theory that Canadian world status suffers from close relations with the United States usually point to the decline in Canada's power-ranking from third (or fourth; opinions differ) in 1945 to ninth (again opinions differ) today.[13] The selection of 1945 as a base period, however, is highly misleading, since this was the temporary pinnacle of Canadian status. If we take a longer perspective, the period 1925-1965 for example, it is harder to support the thesis. World War II is a convenient, if arbitrary, dividing line between Canadian dependence on Britain and Canadian dependence on the United States. During the period 1925-1940 Canadian status, as measured by a recent empirical study, managed to rise from fifty-seventh to fifty-sixth.[14] Although the study does not go beyond 1940, my admittedly cursory scanning of the literature shows no one who has not ranked Canada among the fifteen leading nations in the world since 1945. Canadian world status and dependence on the United States do not appear to vary inversely. Even the alleged slippage from third to ninth can be explained without reference to the United States. The recovery of Europe and Japan from war destruction and the rising influence of Afro-Asian nations suffice as an explanation. One could even argue that 9th out of 120 is a better ranking than 5th out of 60.

Those who see a threat to Canadian independence usually emphasize Canada's power vis-à-vis the United States rather than the world in general. Here again, caution is in order. It is possible that Canadian dependence on the United States with respect to some issues may decrease dependence on the United States with respect to other issues. For example, Canadian dependence on the United States in the area of military security carries with it a certain freedom from American control. The United States will defend North America from attack no matter what Canadians do. Washington cannot make a credible threat to stop defending Canada. James Eayrs has observed that he knows of "no other country in the world which could suddenly stop spending a comparable sum of money on national defense with so little adverse effect upon its security position."[15] Although abolition of Canada's defense budget would increase its dependence on the United States in the sphere of continental security, the money saved could be used to decrease Canadian dependence in other spheres. For example, it could be used to buy back ownership of Canadian industry and thus lessen economic dependence on the United States.

Dependence

Much of the writing on the American threat to Canadian independence focuses on this question: Is political independence compatible with economic dependence?[16]

Economic dependence can conceivably increase the political power of the dependent nation vis-à-vis the nation upon which it depends – at least on some issues. Consider the case of American investment in Canada. The United States has, in effect, placed hostages on Canadian soil. The political influence that can be derived from threatening to expropriate or otherwise harass these investors would not be available to Ottawa without such hos-

10

tages.[17] Furthermore, American corporate investors can be helpful to Canada in influencing the American government. Although Walter Gordon claims that the American government influences the corporations in the interest of United States foreign policy,[18] there is good reason to believe that on many issues influence flows in the other direction. With regard to many issues the most important lobby in Washington on behalf of Canada is likely to be those very American companies who by establishing and operating branch plants in Canada are charged with being a menace to Canadian power.[19]

Although the "Gordonites" may overstate their case, the prize for political naïveté goes to their opponents, who purport to see politics and economics as totally separable.

The anti-Gordonites set up the straw man of a direct, one-to-one relationship between economic and political dependence and then proceed to knock it down. The real question, however, is whether economic and political dependence tend to vary in the same direction, not whether the relationship is one to one. It is easy to show that economic dependence does not lead to "inevitable" and "total" political absorption; but it is harder to show that such absorption will not be probable and partial.

Potential political power is implicit in all international trading relations.[20] It is better to admit this and get on with the argument than to assert that American capital does not acquire voting rights and therefore could not possibly influence the Canadian parliament.[21] Voting is only one of many ways to influence people, whether they be Canadian MP's or American congressmen. Although General Motors does not vote in American elections, it is rarely considered to be politically impotent.

The real problem here is determining the economic costs of various degrees of Canadian political independence and determining what price Canadians are willing to pay. No fruitful discussion of the issue can be based on the assumption that there is no correlation whatsoever between political and economic independence.

Solutions

A number of proposals for solving the problem of Canadian-American relations have been advanced by well-intentioned men on both sides of the border.

11

More knowledge

The most common remedy one encounters is more understanding of Canada by Americans. The appealing ring of this panacea has inhibited critical examination of its probable effects. Would an increase in the American people's knowledge and awareness of Canada reduce friction between the two nations? Most Americans, of course, rarely think about Canada. To the extent they do, they probably have a vague feeling that Canadians are friendly, likeable, and, all-in-all, just about like Americans. Would the situation be improved if the American mass public were to become more aware of the fact that Canada is a haven for American draft-dodgers, that anti-Americanism exists in Canada, that Canada wants Red China in the United Nations, that Canada trades with both Cuba and Red China, that supplies for North Vietnam are being smuggled out of the United States via Canada, and that many Canadians oppose American policy in Vietnam? Perhaps it is not so much the amount of knowledge that matters as the kind of knowledge. A wrong belief that others like them may lead to more amicable relations than a correct belief that they do not.

One might ask whether, as a general rule, it is true that nations which know a lot about one another tend to get along well. Most of the wars fought during the last 200 years have been fought in Europe, where nations presumably are more aware of each other. Although the French acquired knowledge about the Germans during the occupation, it is doubtful that they were any better disposed toward Germany because of it.

One can, of course, justify increased knowledge on other grounds. But before we accept the proposition that more knowledge will lead to less friction, we should ponder the ancient advice on how to treat sleeping dogs. Few people have ever been bitten by a sleeping dog.

Closer relations

The assumption that closer relations are better relations is an axiom for students of international relations in general. It is not surprising, therefore, to find it cropping up as a suggested response to the Canadian-American problem. The lack of semantic precision that typifies the study of international relations is nowhere better illustrated. Precisely what does "closer relations" mean? How would we know whether relations were getting closer?

The Merchant-Heeney Report defined its task as working out

principles which would make it easier to "avoid divergencies in economic and other policies of interest to each other."[22] Yet, this raises several questions: What does divergency mean? Can policies diverge yet not conflict? If we could eliminate all divergence between American and Canadian policies, would we want to do it? Perhaps a certain amount of divergence, and even conflict, is desirable in terms of preserving Canadian independence and/or national identity.

Although George Ball has indicated that the United States government would like both nations to pursue "common objectives in the world at large,"[23] it is difficult to see why this would be desirable from the standpoint of either nation. It is more important for the foreign policy goals of the two nations to be compatible than it is for them to be identical.

More bureaucracy

Whenever political problems arise Americans tend to pin the blame on faulty organization. When the Republicans lose, they reorganize; when the Democrats lose, they do likewise. In international relations there is a similar propensity to assume that more and/or better bureaucratic machinery will solve any problem. The foreign aid agency has been reorganized so many times that most people have lost count. Of course, more advance consultation through improved machinery for inter-governmental cooperation could be harmful only if it drew attention away from the real Canadian-American problems. Almost none of the problems outlined earlier is amenable to solution by bureaucratic tinkering. The problems are more deep-seated and arise from such fundamental facts as the gigantic disparity of power between the two nations. Bigger and better bureaucracy will not even give us symptomatic relief from what ails the Canadian-American relationship.

Quiet Diplomacy

Quiet diplomacy is the favourite response of the professional diplomats to Canadian-American problems – or to any problem for that matter. "Don't rock the boat. Things will turn out fine if you leave everything to behind-the-scenes diplomacy." With regard to many problems, they are probably right, but quiet diplomacy is not always more effective than squeaky-wheel diplomacy. In a discussion of peaceful settlement of disputes, Inis Claude ruefully admits that "states are likely to get what they want if they raise a sufficient fuss, and unlikely to get it if they fail to do so."[24] This observation seems especially apropos if one defines the problem in terms of Canadians being taken for granted. The quickest way for Canada to get the United States to stop taking it for granted is to make trouble. Whatever else one can say about Charles de Gaulle's foreign policy, one cannot say that it has allowed France to be taken for granted by the United States. Most Canadians would regard armed attack too costly as a means of attracting American attention, but it would certainly be effective. Canadians will have to decide what price they are willing to pay to stop Americans from taking them for granted.

Squeaky-wheel diplomacy may be superior to quiet diplomacy in attaining other foreign policy goals as well. Thomas C. Schelling, in his imaginative study of bargaining strategies, has pointed out that publicity may be an asset to one or both parties in a bargaining situation.[25] He argues that national representatives may strengthen their bargaining position by arranging to be charged with appeasement for every small concession. It is thus easier for them to convince the other party that they cannot afford to give in. On most issues publicity would probably help Canada and hurt the United States. The recent controversy over the American-owned Mercantile Bank of Canada is a case in point. When Washington protested proposed Canadian legislation limiting the assets of the Bank, Ottawa rejected the protest in a widely publicized note. The subsequent uproar in the Canadian press and parliament demanded reassurance from the Prime Minister that the Government had no intention of "giving in" or of "retreating before American pressure." This domestic hue and cry made it easier for the Canadian government to convince Washington that it could not afford to compromise on the issue for fear of losing domestic political support. The United States government could counter with no such argument. Not many Americans were even aware of the matter, and if they had been, it is unlikely that they would have rallied to the cause of First National City Bank. Given that the American public is relatively apathetic toward Canadian affairs and given that the Canadian public is relatively sensitive to relations with the United States, one suspects that on many issues Ottawa could strengthen its bargaining position vis-à-vis Washington by publicity. Quiet diplomacy, on the other hand, will probably tend to favour the United States.

Independence

Another frequently mentioned response to the Canadian-American problem is independence. Although this alternative has received much polemical treatment, relatively few attempts have been made to appraise it objectively. In the first place, the alternatives have been vastly oversimplified. Walter Gordon's book, *A Choice for Canada,* is subtitled "Independence or Colonial Status." Here and at other places in the book Gordon implies that there are only two alternatives.[26] There are, however, many points on the continuum between colonial subjection and complete independence. One should distinguish between maximizing independence and optimizing it. When Gordon says that the great majority of Canadians want their country to be as independent as possible, he is clearly choosing to maximize independence.[27] At other times, Gordon appears to favour only as much independence as it is "desirable" for any single nation to have in today's world.[28] Rational evaluation of independence as a policy-alternative requires more explicit recognition that there are degrees of independence and that the maximum degree may not be the optimum one from every standpoint.

Closely related to the oversimplification of alternatives is the failure to consider the economic, social and political costs of various degrees of independence. Walter Gordon usually ignores the question of costs or else implies that there are none, as when he refuses to admit that the Canadian standard of living would suffer from severing economic ties with the United States.[29]

Not only is it unclear how much independence Canada wants and what price it is willing to pay, it is also not always apparent from whom they want to be independent. Although it is often implied that independence from America is the desired goal, no distinction is usually made between the American government and American corporations. Insofar as independence refers to corporations, the Canadian nationalists may be deluding themselves if they believe that "Canadianization" will solve the problem. It might just transform the problem into one of independence of the government from Canadian corporations. Although Canadians complain that American corporations do not behave as good corporate citizens, Americans have filed the same complaint against their own corporations. There is a growing body of literature focusing on the problem of getting giant corporations to behave in accord with the public interest.[30] One must therefore raise the question: To what extent are the Canadian government's problems due to American corporate ownership, and to what extent are they due solely to the nature of giant corporations?

In sum, the question of Canadian independence needs to be stated in a more sophisticated way. One should ask: How much independence, on what issues, from whom, and at what cost?

When a man's reach exceeds his grasp he can avoid frustration in two ways. Either he can adjust his reach or he can improve his grasp. Harry Johnson has advised his compatriots to stop reaching for the unattainable:

> Unlike the citizens of other small countries bordering on large countries, Canadians are not prepared to content themselves with the advantages that can be derived from small size, but set themselves the impossible aspiration of equalling the United States, and, still more impossible, of getting the United States to treat them as equals.[13]

Conclusion

Canadians and Americans have gotten along remarkably well so far. If any two contiguous nations have had smoother relations during the last one hundred years, they have not yet come to the attention of this writer. It is possible that Canadian-American relations can be made even more successful during the next one hundred years. An attempt was made in this essay to further that goal by clarifying the basic nature of the situation, identifying various definitions of the Canadian-American "problem," and briefly appraising some of the alternative responses to the problem. The efficacy of each response, of course, varies with the definition of the problem.

The final point that should be emphasized is the need to keep the Canadian-American problem in a larger perspective. In terms of either United States national interest or of the interests of the rest of the world, improvement of Canadian-American relations is not a pressing problem. The basic root of such problems as do exist is the existence of a small nation next to a super power. As long as things are relatively quiet at the Canadian desk, Washington is unlikely to initiate any radical changes in its policy toward Canada. It is up to Canadians to decide whether the various remedies are worse than the disease. One can get rid of a blemish on the finger by amputating the arm, but few people try it.

Charles Hanly

THE
ETHICS
OF
INDEPENDENCE

Charles Hanly is Assistant Professor of Philosophy at the University of Toronto. Editor of the recent Revolution and Response, *Dr. Hanly chaired the International Teach-In in 1965 and is at present President of the Canadian Peace Research and Education Association.*

Why should Canada pursue an independent course in world affairs when following British or American leadership is usually easy and often profitable? Why should anyone expect Canadians to abandon the emotional luxury of being able to lay blame for the evils of the world on Washington or London? Unfortunately, the satisfactions of the dutiful, submissive ally must be frequently disturbed by uncertainty concerning the wisdom of the course being charted for Canada by the dominant powers in the alliance. Evidence of such uncertainty concerning British leadership in Africa and American leadership in Asia is apparent in editorials of both liberal and conservative dailies, the proliferation of protest groups across the country and open letters to the Prime Minister. This malaise is coupled with and reinforced by a growing demand for a clearer expression of Canada's national interests and definition of our relations with other countries.

17

The Utilitarian Imperative

It is no accident that the current dissatisfaction with the results of a dependent foreign policy is linked to a demand for more independent Canadian initiatives. The misgivings are a product of one of the ethical principles of our culture – utilitarianism. Applied to international affairs, this principle requires that our foreign policy, in serving the interests of Canadians, should also serve, whenever possible, the interests and aspirations of the peoples who are affected by it. It declares that the security and well-being of one nation or society should not be based on the devastation, impoverishment or suffering of another society.

A major obstacle to following an ethical foreign policy is acting on the basis of unthinking loyalty, emotion or ideology. These appeals to stereotypes confuse the understanding of the real forces that are shaping events. They distort and often dehumanize our perception of what are the legitimate interests of those involved in a particular international conflict. Such appeals too often justify compliant condonement of a traditional ally's action when opposition or initiative is required. We Canadians might not be so indifferent about what is happening in Rhodesia if an illegal black African government were treating British colonists in the manner in which Smith's white minority regime has been treating Africans. Underlying the ideological approach to policy-making are the affiliations that Canada has developed with its two traditional sources of direction, the United States and Great Britain. Consequently, the question of independence versus affiliation in foreign policy is raised as soon as our automatic support for an American or British policy clashes with the utilitarian imperative of seeking the greatest good of the greatest number. The Suez crisis of 1956 and its aftermath will serve as an illustration.

Because Canada is a small power it is in our interest to establish that the more powerful nations should not use their military superiority to arbitrarily coerce less powerful nations. The British and French governments perceived the nationalization of the Suez Canal by Egypt in 1956 to be a physical threat to their national interests. Consequently, in league with Israel, they embarked on a military expedition to take possession of the Canal zone. The Canadian government was concerned about the rights of Egypt, as a small, newly independent power, to run its own economy and recognized the danger of the British and French action in provoking a Soviet counter-intervention. In cooperation with other

18

countries Canada utilized the United Nations to halt the Anglo-French assault on Egypt and to gain acceptance for UN troops which could secure peace in the area, guarantee the safety of Egypt and elicit Egyptian assurances of universal access to the canal. Canada's Suez policy met the requirements of the utilitarian principle, since it furthered Canada's international interests by supporting the autonomy of another small power, Egypt, while at the same time securing the most important national interests of Britain and France – access to the canal for shipping.

The Canadian action during the Suez crisis sharply etches an essential aspect of the independence question. Given our historical loyalties, our racial and religious affinities and our ideological outlook, it would have been easy and, in a sense, "natural" for Canada to support the Anglo-French invasion of Egypt. Many Canadians were in fact dismayed that our UN representative was not only opposing Britain but had initiated a plan for United Nations action that won the support of the Soviet Union. Pearson was publicly condemned by Conservative politicians at the time for aiding the cause of world communism. But in reality our policy-makers were reaching beyond habitual considerations of racial or ideological kinship to embrace the legitimate needs and aspirations of other peoples. Of course, not all aspirations that a society may develop are legitimate, as for example the drive for world conquest by Nazi Germany. A judgment concerning legitimacy of the other countries' aims, difficult though it is to make, is implicit in most major policy decisions. Such judgments should be impartial, but impartiality is often impaired by fixed ideological affiliations. In the Suez crisis Canada chose to disengage from the emotional patterns prescribed by our traditional loyalty to Great Britain and in so doing made a useful contribution to world affairs.

But failures are instructive too, and the Middle East crisis of 1967 resulted, at least in part, from the failure to gain right of access to the Suez Canal for Israeli merchant-shipping and the failure to secure Israel's agreement to have United Nations troops stationed on their territory. In retrospect Canada seems to have resigned the role of United Nations policy initiator and gadfly concerning Middle East problems too readily. Certainly, Mr. Pearson was fully aware that the UN peace-keeping operation was only a means of buying time during which the underlying sources of conflict between Israel and the Arab States could be removed by negotiation. Perhaps the explanation of this resignation is to be found in the fact that Canada's success in 1956 was dependent 'upon US and Soviet support for our policy. Consequently, the limitations of Canadian policy were defined by the extent of American and Soviet support for a permanent settlement. If so, the lesson is clear. If Canada is to be more effective in the future, it will be necessary to find ways and means of securing US support for Canadian initiatives as well as ways and means of acting effectively when US support is not available.

Further policy implications can be drawn from the utilitarian principle. Our racial kinship with the white Rhodesians and our traditional support for British policy in Africa notwithstanding, it would be wrong for Canada to pursue a Rhodesian policy that is detrimental to its majority African population. Despite our ideological differences with China and some uncertainties concerning China's international goals, it is right for Canada to sell wheat to China. Not only has this brought prosperity to the farmers of Western Canada, it has also contributed to economic development within China making it possible for the Chinese to eliminate famine from their society, and may for this reason, contribute toward the establishment of peaceful and cooperative relations with China in other areas in the long run. Finally, our religious, racial, and ideological kinship with the US does not in itself ever justify our support of an American policy if that policy in our own judgment is mistaken.

Following American leadership is too often premised on the true but irrevelant idea that we Canadians are basically the same as the Americans. On the contrary, we are morally obliged to oppose friends and allies such as Britain and the US when we find that their policies and actions are running counter to either our own interests or those of other nations adversely affected by British or American actions. In particular, concerning the war in Vietnam, the utilitarian principle requires us to ask two questions which may be stated in their most basic form as follows: Is a unified communist Vietnam allied to China a threat to the security and well-being of Canadians? and, Is a communist take-over in Vietnam a greater threat to the well-being of the Vietnamese people than the continuation of the war? If our answer to both of these questions is No, then we have no alternative but to oppose the war, unless our opposition would so damage our relations with the US that our own national well-being might suffer at the hands of a disappointed, angered and vastly more powerful neighbour with whom we are linked by many mutually advantageous dependencies.

The war in Vietnam is now a focus of the underlying dilemma of Canadian foreign policy: affiliation versus independence. The crux of the dilemma is our emotional support of Americans, which is at odds with our disagreement with US policy. There can be no doubt that a majority of Canadians feel an emotional bond of social and ideological kinship with the Americans which, reinforced by our economic ties, establishes a strong tendency to support any major American action, especially when the American policy is presented as halting the spread of communism. This climate of opinion is reflected in the reluctance of the New Democratic Party to make its declared opposition to the war in Vietnam an important election plank – a reluctance born of the discovery that it is not a popular issue. Many Canadians do not want Canada to be at odds with the US on any major issue. Consequently, Canadian governments have to take this climate of opinion into account in forming its policies.

However, counterbalancing our basic pro-American reflexes is our different attitude towards the cold war. Canadian governments have perceived the cold war differently than have recent US governments. Even Kennedy during his short term in office was unwilling to run the political risks involved in according China diplomatic recognition. In contrast, two of our governments, one Liberal and the other Conservative, have *sought* to extend diplomatic recognition to China and were deterred not by an adverse public opinion but by US pressure. Furthermore, our economic interests diverge from the US and impose on Canada an attitude toward the cold war that differs sharply from the American. If the US can afford large agricultural surpluses, Canada cannot. Our ability to sell western wheat to China, the Soviet Union and Eastern Europe has helped bring a vitality to the prairie provinces that they have not enjoyed since before the depression. These sales have also brought about a substantial reduction in our balance of payments problem. Thus, while both Liberal and Conservative cabinet ministers have been winning votes at the polls by arranging for the sale of our non-strategic products to communist countries, successive American administrations have been using the Trading with the Enemy Act as a weapon in the cold war not only to inhibit the growth of military power in communist countries such as China and Cuba, but also to arrest their economic development and undermine their governments. Consequently, Senator Fulbright's minority position in the US comes close to expressing the views of a majority of Canadians, views

21

that would be official Canadian policy were it not for the fact that the US government persists in its hostile attitude toward China.

Consequently, the dilemma of our foreign policy is essentially this: most Canadians do not want to be in conflict with the US, but many do disagree with American cold war strategy. A major feature of Canadian policy ought therefore to be a contribution to a more adequate Western assessment of the cold war.

But what are we going to do about it? The need for a greater Canadian contribution to international developments returns us to the problem of affiliation or independence in foreign policy and debate on how Canada can maximize its influence.

Independence or Affiliation?

Canada can choose between two basic strategies for its foreign policy: affiliation or independence. Canada is not alone in being confronted by these alternatives.

The USA and the USSR have emerged as the giants in relation to which all other countries, including France and China, are small powers. The affiliation strategy requires a small power to adopt a great power as its leader in international affairs. The small power will then seek to acquire some measure of influence over the course of events through its relation to a great power – an influence which it believes it could not have on the same events if acting independently. To augment its influence the small power will support the major policies of the great power to which it affiliates and refrain from taking initiatives of its own that would create open conflict. If the small power disagrees with the great power, it will neither openly declare its opposition nor do what it can to counteract the policy; it will, instead, seek to use its general support of the aims of the great power as the grounds for claiming the right to have its views taken into consideration by the decision-makers of the great power. Independence of action is limited to those areas in which the interests of the great power are not at stake. Britain's rapid decline as a great power after the war has been completed by her adoption of the affiliation strategy toward the US. Canadian foreign policy is also grounded at the present time in an affiliation strategy toward the United States which provides the major premise for quiet diplomacy.

There are two types of independence strategy which can be conveniently named the middle power and the small power independence strategies. The crucial difference is the possession of an independent nuclear capability. France and China are independent middle powers with a modest nuclear deterrent sufficient for self-defence and an independent foreign policy, but are without enough military, economic or political power to compete with the giants on equal terms. Yugoslavia, Sweden, Mexico and Pakistan are examples of countries that are following small power independence strategies. Independence requires above all the determination to act in each situation as national interest and circumstances may dictate, whether alone, in cooperation with other nations great and small or through alliances.

Alliances such as Nato and Norad should not be treated as sacred obligations but as expedient means of achieving specific goals whose validity is subject to constant review. Accordingly an independence strategy also implies some degree of cold war neutrality.

Canada, or perhaps more correctly, English-speaking Canada, is pre-disposed by habit to adopt the affiliation strategy. During the early years of the nation, Canadian foreign policy was decided in Whitehall. British interests were Canadian interests and British wars were Canadian wars. After the Second World War Canada enjoyed a brief moment of quasi-independence as the honest broker for the Anglo-American partnership. But Britain's rapid decline accompanied by American ascendency has rendered such a role superfluous. And Canada's last act of affiliation to Great Britain has been to follow Britain in adopting an affiliation strategy toward the United States. French Canadians have been the major force working in the direction of independence from Britain and they continue to exert a pressure in the direction of independence from the US. Most of the new Quebec intellectual and political leaders are acutely aware of the problems of nationality. They can empathize with the nationalist aspirations of other peoples and this empathy generates an opposition to imperialism in any form and in particular to American military interventions in Latin America or in South-East Asia. But this pressure is not as great as it might otherwise be in the area of foreign policy because of the strength of traditional French-Canadian catholicism which is similar in this respect to English-Canadian protestant fundamentalism: any rigidly dogmatic religious position strongly reinforces war-like attitudes, particularly a militant opposition to communism.[1]

However much our historical and religious heritage suggests that we pursue an affiliation strategy, I think that Canada has greater potential. An independent foreign policy might well have the effect of uniting Canadians in a shared pride in our national contribution to world affairs.[2] But outweighing this consideration of national need is the danger and futility inherent in our pursuit of the affiliation strategy.

When viewed from the standpoint of the international system and its current needs, the affiliation strategy is regressive rather than constructive. It perpetuates a dangerous ideological polarization of nations even at a time when there has been some reduction in the ideological cohesion of the Soviet Bloc, as evidenced by the offer to disband the Warsaw Pact in exchange for the dismantling of Nato. This relaxation has been facilitated by a decrease in the threat represented by a united, American-dominated West Europe, resulting from the emergence of an independent France. As the American threat has diminished, Eastern European countries under the pressure of internal difficulties have been able to experiment a little in the direction of liberalizing their economies and societies. Just as we feel more secure in a world in which communist countries are able to disagree among themselves and follow independent courses, so we can expect that the communist countries will feel more secure in a world in which capitalist countries do not form a monolithic bloc implacably opposed to their existence. The current phase offers us an opportunity to begin the work of replacing the inherently dangerous system of threats upon which the relations between capitalist and communist countries in the past have been based with new forms of mutually advantageous co-operation. If Canada is to maximize its contribution to this desirable international development, we must abandon our affiliation strategy and the chronically quiet diplomacy by which it is pursued in favour of independence. And if our independence is to be credited it must be made manifest by well-defined declarations of policy backed up by specific actions.

The affiliation strategy is not only regressive, it is also futile. It is premised on the assumption that by being a "good ally" (one that does not oppose any major policy of the US), Canada will acquire influence in Washington. But any senior American government adviser such as Bundy or Rostow always has more influence on decision-making than the Canadian ambassador who represents the people of Canada – unless our ambassador has a bargaining position. Failing this our ambassador has less influence than, for example, Galbraith, a former Canadian, because Galbraith is a leading opinion-maker of the American intellectual élite, which is a segment of the voting public in the US. To be sure, Canada's relations to Cuba prior to the Bay of Pigs and our information about the domestic politics of Cuba enabled the Canadian ambassador to offer correct information to the Kennedy administration. Had the American decision-makers been acting rationally, this would have deterred them from that bizarre misadventure. But Kennedy acted on the misinformation of the CIA. His reaction to the ensuing fiasco was not to rely in future on Canadian advice and information. It was the reaction of any responsible American president: he improved the American services that feed information to the President.

The US attitude to its own leadership position in the western alliance and its disregard of the Canadian government's views on matters of grave Canadian concern was vividly illustrated during the Cuban missile crisis. Diefenbaker delayed Canada's declaration of support for American actions against the installation of missiles in Cuba pending further information concerning the threat and the American plan for dealing with it. Canada was chastised for the delay in declaring support, although Diefenbaker was only carrying out his responsibilities as Prime Minister of Canada in a situation that contained the threat of an immediate escalation into nuclear war with the Soviet Union. There was never any question Kennedy's consulting the Canadian government for its view of the crisis and of how it should be handled. There was not, apparently, even much information flow from Washington to Ottawa on this crucial issue. It would appear, then, that quiet diplomacy does not achieve its objective, namely, the kind of mutual consultation that could lead sometimes, if not often, to a real adjustment of US policy to Canada's view of the situation. To be sure, the critic works under a serious handicap because it is in the very nature of quiet diplomacy to leave Canadian foreign policy objectives somewhat ill-defined, at least, publicly. In addition the diplomatic activities by which they are pursued are largely secret. Consequently, a citizen who wants to appraise the success of the strategy must base his assessment on rather scant, if perhaps telling, indicators. Subject to the margin of error resulting from this handicap, it appears that the affiliation strategy and the quiet diplomacy by which it is pursued have been ineffective.

To be sure, Canadian foreign policy has not been uniquely premised on the affiliation strategy. During the past twenty years independence has been practised on at least three specific issues: the negotiation of the Korean Truce in 1953,[3] the sales of wheat to China and our relations with Cuba. However there has been a consistent failure to achieve certain general and specific objectives of a foreign policy based on Canada's perceptions of the world and our place in it. Canada has failed to develop, especially in our American ally, a politically flexible and militarily cautious accommodation with the communist powers. Nor do we yet have an adequate approach to the economic, social and political needs of underdeveloped countries and, in particular, to the revolutionary unrest that results from them. These general failures of our foreign policy are sharply focused in two specific issues: China and Vietnam.

The low degree of Canadian independence in foreign policy can be measured today by our continual failures to extend diplomatic recognition to China and to be outspoken in our criticism of the US prosecution of the war in Vietnam. To analyse the sources of one failure is also to have analysed the sources of the other. Let us again consider Vietnam. Whatever one's understanding of the events that immediately precipitated the US involvement in the war, two things are clear: the war originated in a struggle *indigenous* to Vietnam to remedy socio-political ills and reunite the country; given the current and predictable course of the war a National Liberation Front victory in South Vietnam, while no doubt undesired by many Vietnamese, especially the Saigonese, is nevertheless more in the interests of the Vietnamese people as a whole than the further devastation of the nation. Canada's affiliation to the US is evidenced by the way in which the Canadian representatives on the ICC have acted, by the silencing of Walter Gordon and his cabinet colleagues who share his views, and by our complete failure to influence the US to seek a negotiated settlement, rather than a military victory.

The general futility of this policy has already been established. Its particular futility in relation to Vietnam emerges very clearly in connection with the problem of achieving a cessation of the bombing of North Vietnam. It is clear that the Canadian government would like to see a negotiated settlement of the war in Vietnam. Canadian diplomacy has been aimed bringing negotiations about. Furthermore, Canada has a unique asset – a Canadian who is respected in Hanoi in the person of Chester Ronning. In the summer of 1966 Ronning talked to Ho Chi Minh and was told that if the US undertook an unconditional cessation of the bombing of North Vietnam, he would undertake unconditional negotiations with the US. However, the US wanted a corresponding decrease in North Vietnam's support for the NLF in the south as a *quid pro quo* for the cessation of the bombing. Failing this they planned a further escalation of the war. Ronning's diplomacy failed and escalation has continued. Here was a clear opportunity for an active mediating role to achieve the negotiations, which are the declared objective of Canadian policy. Yet as soon as the US rejected the proposal, Canada stopped being the intermediary and instead fell into step and endorsed the idea that North Vietnam must make some reciprocal reduction in the level of military activity.

Are there any limits to Canadian support for the war despite Canada's declared preference for a negotiated settlement of the war? Is there any point at which the Canadian government will have to say that the US has passed up too many opportunities and Canada, however reluctantly, will have to seek other, more public means to end the war (cooperate with France to bring pressure on the US to negotiate, for example) than the strategy of affiliation allows? In any case, Canada's failure to influence the conduct of the war in any material way by means of affiliation and quiet diplomacy demonstrate the bankruptcy of this approach to international affairs. We are the sheep and the State Department is the shepherd.

The alternative is a strategy of independence which would be pro-American as far as possible but would not rule out taking a public position in opposition to the US whenever the issues and circumstances demanded. Independence in foreign policy in 1968 requires at least two policies: a) Canadian diplomatic recognition of China, followed by vigorous efforts to get China seated at the UN; b) the open advocacy of a de-escalation of the war in Vietnam involving, at least, the cessation of the bombing of North and South Vietnam and, if that fails to produce negotiations, the withdrawal of US forces to limited fortified areas where they would remain to protect the interests of their allies among the Vietnamese until a satisfactory political settlement is reached. Such a policy successfully pursued would more effectively combat communist world domination than America's current counter-insurgency strategy.[4] For the de-polarization of the cold war would have the effect of disconnecting the now dangerously united forces of communism and nationalism as manifested in the proliferation of National Liberation Front movements. However, Canadian policy should be based on the willingness to accept the occasional expansion of communism, especially in backward and impoverished societies that are being denied even some modicum of social justice by their ruling élites. Such expansion would reduce the overall international dynamism of communism and the new communist societies that might result would not be, in all likelihood, much of an advertisement for world communism.[5] This tactic, if successful, would buy time during which China could pass through her initial phase of revolutionary zeal, allowing other indigenous cultural and social forces to assert themselves, paving the way for the kind of co-existence with the West that is now rapidly emerging as a possibility with the Soviet Union. Because of our lesser involvement in the cold war, Canada should have, and I think does have, a capacity for a more dispassionate perception of world ideological conflicts than our American neighbours. We also have our own economic and political interests to serve. Consequently, branch plant diplomacy is not good enough for Canada. It is time for Canada to convert our foreign policy strategy from affiliation to independence.

Peyton Lyon

QUIET
DIPLOMACY
REVISITED

Peyton Lyon is Professor and Chairman of the Department of Political Science at Carleton University. A former diplomat, Dr. Lyon is the author of The Policy Question *and* Canada in World Affairs.

We would be more influential in world affairs, as Mr. Hanly and many other Canadians contend, if only we had the courage to display our independence more boldly. Alas, the contrary is closer to the truth. If our stress is on independence in an increasingly interdependent world, this can only be at the expense of Canada's ability to exercise a moderating influence upon the decisions of other governments.

It was back in the bad old days of the "Cold War" that I became a convert to the belief that for Canada the best foreign policy is one that makes the most of its unusual relationship with Washington, something that can best be accomplished by tactics now generally described as "quiet diplomacy." The world has changed, and continues to change. We have become more conscious, moreover, of the internal threat to Canada's survival as a federal state. In the light of these developments, it is reasonable to ask if Canada's foreign policy, however successful in the past, is not now in need of an overhaul. I propose to review the case for quiet diplomacy and to reassess its validity at the beginning of Canada's second century.

I shall skip lightly over the direct benefits to Canada, mostly economic, of smooth relations between Ottawa and Washington. In so doing, I do not wish to imply that there is anything improper about taking into account the impact upon Canadian living standards of different foreign policy options. Some of my academic colleagues seem to believe that our activity in world affairs should be all "knight errantry"; they refuse to face up to the possibility that the foreign policy that does the most for the material well-being of Canadians might also be the policy that enables Canada to make its best contribution to world peace. If a policy doesn't hurt, they seem to feel, it must be reprehensible. If we accept democracy, however, we cannot simply disregard the evident wish of the majority of Canadians, high-minded academics included, not to be left too far behind their opulent neighbours.

My main argument for a policy of close alliance with the United States is not that it is good for Canadian living standards or national independence. Rather it is based on the following propositions.

The United States, the wealthiest and most powerful country on earth, is a significant factor in almost every situation, whether it chooses to act or not to act.

Geographic and cultural factors give Canada the opportunity to exercise more influence in Washington than is exercised by any other country of comparable power.

This influence, in favour of diplomatic flexibility and military caution, has generally been on the side of sanity.

Canada, by exploiting its close relations with Washington, exerts greater influence in world affairs than it could through its relations with any other country or group of countries.

The belief that Canada has a special standing in Washington, access to American intelligence and insight into American thinking is a source of strength in Canada's dealings with other countries, including the neutrals and Communists; it is scarcely ever a handicap.

The fact that Canada has its own views and determines its own policies can be demonstrated without prejudicing good relations with Washington by the public airing of every difference.

A policy of seeking to influence world affairs through close alliance with Washington and quiet diplomacy is easy to support if one believes, as I do, that post-war American foreign policy has been basically responsible; that, despite errors in judgment in Washington and occasional excesses, the world is a better place than it would have been had the Americans reverted in 1945 to their traditional isolationism. It does not follow, however, that the policy of close alliance should be rejected if one believes that the Americans are generally misguided. Quite the contrary. It is for the very reason that the Americans are capable of making mistakes, with tragic consequences not only for themselves but for Canadians and the rest of the world, that we should seek to maximize our influence in Washington. The *more* one worries about the propensity of American policy-makers to make mistakes, and the greater one's confidence in the superiority of Canadian motives and wisdom, the *more* one should favour policies designed to increase the effectiveness of the Canadian voice in Washington.

The case for alliance and quiet diplomacy is vulnerable if it can be demonstrated that Canadians are never in fact able to bring significant influence to bear upon American policies, except perhaps in bilateral matters, or that we could exert more influence in Washington if the alliance were looser and differences of opinion more openly expressed. Although the existence of influence is always difficult to demonstrate, and still more difficult to quantify,[1] both propositions are highly implausible. The conviction of almost all Canadians who have represented Canada in Washington is that our influence is significant, even though it varies greatly from issue to issue. They also believe that the elementary rules governing the relations between friends do apply. Our official views, for example, are more likely to be received sympathetically if we do not appear to question the ultimate goals or sincerity of the Americans, or give the impression that we are playing up our differences merely to demonstrate our independence. There are occasions when it is desirable to air our differences or offer advice in public, but such occasions should be kept to a minimum, and the reasons for breaching the normal rules should be obvious.[2] Canada's ability to influence American policies is greater if its stake in the problem or area under consideration is obvious; the

31

fact, for example, that we have troops in Europe does make it easier for us to gain a meaningful hearing in the American discussion of European problems than in the formulation of American policies towards Latin America. The impact of Canadian views also bears some relationship to their soundness, and the persuasiveness of the men seeking to put them across; there have been occasions when no foreign government could comprehend what it was that Ottawa wanted them to do.

The relationship between Canada's alliance with the United States and its ability to influence international developments is illustrated by its role in disarmament negotiations. Canada has been a member of almost every disarmament commission since 1945; during much of this time it was the only participant without great power status. Canada received this assignment in the first instance because it had participated in the development of the atom bomb; it is now active in the Geneva talks because of the expertise it has gained and also because it is a member in good standing of the Western alliance led by the United States. Canada's most useful contribution comes during the planning sessions of the western delegations when it has the opportunity to encourage its allies to be more imaginative and daring in seeking agreement with the Soviet Union. The Canadian delegation is also consulted by the neutral and Communist representatives on the assumption that it has more influence with Americans and insight into their thinking. If Canada cut itself off from the intimate consultation customary among close allies and the exchange of intelligence, it would be less able even to understand the points at issue.

Similarly, Canada's ability to influence nuclear planning has been enhanced by its share in developing the weapons systems and by its membership in Nato. It is, of course, illusory to expect that a country like Canada could ever have decisive influence at a moment of such supreme crisis that a nuclear exchange might be launched; it is not too much, however, to aspire to a share in the contingency planning that might largely predetermine the ultimate decision. Such sharing can seldom be publicized, and it cannot be effective unless the smaller ally retains the confidence of the nuclear power and has knowledge that can scarcely be obtained without some participation in the management of the weapons. Canada, through its membership on the seven-nation Nato committee on nuclear planning, is presently engaged in discussions of the desirability of installing an anti-ballistic missile

32

system. Canada can only wield influence in these matters if we nurture our special relationship with Washington.

The outsider is perfectly entitled to be sceptical about claims by Canadian politicians or civil servants that they have influence in the making of American foreign policy. Obviously it is in the Americans' interest to keep Canadians from becoming too discontented. They may simply be flattering us by going through the motions of consultation and taking, or appearing to take, our advice on some secondary matters. On the other hand, the outsider should recognize that, in addition to the inherent difficulties in quantifying influence, the practitioners of Canadian diplomacy are handicapped in documenting their case by the Official Secrets Act, natural modesty and the awareness that boasting about their success in influencing foreign governments is likely to make it more difficult for those governments to heed their advice in the future.

To publicize quiet diplomacy, indeed, is a contradiction in terms. The *Globe and Mail* was quite right to poke fun at "the quiet diplomacy which is so loudly championed by Mr. Pearson and External Affairs Minister Martin."[3] Both have impaired the effectiveness of Canadian foreign policy by hinting, under pressure, that they express much graver misgivings to the Americans in private than they do in public; it is then left to the hearers to guess what these misgivings are – and they often guess wrong. Although the Merchant-Heeney report was full of irrefutable common sense, its publication was also a tactical blunder; by focussing attention on quiet diplomacy, and even lending the doctrine a degree of official sanction, it discouraged observers from taking any Canadian pronouncement at face value. That is not entirely unreasonable because Canadian views, in line with quiet diplomacy, should often be understated in public. The difficulty comes whenever it is automatically assumed that the government is speaking its mind when its expressed views coincide with those of the observer, but must be dissembling when they do not; for example, anti-American critics assume, incorrectly as it happens, that the government can only be expressing its true beliefs when it is damning Washington.

In the same *Globe and Mail* editorial, Mr. Pearson's description of certain proposals by U Thant as "unrealistic" was assumed to be "quiet diplomacy" masking Canada's "independent" assessment even though the Prime Minister had first expressed the same thought in a conversation he assumed to be off-the-record. Furthermore, after referring to Mr. Pearson's Philadelphia speech, in which he departed from "quiet diplomacy" by publicly recommending a pause in the bombing of North Vietnam, the *Globe* commented: "It would now be easier to have some faith in Ottawa's quiet diplomacy if there had been some change for the better in the intervening period." In other words, quiet diplomacy was damned because Mr. Pearson's most famous departure from it failed to produce results, or at least the results that the *Globe* wanted! There may be some truth in the report that Mr. Johnson's irritation was due in large measure to the fact that he had already decided upon a pause in the bombing but refused to be put in the position of appearing to act at the behest of another government. Mr. Pearson's lapse from quiet diplomacy may thus have delayed the implementation of the very policy he recommended. Certainly all governments are resentful when foreign leaders appear to take the side of their domestic critics. A former senior member of the Department of External Affairs has written:

> On issues in which Canadian interests are remote, or indirect, or where we are taking no responsibility, as is the situation in Vietnam, public diplomacy may be the very worst tactics because it inevitably rouses the national ego on the other side. Back seat driving in diplomacy may have much the same effect as in motor driving – it arouses the emotions and makes for recklessness on the part of the driver. Canadians may derive emotional satisfaction by public or platform diplomacy – like the Pharisee they can thank God they are not as other nations are – but such tactics may well be counter-productive. I much suspect that all the public criticism of US policy outside the US has had the effect of solidifying support in the US for the Johnson policies.

The public hears about some Canadian diplomatic initiatives but has little conception of the number and intensity of our efforts to influence American decision-makers at all levels from desk officer to President. Even when Washington persists in policies that many Canadians consider misguided, it remains entirely possible that the Americans would have pursued these policies with greater vigour, or launched other misguided policies, but for Canadian representation. Until all the files are open, and perhaps not even then, quiet diplomacy cannot be branded a success or failure simply because American policies do, or do not, come up to the critic's standard of perfection.

The case for quiet diplomacy rests essentially on common sense, the testimony of experienced diplomats and knowledge concerning the normal behaviour of human beings. Not everyone will accept this as an adequate basis for judgment. It is especially unconvincing if one believes, with James Eayrs, that every diplomat places his conscience in cold storage when he reports for duty, and soon loses the capacity to recognize the truth. I can only offer several impressionistic generalizations acquired during six years as a junior diplomat and eight as a university teacher: there seems little to choose between the two professions in terms of intelligence; but the Canadian diplomat, in my experience, is less likely than the academic to be concerned about personal advancement, status, prestige or even matters of protocol; he is more concerned with substance and more likely to question the validity of his premises and the value of his contribution to the general good. I don't expect everyone to accept this appraisal, and the case for quiet diplomacy does not necessarily fall if it is rejected. I must say, however, that I am astonished by the arrogance of some of my academic colleagues who claim, on the basis of one-sided experience, superiority to the diplomat in both morality and the ability to discern the truth about the complex relations of men and nations.

Scepticism, moreover, works both ways. Whenever I become discouraged about the difficulties in the way of demonstrating the achievements of quiet diplomacy, I console myself with the thought of how much more difficult would be my task if I had to show how a policy of non-alignment and tub-thumping diplomacy would augment Canada's influence in world affairs. What unaligned country exerts significant influence upon the policies of the super-powers? Collectively, the unaligned nations are now enjoying a field-day in the United Nations; even if one takes seriously votes in the General Assembly, however, it is hard to believe that the addition of one further member to the ranks of the unaligned would make much difference. Undoubtedly the departure of Canada from the US-led alliance system would create a momentary sensation. It might be applauded in the press of some nations. Within a brief period, however, the influence of Canada, even with the neutral and communist countries, would almost certainly decline. The assumption that Canada is more influential in Washington than most other countries is one of our strongest diplomatic assets; we could not recoup the loss of this asset by seeking comparable influence in any other capital, or group of capitals.

Although few Canadians appear to favour neutralism, many demand a much more independent line within the Atlantic Alliance. It is difficult to conceive a less rewarding policy in terms of influence; we would not escape the stigma (if such it is) of membership in a military alliance but, by antagonizing the other members, we would lose the ability to influence their policies that alliance membership generally brings. De Gaulle, it is true, has had remarkable success in getting France onto the front pages of the world's newspapers and he has not been wrong on every issue; we should welcome, for example, his belated reconversion to the proposition that the western nations should seek to improve their relations with the Communist countries. On the other hand, France under de Gaulle could almost certainly have had a greater and more constructive influence over the mainstream of international affairs had she conducted herself as a better ally.

Even if one takes a more generous estimate of recent French influence, it does not follow that similar tactics by Canada would be productive. Our geographic location, at least during the present phase in weapons technology, does not give us anything like the nuisance value possessed by France. We invite ridicule when we try to augment our influence by threatening to be awkward.

From the point of view of maximizing influence where it counts, and also economic well-being, there is no doubt that quiet diplomacy has served Canada well. But these are not the only goals of foreign policy, nor even necessarily the most vital. How does quiet diplomacy contribute to the attainment of Canada's other goals?

The most serious political problem now confronting Canada is the threat to its survival as a federal state. Canada may need to solve its *internal* international problem before it can resume its most useful role in international affairs. We may need to save Canada before saving the world. Given the seriousness of the threat to national unity and the fact that our ability to help other peoples will diminish if Canada disintegrates, I would favor substantial changes in our foreign policy if I thought that this would strengthen our sense of national identity, pride and cohesion.

The relaxing of world tensions since the Cuban crisis of 1962, moreover, makes it easier to contemplate a reduction in Canada's moderating influence in world affairs. In spite of Vietnam, the Soviet and American governments continue to work for détente.

The situation in Asia, while ugly in the extreme, seems unlikely to embroil the world in nuclear war, and Canada is not considered to have as great a stake in Asia as in Europe. The shift in West Germany's Eastern policy is decidedly encouraging. Many hurdles remain and quiet Canadian diplomacy might be helpful in persuading reluctant allies that they should not allow national interests narrowly defined, or injured pride, to upset the reassuring trend towards a European settlement and a non-proliferation agreement. On the other hand, it can scarcely be contended that it is as important as it once was that Canada's leaders give first priority to the solution of global problems.

With relatively easy conscience, we should be able to give first priority among our foreign policy objectives to the strengthening of national unity, even though this might well mean the adoption of policies that do more to overcome Canadian complexes than the difficulties of the international community. But can foreign policy really contribute to this goal?

Canada received world-wide acclaim for its foreign policy at the time of the Suez crisis in 1956; this was the fruit of years of quiet diplomacy that had won the confidence of all the principal parties to the dispute.[4] The acclaim may have strengthened our pride in being Canadian and, indirectly, national unity, but the evidence is inconclusive. It certainly increased Canadian expectations and the pressure on the government for spectacular diplomacy. Ironically, the impact of the acclaim for Canada's Suez performance was to create a popular demand that made more difficult the maintenance of the tactics that had earned the acclaim. The increase in the clamour for diplomatic achievements that can be publicized coincided with a significant decline in the relative strength of Canada's diplomatic assets. The result of this rising demand and declining assets was a tendency, that has persisted, to substitute posture for policy.

The prospects for a repetition of the post-Suez acclaim, even if Canada again practises quiet diplomacy as skilfully, are not great. The world stage is more crowded. While a quiet Canadian contribution can still be useful, it is less likely to be noticed. And if our diplomatic efforts are not noticed by foreigners, Canadians are unlikely to conclude that they are worthwhile. Whatever it might do for the general good or the Canadian standard of living, quiet diplomacy does precious little for the national ego. Popular support for quiet diplomacy may require more maturity, and understanding of international relations, than most peoples possess.

On the other hand, raucous diplomacy, by diminishing influence, is likely to be self-defeating even from the point of view of promoting national pride and unity.

Canadian unity would certainly be strengthened if Canadians could be convinced that their country is something more than a pale carbon copy of its more powerful neighbour. The demand for policies that demonstrate both Canada's independence, and its uniqueness, is difficult to satisfy, however, without abandoning quiet diplomacy – something responsible Canadian politicians and diplomats are reluctant to do because they appreciate the probable costs in influence as well as economic well-being. Satisfying the demand might even require them to subscribe publicly to opinions about American policies that they do not in fact hold. Too often it is assumed that if Ottawa takes a stand similar to Washington's, this can only be the result of dictation, or at least of an attempt to curry favour. In fact, Canadian and American experts see many situations in much the same light because they have access to much the same information and, as North Americans, they are much the same kind of people. In many respects, moreover, the interests of the two countries are virtually identical.

Semi-informed Canadians tend to take for granted that their misgivings about the American presence in Vietnam are fully shared in private by the Canadian government. There is little basis for this assumption. On the contrary, there is reason to take seriously the many official Canadian declarations of general sympathy for American aims in that troubled land. Douglas Fisher and Harry Crowe reported recently that they have been often told in conversation with External Affairs officials that:

> There is something close to unanimity among all External Affairs men who have been stationed in Southeast Asia in the past decade. They're all for the Americans in Vietnam and the role they are trying to carry out.

In short, among the Canadians who know the situation best, sympathy for the American position is the greatest. Fisher and Crowe were on shaky ground, however, in attributing the generally pro-American attitude of External Affairs officers almost solely to a materialistic concern to promote the economic well-being of Canada.[5] Certainly the Canadian officials who serve on the International Control Commission in Vietnam consider it their duty to report objectively; while ICC reports have been critical of both sides, the Canadian assessment, as expressed in the controversial

38

majority report of 1962, is that the original transgression was Communist, and that the principal blame for the continuation of the fighting lies in Hanoi. Canadian officials primarily concerned with Far Eastern affairs may, at times, be critical of American tactics; they may feel, as I do, that the bombing of the North is counter-productive, or even that the Americans showed bad judgement in becoming so heavily involved in Vietnam. I should be astonished, however, to learn that they considered the Americans censurable on moral grounds, or wanted them to disengage before a new settlement has been negotiated that is consistent with American commitments to the South Vietnamese. Mr. Paul Martin, it is true, has recently become more guarded in his expressions of sympathy for American policy in Vietnam.[6] This probably reflects a genuine difference of opinion with Washington about the wisdom of the bombings in the North. Even more, I believe, it is the result of an ambitious politician's understandable tendency to respond to articulate domestic opinion, whether he agrees with it or not, especially in situations when he might otherwise appear subservient to Washington.

Not long ago I heard a prominent Member of Parliament explain that what we need to keep Canada viable is a good anti-American binge about every five years. Certainly, in seeking to cement national unity, policies that fan anti-American sentiment and apprehension about American dominance, would seem of obvious utility. Such policies, however, can easily turn out to be counter-productive. Messrs. Diefenbaker and Green experimented with a Gaullist *politique de grandeur* and went far to disrupt relations with Washington. I am not aware that the results accomplished very much for the unity of Canada, or even of the Conservative Party. Similar policies, conducted with skill, might conceivably be more rewarding, but it is unsafe to assume that the Canadian masses are as susceptible to anti-Americanism as the Canadian intelligentsia.

A more promising approach is to adopt policies that point up the different characteristics and roles of Canada and the United States, without causing serious friction between Ottawa and Washington. We are already pursuing such a policy in our support for United Nations peace-keeping. From the point of view of our identity complex, it would be comforting if we could count on a steady series of dramatic crises in which Canada's boys in green will be welcome. Unfortunately this is not the case; the expulsion of the UNEF from the Gaza Strip has raised grave doubts about the future of UN peace-keeping, and some experts predict that the likeliest demands for peace-keepers in the future will be such that many Canadians will be opposed to participation. It is also doubtful that Canada can accomplish much within the United Nations to establish peace-keeping on a more secure basis; our leadership during the misguided attempt to secure a legal solution to the financial difficulties, essentially a political problem, has rendered our activity suspect to France, the Soviet Union and the other members who share their views. This is not to suggest that Canada should abandon its enthusiastic support for peace-keeping. Rather it is to caution that the role may not be as satisfying to Canadians in the future.

Canada should nevertheless proceed quickly with the unification of its armed forces. This will improve their efficiency for peace-keeping without destroying their usefulness within Nato. Even if the fighting effectiveness of the forces is reduced (an unlikely development), the experiment will not have been wasted. Because Canada's forces are not crucial to western defences, our allies are pleased that we are doing the pioneering. If unification is a success, other nations are likely to flatter us by following. Succeed or fail, the fact that we are attempting something that is forward looking, and has not been achieved elsewhere, should do wonders for our identity complex.

Such measures, while useful, are unlikely to satisfy fully the clamour for demonstrations that Canada is independent of, and different to, the Great Republic. This demand will be difficult to meet without creating friction with Washington. Indeed, unless there is a great deal of noisy friction, the skeptics will not be convinced that Canada is really exercising its independence.

Satisfying the demand for a posture of greater independence in Canada's foreign policy would thus almost certainly mean a reduction in Canada's influence in world affairs. The price might well be worth paying, I have suggested, if it were to make a significant contribution to the preservation of Canadian unity. This, however, is at best uncertain. Indeed, for most countries, most of the time, foreign relations bring more frustration than gratification, and we would be unwise to count on spectacular success in world diplomacy to bolster domestic unity.

We would be even more foolish to abandon a foreign policy that has been generally helpful, and admired by foreign experts, for a new policy that might well prove to be counter-productive, even in helping Canadian intellectuals to overcome their inferiority complex. The case for quiet diplomacy may not be as compelling as it was during the cold war. I don't believe that it is. On the other hand, the case for a tub-thumping, moralistic approach – one that puts more emphasis on the appearance of rectitude and independence than the reality of quiet influence – has not as yet been established. I doubt if it can be unless we adopt the escapist premise that the over-riding purpose of foreign policy is to be ostentatiously on the side of virtue, regardless of practical consequences. Is the world sufficiently secure for such luxuries?

A. F. W. Plumptre,
A. E. Safarian,
Pauline Jewett,
Abraham Rotstein

RETALIATION: THE PRICE OF INDEPENDENCE?

A. F. W. Plumptre, a former senior civil servant, is at present Principal of Scarborough College. Mr. Plumptre taught for some time at the University of Toronto and has published Central Banking in the British Dominions.

A. E. Safarian is Professor of Economics at the University of Toronto. A former Head of the Department of Economics and Political Science at the University of Saskatchewan, Dr. Safarian has published two books, The Canadian Economy in the Great Depression *and* Foreign Ownership of Canadian Industry.

Pauline Jewett is Professor of Political Science and Director of the Institute of Canadian Studies at Carleton University. A former MP, Dr. Jewett was part-author of Canadian Economic Policy *and contributed an article to* Voting in Canada.

Abraham Rotstein is Assistant Professor of Political Economy at the University of Toronto. Former President of the University League for Social Reform and at present co-editor of Canadian Forum, *Dr. Rotstein has edited* The Prospect of Change: Proposals for Canada's Future *and (in collaboration with Karl Polanyi)* Dahomy and the Slave Trade.

That the Canadian-United States relationship is a unique one is a readily accepted notion. Identifying the principles which compose this relationship is not such an easy task. We are concerned here with the factors which may limit the policy-initiative of the Canadian government. The recent Mercantile Bank affair brought to the surface once again the fear that retaliation is a restraining influence on Canadian action. Is the reality of retaliation, in fact, an influence on Canadian policy-making? Is the fear of retaliation a constant cloud in the back of decision-makers' minds? If the answer to these two questions is Yes, then how does the threat influence the calculations of our senior officials? Is the consequence to restrict Canadian action or stifle it? The round-table participants below address themselves to these questions.

A. F. W. Plumptre: Tit for Tat

The basic difficulty in dealing with the question of retaliation may well lie only partly in the concept itself but equally in the closely related notion of "an independent foreign policy." The more "independent" (in some sense) our policy becomes, the more likely it is to provoke "retaliation."

I have spent much of the past twenty-five years in various official positions in Ottawa, Washington and Paris. Throughout that period I was trying to help formulate and execute something that could with justice be called an independent Canadian foreign policy. And yet I can only remember two or three occasions, in regard to rather specific issues, on which either the word or the concept of "retaliation" against Canada entered into consideration.

How did this come about? I and others like me, were we simply "innocents abroad"? I would like to think not. But I can only make myself understood by a further look at the concept of an "independent" foreign policy.

In the inter-war decades while Canadians worked for a policy that was in one sense "independent," we were, in another very important sense, working on behalf of Canada to create an international order in which no country would ever again have an "independent" foreign policy. The warnings of the past were all too apparent.

After the war, however, Canada as a nation played a role far beyond its size and its years in building the post-war structure of international collaboration and cooperation – in building the UN itself, in building its various specialized agencies and in building a host of other international bodies, formal and informal. All these were designed to prevent a recurrence of the dangerous, dog-eat-dog type of national independence as well as to dispel illusions of peaceful independence that always went with neutralism and isolationism. All were designed, some no doubt better than others, to allow national aspirations to work themselves out, but within an internationally agreed to framework.

Does this mean that Canada has bound herself in with a series of international institutions and international agreements in which someone else, great or small, has more influence than we have? Facing the facts frankly, the answer to this question must be Yes. We Canadians have worked, along with others and with no little success, towards an explicitly interdependent world where national authority is exercised within a framework of codified international arrangements and agreements.

A framework of international agreements and arrangements, formal and informal, today provides the foundation of the foreign policy of every country, including Canada. Further, every country has its own representatives abroad – not only its striped-pants team but in many cases its cloak-and-dagger team and always its unofficial representatives in the form of press men, business men, financiers, tourists and many others all of whom form part of the complex web of international relations.

Accordingly, most governments, and certainly a government as well-served as the Canadian, will always formulate its foreign policy in pretty full knowledge of what the effects of its policy, what the repercussions of its policy, will be abroad. It will indeed weigh the pros and cons of each action, and weigh them carefully. The repercussions of its actions abroad may be in Government circles; in business or financial circles. But I do not think we should generally use the word "retaliation" to describe such repercussions. They are simply part of the day to day assessments involved in judgement-forming and policy-making. In some ways the conduct of external affairs resembles a game of chess. Each move takes into account all previous moves by *both* players, and their possible future moves; but it is a mistake to describe any particular move as retaliation for the last one.

I suggest that the word retaliation is properly reserved for something different, a tit for tat that must be unpleasant for the recipients.

Put in this crude way, the danger of anything deserving the name retaliation is minimal. "Pressure," yes; "retaliation," no.

If Canada adopts a measure like the magazine tax that is clearly unwelcome in various quarters in the United States, we may be reasonably sure that certain identifiable forces will be set in motion against us. This possibility may well affect the outcome of a disagreement between ourselves and the Americans in GATT or in some other international arena; but the process is not well described as "retaliation." A country moves purposefully, yet somewhat cumbersomely, towards its objectives. It is neither within its power nor its purpose, in most cases, to "punish" or to "slap back at" other countries that get in its way. Retaliation is a game that Latin American dictatorships might play with each other; but it is not really a game for grown-up countries.

At the same time, I suspect that bilateral aid (i.e. direct country-to-country aid that does not go through some institution such as the World Bank) is the field where the notion of retaliation comes closest to finding a fit. This is precisely because such bilateral aid is not, at least as yet, provided under the protective coverings of an international agreement. Since there is no such cover the arrangement is wide open to charges such as retaliation. For example, the Ceylonese government nationalizes certain US oil interests and the flow of US aid to Ceylon is immediately cut off, at least for the time being. It is, perhaps, reasonable to describe this as retaliation. Nevertheless, it is important to recognize that the US agency that actually takes the action will probably not do so because of its sense of outrage or antipathy towards Ceylon but only in order to ensure that the total amount of aid voted by Congress in the future, including aid for Ceylon, will not be jeopardized by this particular Ceylonese action.

Canadians, particularly Canadians of the post-war generation, may need to be reminded how extremely careful the Canadian Government was throughout World War II to keep off the list of countries that received US aid – a list that in the end included all or virtually all of the other allies of the United States.

However, our independence of the American aid programme does not render us impervious to the results of other American actions; far from it. And in this regard we must remember that the US government can hurt Canada unintentionally as well as intentionally – like the big pig that just rolls over onto the little piglets. For the piglet, life, liberty and the pursuit of happiness can only be bought at the price of eternal vigilance.

Returning to our example of the magazine tax, we were really less exposed to the danger of damage through American action under the complicated and cumbersome legal procedures of GATT than under the day-to-day disposition of routine business in Washington. There can hardly be a day, and never a week, in Washington when some US official is not taking action to ensure that some Canadian interests under this treaty, or that agreement, or some non-recorded but gentlemanly understanding, are being protected. In Washington, as indeed in Ottawa and every capital, the erosive rats are always nibbling away. However, there are always borderline cases, matters for judgment. And in those cases the judgment may be affected by whether the wind is, at the moment, blowing in favour of Canada or in the opposite direction.

I do not remember whether, at the particular moment when we announced our magazine tax, there were on their way through Congress any bills that were designed to give new support to US interests at the expense of Canadian – for example whether our lead and zinc exports, or our exports of motor-car parts, or any other of the Canadian exports that are under perennial attack in Congress were under attack then. If so, one can guess that the bill, whatever it was, got a little farther along the Congressional path before it was killed than it otherwise would have done. Perhaps it even got as far as President Eisenhower's desk for his signature or his veto. One can see him reaching for the red pen to record a veto. At that very moment Henry Luce of *Time* calls to alert him to the new infamy that is abroad in Canada. So he puts back the pen, telling his aide that this one will have to have some more thought. Then he ruminates on the state of his political situation wondering whether he can afford to continue to protect Canadian interests if Louis St. Laurent is going to stab him in the most sensitive section of his press. Very human. But is he pondering "retaliation"? Again, the word does not fit either the facts or the feeling of the situation.

If we did decide to call it "retaliation," we would have to recall that we are really in as good a position to retaliate against the United States as they are against us. Not only do their exports to us far exceed our exports to them, but we have all those lovely investments of theirs to stick pins into – publishing houses, oil companies and many, many others. Just as in Washington there is a long queue of people lined up to get something for themselves at the expense of Canadians, so there is a similar line-up in Ottawa of Canadians who would like to get something at the expense of Americans.

And yet, even this is the wrong way to look at the matter. It is true that there are erosive rats at work all the time in each capital to undermine our international agreements. But these are entered into because, on balance, each agreement in each country helps more than it hurts. In the long run, the successful erosion of treaties by the rats in Ottawa would hurt Canadians as much as Americans. Similarly, erosion in Washington would hurt Americans as much as Canadians. This is why each country supports each agreement.

So, after all, when he picks up his red pen again and vetoes the anti-Canadian bill before him, President Eisenhower is acting for the US interests involved and not for the Canadian interests. And if that is so, what has become of the last vestiges of the concept of "retaliation"?

A. E. Safarian: The Web of Repercussions

A few months ago I asked a senior American diplomat who has had a lot to do with Canada whether retaliation was involved in a particular action that the United States had taken. He replied that diplomats did not use such coarse words or think in such simplistic terms as "tit for tat" in Canadian-American relations. Later, however, he admitted, that occasionally the USA had "reacted" to a Canadian initiative.

It seems to me that, while very effectively destroying the simplistic theory of retaliation, Mr. Plumptre has gone on to build a much more dynamic model of the complex relationships between the two countries which would urge even more vigilance in our dealings with the United States. It suggests a degree of extended involvement across the board that is much *more sensitive*, and in certain circumstances could be much more damaging, than too simple a concept of retaliation would imply.

One point which needs to be emphasized is that possibly the old-fashioned, simple kind of retaliation has not entered too often into Canadian-American relations in the last couple of decades because on most of the major issues of policy we have gone along with the United States, largely because we found these policies to be in our interests as well. I refer here to the international organizations, economic and otherwise, which were established just after the war and to such things as broad military policy and trade policy. We have opted too for a certain kind of orderly rules-regulated world in the past two or three decades, and it is because of this and because we have found ourselves on parallel courses that the concept of retaliation as such has arisen only on relatively few occasions. One wonders what would happen if Canada opted for policies which were radically different from those which the United States favoured on the world scene; policies which affected not merely such mundane matters as trade but international relations in general, and which were followed by a full re-orientation of economic and other ties. I am not suggesting that we take such an initiative but simply suggesting why direct and explicit retaliation has been relatively rare in dealings between the two countries in the past couple of decades.

But beyond the simple model of retaliation there is the possibility that what we do or do not do in one area of policy may have an effect on a totally different and ostensibly unrelated area of policy. Eventually you have a complete web of inter-relationships with numerous tensions and the possibility of explosion or pressure or repercussions. These inter-relations suggest certain thoughts about policy-making in this area. It seems to me that this extensive web presents certain *costs* and also presents certain *opportunities*, and that the wise policy-makers must find ways of reducing the costs and maximizing the opportunities. The costs, of course, are those which come with interdependence, for you give up the freedom to undertake certain kinds of manoeuvre. On the other hand you secure certain kinds of opportunities which you can use, and there is some question in my mind whether Canada has been capitalizing fully on these.

In terms of the problems of interdependence, you do rely on other people to be as thoughtful and ethical as you yourself are. They must make the right kind of move as they consider or play the chess game, as they look at the moves and counter-moves, and they must have thought out the consequences of these moves fully before making them. Because we cannot take this for granted, this web of interdependence becomes very painful at certain points. Take the Interest Equalization Tax affair of the early 'sixties when the Americans were thoroughly exasperated with us for reasons which were sometimes deserved and sometimes not. It was in that context that, if not retaliation, at least an enormous degree of thoughtlessness must have occurred on this particular point. You must remember that the Americans had had a balance of payments problem for years before the July 1963 Interest Equalization Tax was announced. There may have been somewhat enlarged capital flows to Canada than in the previous year but the gold outflow from the United States and the pressure in her balance of payments, had gone on for years. You must also remember that the American authorities had been talking in general terms about the possibility of restraining capital outflows for at least two years prior to that. One must ask why they decided to use this particular technique of control of capital outflows at this particular time, July 1963, *knowing full well* what the implications for Canada would be. I am afraid I cannot accept the suggestion that they did not know how seriously this would affect Canada. We have had to finance a very substantial current deficit by capital inflows in every year (bar one) since 1950. If the capital inflow is cut off suddenly all sorts of trouble follows at once in the exchange market and in the money market generally until we find an equivalent amount of foreign exchange. There are ways of doing that, though most are painful (particularly to the Americans!) if required suddenly. Moreover, the major consequences of the American tax would be felt most immediately in just two countries, Canada and Japan; so that it seems to me that no great amount of expertise was required to anticipate what the immediate effects would be. It may have been colossal thoughtlessness or incompetence and not outright retaliation, but it was done in a context in which we had set a precedent by interfering with the flow of capital through Mr. Gordon's June 1963 budget. The Americans may well have felt this freed them to experiment with controls on the flow of capital too.

Consider also the implications of the great disparity of strength between the two nations. The big pig may not be thinking of doing damage but if he rolls over on the piglet – that's it. In this kind of situation we must be not only eternally vigilant, on all fronts, but we should also be extremely competent on all fronts and I would say that we must be even more competent than the Americans a good proportion of the time in areas which concern us greatly. I am not sure that at the senior level of the federal government the quality of our officials has kept pace with the demands of this increasingly more complex and interdependent world. It used to be at one time that Canadians really had the confidence, on quite objective grounds, to handle the big international tasks. Quite a few of them do not now appear to have that confidence among our politicians and in the senior levels of the civil service. I cannot explain this, though I think perhaps the Diefenbaker years had something to do with it, along with minority government and the relative strength of the provinces. Perhaps we are not drawing on the full range of Canadian talents for the senior levels of our most important positions. In several major areas of economic policy on the domestic and international fronts, for example, we have not done as well in the past decade as we can or ought to.

There are also opportunities to be found in this web which we are learning to exploit and that we have got to learn much more about. Sometimes they arise in the most peculiar way. One of the things that has always puzzled me is how we ever got the Automobile Pact through. When you look at that deal (and not whether Canada should have made it, which is another question) it is remarkable that we ever got the Americans to agree to it. It is not every day you can go down there and get them to present you with two or three per cent of their market. It may be that the Americans simply did not want to get involved in a trade war with Canada. If that is true, then we have an awful lot more bargaining power down there than I ever thought we had. That may be part of it. There is also a story going around that the President of the United States was far happier about the deal with Canada after we agreed, independently of these negotiations, to send our troops to keep the peace in Cyprus. That may be an apocryphal story. Moreover, I would not want for a moment to suggest that the Canadian authorities would or should tie their peacekeeping efforts with the UN or otherwise to a specific problem with the United States. We do not operate that way. But I am quite sure that, within this large web, some kinds of trade-off might work towards more than one of our objectives. Here, in brief, countermoves, pressures, and possibly on occasion if not retaliation, a hint of retaliation, might make this system work more to our advantage.

The retaliation of "tit for tat" may be too simple for today's world but the web of interdependence and all it implies is the basic reality overshadowing the bargaining of complex relations at all the levels between Canadian and American governments.

Pauline Jewett: The Menace is the Message

It has been suggested by Mr. Plumptre that the term "retaliation" means something outside the law, a lawless act. If this *is* its meaning, then I should not be using the word. But I think the term "retaliation" should and does apply to lawful situations, to acts that are well within the law. Certainly this is how it is understood in political circles. I cannot, of course, speak for all political circles, but I do recall very well the use of the word "retaliation" on many occasions, within my own party and in Parliament, while

I was a Liberal MP. It was used chiefly in the context of Canadian-American relations when the fear was expressed that the US would "retaliate" against Canada, through some specific act or policy (quite legal), should Canada pursue a certain course of action.

I could give several concrete examples of this but the most vivid in my memory concerns the magazine legislation of 1964 which excluded Canadian advertisements in American journals from tax exemption and so gave Canadian journals protection. The Liberal caucus was generally in favour of this legislation and also in favour of having it include *Time* and *Reader's Digest*. There was only one individual strongly opposed to the latter and he had *Reader's Digest* – a large employer – in his riding! The cabinet, I gather, was a bit more split, being closer no doubt to political reality. The "political reality" in this instance was, quite simply, fear of American retaliation. Members of caucus had it explained to them by members of cabinet that, should the government go ahead and include *Time* and *Reader's Digest*, Washington (in response, no doubt, to domestic pressures) would "retaliate" against us. A tentative agreement on some particular matter (automobiles perhaps?) would not go through. Or the President would cease supporting us vis-à-vis Congress with respect to some proposed Congressional act.

Maybe we politicians are just naïve. After all, we are not in the State Department or External where people "know" that these things are not going to happen. But I can only say that the fear was there and that past experience had shown that it was justified. Professor Safarian notes that there have been few occasions when we suffered the act of retaliation. But there have been a sufficient number of times when we feared its possibility that the threat of retaliation has conditioned governmental attitudes into general timidity.

What concerns one most about all this is the mesmerizing effect it has on Canadian policy-makers. Instead of doing things that they think are desirable or that the Canadian public may want done, our policy-makers do things that the American public or the American government or powerful American pressure-groups want. Not always, of course. Not on bread-and-butter issues like selling wheat to China. But on broader matter of foreign policy like *recognizing* China or the war in Vietnam, our governments waffle. They do not take the positions that either their own judgment or, in many instances, Canadian public opinion demands.

Canadian politicians frequently *do* have views substantially different from those of their American counterparts. I could not help noticing this when I was a member of the Canada-US Interparliamentary Group. The Canadian MPs and the Senators taking part in the discussions found themselves — regardless of party — in substantial agreement on a number of subjects — the cold war, China, Nato, Cuba, and so on — and in substantial disagreement with the American Congressmen and Senators taking part, Democrats and Republicans (barring Wayne Morse). Both sides noticed this difference in attitudes. Similarly, Canadian public opinion is frequently at odds with American. One can look at the polls, for example, on China or, more recently, on Vietnam, and compare. Or one can look at the different attitudes taken by the churches in the two countries on these and other matters.

I despair of our ever transcending our caution. We *do* have a different view about a variety of matters but because of our fears (and our chief fear nowadays is the fear of American retaliation), we rarely take positions reflecting our own judgment or responding to public opinion in our own country. Our caution does a great disservice not only to ourselves internally but, most serious of all, to an independent, creative contribution to world problems.

Abraham Rotstein: Retaliation and Independence

To confront the question of retaliation head-on, I would accept a great deal of what Mr. Plumptre has said about the chessboard analogy but I am not sure how he reconciles this with the type of world he describes, which reminds me of the sweet reasonableness of the League of Nations in the 1930's. To go on to the question before us: Is retaliation a face of life on the international scene or not? I think there can be no doubt. The American presence in South Vietnam and the bombing of North Vietnam is a response, so the Americans claim, to the invasion from the North. As such it is retaliation while being at the same time a defence of their own interests. The fear of retaliation in turn by China is very strong. To take a less dramatic instance, we in Canada decided to bring the Duke of Edinburgth to our 1967 celebrations at Vimy without consulting the French, and so de Gaulle responded by not sending an official French representative. There are countless other instances. I think there is no doubt that among the facts of life on the international scene, retaliation is one of the most consistent and pervasive.

At the same time we must also take seriously the fact that retaliation has not been a feature of Canadian-American relations. This hardly allows us to conclude, however, that it will necessarily be ruled out in the future. We have enough instances of the Americans using retaliatory devices in their relations with other countries to know that it is a common instrument of US policy. Their external aid to Egypt moves up or down every six months depending on the political climate; trade concessions to the Communist bloc are alternatively granted and withdrawn. American economic relations with Poland and Yugoslavia over the years are clear examples of the use of policy to reward or punish other nations for their behaviour. These techniques are used effectively by the Americans to secure their own interests and justifiably so.

In their relations with Canada, the point is simply that that part of the chess-board has not been brought into play. Together, we operate on a narrower area of the board. Canada does not do things which might provoke retaliation. The Americans in turn are very leery of engaging in any actions which would set the retaliatory process in motion. Those powerful chessmen on the board have not been brought into play and perhaps will not be used in the future if the old patterns persist. The levels of independent initiative and risk that have been taken by Canadian policy-makers in the past have not been high, and, therefore, a series of retaliatory steps has not been necessary. I suppose that the pattern is governed by what Professor Fred Watkins at McGill used to call "the law of anticipated reactions": a policy is decided in terms of expected responses from those it will affect.

But if Canadians become restless with the old pattern of docile (or voluntary) compliance with American foreign policy, we cannot assume that retaliation may not become an important factor in our future relations. The question which I personally find interesting is this: What are the prerequisites given this relatively benign situation in which we find ourselves for carrying on an independent Canadian foreign policy? The kind of independent policy I have in mind may not be very different from what Escott Reid has called an "effective" policy. In order not to beg the question, however, I would ask: What conditions are necessary to permit us to take foreign policy initiatives which may have economic repercussions in our relations with the United States? The issues I have in mind, for example, are China and Vietnam.

I would like to suggest that there are three important requirements to make an independent Canadian foreign policy possible. The first is the development of support for such a policy among

Canadian public opinion. The present state of Canadian public opinion is, on the whole, uninformed, too fearful and reticent; this makes an independent policy difficult for domestic reasons. I regard as very promising, therefore the emergence of such groups as the United Church in an active role in foreign policy pronouncements. I think there should be other groups: university professors, trade unionists, women's groups, etc. I think public opinion should be conceived (potentially) as a network of such groups rather than what we sometimes think of – a collection of well-read individuals.

In this regard it is important to pay more attention to the use of media in the formation of public opinion formations. I found, for example, that an unusual feature of present-day life in Ottawa, is the role played by Executive-Assistants to Ministers who are not bound, as I understand it, by the oath of secrecy. They are the ones, therefore, who can originate leaks to the press and thus create some public interest and support for a certain policy. Press leaks have also been used in Canadian-American relations such as the Mercantile Bank case. If there is a deliberate press leak, public opinion may become aroused, and if I were sitting at a desk in the US State Department, I would take this to mean that here is an issue on which the Canadian government is going to take an independent line and is not going to back down. I would suggest that if we want an independent foreign policy, some of these *ad hoc* and informal techniques should be looked at closely. An articulate and informed Canadian public, aware of the issues, is the first important prerequisite to an independent foreign policy. Any Canadian government which set out on an independent course and got into continuous trouble with the United States, would not last long. The Canadian public in its present condition would not tolerate such a policy.

The second prerequisite is to survey in advance the possible countermoves that may be made by the United States and to have prepared policy-positions on which to fall back. The most serious critique I have with regard to our relations with the United States, is that these relations are presently viewed as an "all or nothing" game. I mean, in effect, that the web of relationships is very wide and should the web be damaged by some retaliatory move from the United States we are utterly unprepared to deal with the consequences. We have no clear idea where we are most vulnerable nor what we would do in the event of any specific act of retaliation. I find it incredible, for example, that when the US guidelines policy was instituted in 1965 (which had nothing to do with retaliation), the Canadian government was utterly unprepared to cope with the situation. There were no prepared positions, and it came like a bolt from the blue creating general panic and confusion. A second requirement for independence, therefore, is a far more sophisticated approach to research, policy-planning and prepared positions on every important issue where the chessmen may be brought into play. We may then discover that this is not an "all or nothing" game, but that there are limited risks, that we can assess potential costs, and that we know how we will act in particular contingencies. It should not be difficult to estimate the cost of retaliation on oil concessions, the lumber agreement, the automobile agreement, etc. We would then know what we may be in for and should examine the kind and the cost of the alternatives open to us.

The third requirement is for a more sophisticated view of American public opinion itself. If we realized, as so few of us do in Canada, the many different levels of foreign policy formation in the United States, we might deal with the Congress or the Senate in our own interests, and also with other relevant groups in the policy-formation process in order to back up any moves we might make toward an independent foreign policy. I am advocating a skilful and enlarged use of diplomacy on many levels to back up genuine moves to independent positions.

I should mention one assumption in the above remarks. There is no merit in ruffling the feathers of the eagle for its own sake. Nothing that I have said here implies such gratuitous activity. I am simply talking about a greater degree of elbow-room in the world for Canada, about a much wider horizon toward which we would be able to move. My plea is for a solid appreciation of the fact that there would be costs, of precisely what these costs would amount to and how we could cope with the consequences. If politics is the art of the possible, it remains to extend our view of the possible.

Denis Stairs

CONFRONTING
UNCLE
SAM:
CUBA
AND
KOREA

Denis Stairs is Assistant Professor of Political Science at Dalhousie University. Rhodes Scholar and graduate of Oxford, he is at present doing research on Canada's role in Korea.

Whatever one thinks of the content and execution of Canadian foreign policy, one must grant at least that it adds a little vigour to an otherwise vapid political community. Canadians in general are renowned for the flaccid indifference with which they conduct their political affairs; but raise before them the issue of their relations abroad and they at once assume the guise of warriors in combat. The battle rages with special fury when the influence of Washington over policy-makers in Ottawa is the subject in dispute, and to enter the fray at such a point is therefore to risk the most grievous slings and arrows. The venture is justified, however, by the importance of the issue, for it is a pivotal determinant of Canada's freedom-to-choose in international affairs.

The quarrel actually involves not one question but several. When you ask whether Canada should adopt in a specific case a policy opposed by Washington, the first thing you need to know is whether it will be effective in achieving some or all of its objectives in spite of American hostility. If the answer is No, then the policy presumably must be shelved; but if the answer is Yes, then a second and third question follow: (2) What sacrifices – including sacrifices induced by the disapproval or even in extreme cases the retaliatory action of the United States – will the policy require on the part of Canada? and (3) Do you place a higher value on the objectives you expect to achieve than on the sacrifices your policy will incur? The answers obviously will vary considerably from one case to the next, and the last of the questions is essentially normative in character. The first two are empirical, however, and require judgments about the future consequences of your policy. The accuracy of these judgments will depend upon your understanding of the implications of the international relationships concerned, and this in turn will derive very largely from your knowledge of what happened in previous cases of a similar kind.

Here, then, is the rationale for the case-study approach adopted in this paper. It is true of course that history can be a mischievous teacher and that the precise circumstances of past cases may not be duplicated in the present or future. It is true also that a full and systematic treatment would require the testing of a large number of possible conditions and reference to many more cases than two. Even the two slight cases that follow, however, may cast a little light on the subject and at least draw attention to some of the difficulties it presents. Both have been drawn from the post-1945 period, and they have been selected as tests of the limits of Canada's independence abroad, precisely because in each instance Canadian policy was in diametric conflict with the interests of the United States.

Case I – Canada, the United States and Cuba

In brief outline, the facts are these. Following Fidel Castro's seizure of power in January 1959 the United States imposed a steadily increasing series of restrictions on Cuban-American trade – restrictions which were ostensibly in retaliation for Havana's seizure of American-owned properties in Cuba, but which were given added legitimacy in the United States by the growing conviction that Dr. Castro was guilty of cavorting with "communism." By mid-October 1960 the Washington authorities had declared an embargo on the shipment to Cuba of all commodities except non-subsidized foodstuffs and medical supplies.

Havana responded by nationalizing a large number of American-owned companies, by extending and broadening its formal diplomatic relations with the Soviet bloc, and by concluding important agreements for the sale of sugar to the Soviet Union. Official diplomatic relations were finally terminated by President Eisenhower on January 3, 1961. In the following March President Kennedy reduced the quota for Cuban sugar imports to zero and the rupture in Cuban-American relations was complete.

Since then the relationship has been the source of a number of dangerously volatile international crises. The high points have included the attempted Bay of Pigs invasion in April 1961, the subsequent negotiations for the release of the captured invaders, the expulsion of Cuba in January 1962 from the Organization of American States (OAS), President Kennedy's extension of economic sanctions in February of the same year to include a boycott of all Cuban imports, the Cuban missile crisis of the following autumn, and finally the release in December 1962 of the Bay of Pigs invaders in return for $54 million in drugs, medicines and baby foods. To this day each side accuses the other of fostering sinister and subversive activities in Latin America at large, and there is no immediate prospect of an attempted *rapprochement*.

Under ordinary circumstances Washington's quarrel with Havana might have had little to do with Canada. The situation was complicated, however, by the fact that the Americans had resorted to economic sanctions as a statecraft technique in the pursuit of their Cuban policy. It is an elementary axiom of international affairs that economic sanctions are effective only to the extent that their application is widely endorsed by the international community. If the Americans were to succeed in intervening Cuba's foreign transactions entirely and not merely divert them to other countries, they had to win the co-operation of other actual or potential participants in Cuban trade. The result was that the US Government exerted considerable pressure on its allies to join in the economic isolation of Dr. Castro's regime.

For a number of reasons the pressure on Canada was particularly intense. Perhaps the most important was the similarity between the Canadian and American economies, for no other country could replace so effectively the United States as Cuba's chief supplier of manufactured goods. The American policy was designed to weaken the foundations of the Castro regime by undermining the efficiency of the Cuban economy. It could reasonably be expected, for example, that as Cuba's cars, trucks and buses broke down and replacement parts became more difficult to obtain, the Cuban people would suffer some irritating inconveniences. Public transportation systems would cease to function effectively, taxis would begin to disappear, private cars would have to be junked and distribution problems would multiply. In time the Cuban citizenry would become disillusioned with Premier Castro's government, and with luck it would come tumbling down. But clearly this could happen only if no other country replaced the United States as a source (in this instance) of automotive machinery and parts. Of all the possible alternative suppliers Canada was the most threatening because Canadian automotive products were in most cases identical with those manufactured in the United States. A Havana taxi that had been imported from Miami could be repaired or replaced by products obtained from Oshawa and Windsor. If this were to happen on a large scale, the net effect of the American embargo would be the enrichment of Canadian industry.

There was an additional danger that commodities produced in the United States would be exported first to Canada and then reshipped to the Caribbean. Our famous 4,000 miles of "undefended border" would be transformed into a vast gap in the power of the United States to employ economic sanctions against an "enemy" state. The problem was particularly acute in this instance because scrutiny of the movement of goods between Canada and the US is much more relaxed than in the case of either country's trade with other powers.

The Americans could argue also that even if Ottawa did not believe economic sanctions would weaken Premier Castro domestically, it must certainly agree that they would diminish his impact abroad. Cuba, the Americans maintained, was exporting revolution to Latin America. The Castro regime was therefore a threat to the entire hemisphere since it endangered the "western" diplomatic orientation of the Latin American Republics. Trading with Havana could only fortify the Cubans in the pursuit of their revolutionary task, and surely this was an eventuality that Canada was as eager to avoid as the United States.

For observers who are not privy to the documents of the Department of External Affairs it is difficult to determine precisely how severe the American pressure actually was. There can be no doubt, however, that it was considerable. The Canadian Press reported on December 11, 1960, for example, that Bradley Fisk, the American Assistant Secretary of Commerce for International

Affairs, had revealed that Secretary of State Christian Herter had tried in vain to obtain Canadian participation in the October embargo against the Cuban regime. "We will keep working on it," Fisk said. "We will respect Canada's sovereignty in every way, but we will keep reminding Canada of our mutual interests in the fight against communism."[1]

The pressure continued under the Kennedy administration. In February 1962, for example, Secretary of State Dean Rusk indicated that he hoped Canada and other nations would follow the OAS in isolating Havana from the Western Hemisphere. "Dollars and foreign exchange are being used by the Castro Government," he said, "to promote subversion in other countries."[2] In the following March Senator Wayne Morse accused the Canadian government of refusing "to co-operate . . . in stopping her trade in strategic goods with Communist Cuba," and Senator Kenneth Keating commented that is was impossible to understand why a country "willing to supply troops for the defence of freedom should not be willing to make economic sacrifices for the same objective."[3] American newspapers were equally critical and Cuban refugees were infuriated. On January 15, 1961, 175 Cubans demonstrated at the Canadian Embassy in Washington against the trade policy of the Diefenbaker Government. In what must have been a refreshing treat for normally neglected Canadian diplomatists they chanted, "Down with Canada," and displayed placards reading, "Free Cuba protests Canada's Aid to Castro."[4] On another occasion a leader of the exiles, José Miro Cardona, complained that the Canadians were "the Phoenicians of America. Their ships and their cargoes go where there is business to be done."[5]

In essence Cardona was right. In spite of American pressures to the contrary, the Canadian government has maintained "normal" trading relations with the Cuban Republic, qualified only by regulations designed to prevent the trans-shipment of American goods to Cuban buyers over Canadian soil and by prohibitions on the sale to Havana of certain commodities having an accepted strategic significance. As early as November 22, 1960 – about one month after the application of the American embargo – the Canadian Minister of Trade and Commerce, George Hees, told the House of Commons that "Canada's trade and trading relations with Cuba are completely normal [except for] the regular restrictions that are placed on strategic materials going to any country."[6] Three weeks later Prime Minister Diefenbaker issued a somewhat longer statement in which he said in effect that Cuba was not being treated as a special case. The government wanted "to maintain the kind of relations with Cuba which are usual with the recognized government of another country," although it would not encourage "the bootlegging of goods of United States origin." It hoped "that in so far as mutually beneficial economic relations are maintained or developed, conditions in Cuba may be eased and the general relations of western countries with Cuba may be promoted."[7]

Here was a fundamental divergence of views. The American position was that the Castro government was beyond redemption and therefore had to be eliminated. Economic sanctions comprised one of the weapons in the US arsenal and moral as well as political and strategic considerations required that it be used. By contrast the Canadian view was that Premier Castro was probably in power to stay and that in any event the most constructive policy would be to maintain friendly relations with the revolutionary government. Nothing could be solved by alienating the Cubans entirely; indeed it was probable that harsh treatment would serve only to drive them even more deeply into the communist camp.

On the other hand the Government refrained from giving Canadian businessmen any special encouragement to engage in Cuban trade. As Mr. Diefenbaker said, they would "have to make their own judgments on the prospects for advantageous transactions." Nor would Ottawa allow this country to become an escape route for American interests wishing to circumvent the regulations of their own government. To that extent Canada's willingness to conduct its policies in opposition to those of the United States was ultimately limited. In the circumstances, however, these were the limitations of neutrality rather than of dependence. Had Ottawa sanctioned the subversion of American policy by allowing Canada to become a smugglers' alley, then even the most virulent critic would have had to admit the justice of any consequent American outcry. Nevertheless Canadian policy was in fundamental conflict with that of the United States and still is. Neither the 1962 missile crisis nor the succession of the Liberal government produced any change in the Canadian position.

Parenthetically it should be observed that the government's policy has not resulted, as many Americans have claimed, in the enrichment of the Canadian economy. It is true that in some years our exports to Cuba have substantially increased, but in 1960,

1962 and 1963 they averaged less than in the years before the revolution. Trade statistics for recent years show very considerable increments over the pre-revolutionary average, but these appear to be the result primarily of wheat-sale agreements with the Soviet bloc, and in any case average less than one-tenth of pre-1959 exports to Cuba by the United States. In all years, moreover, the pattern of trade has been balanced very heavily in Canada's favour, which means that Canadian dollars cannot be helping directly to finance the export of Dr. Castro's revolution. Indeed the lack of foreign exchange has been the main factor limiting the volume of Cuban purchases in Canada.

It is worth noting also that the purely diplomatic aspect of Canada's Cuban policy has similarly differed from the American. Ottawa, unlike Washington, has continued to maintain formal diplomatic relations with Havana, and the publicly available information indicates that communication between the two capitals has been friendly and useful. Canadian business interests in Cuba, for example, have been treated very differently from those owned by Americans. In particular on those occasions when Canadian assets have been nationalized by the Cuban government, the ensuing negotiations have been conducted in an atmosphere of accommodation and the Cuban authorities have granted full compensation in the form of hard American dollars.[8]

Ottawa's independent policy was effective to the extent that its immediate objective of maintaining amicable diplomatic and trading relations with Premier Castro's government was achieved. Whether it also advanced the longer-range purpose of reducing Havana's political and economic dependence upon the Soviet bloc is more doubtful, and certainly the Canadian position has done nothing to mitigate tensions between Cuba and the United States. There is no evidence that Canada's independent views resulted in any permanent damage to Canadian-American relations, although they may have contributed to the general animosity between the Kennedy and Diefenbaker administrations.

Case II – Canada, the United States and UNTCOK

The background for the second case is more remote and so will require more detail. After the end of the war with Japan, the United States and the Soviet Union divided the Korean peninsula for occupation purposes at the 38th parallel, with the Americans in control of the South and the Soviets in charge of the North. Originally it was planned that a united and independent Korea would be established "in due course," but as the cold war grew more bitter cooperation between the two occupation administrations proved impossible. This unfortunate development was embarrassing for the American government, partly because it was under pressure by the South Koreans to make good the wartime promise of genuine independence, and partly because it wanted to withdraw its troops from what had become an expensive and vulnerable theatre. In September 1947, therefore, the Americans took the matter before the United Nations. There, in spite of Soviet opposition, they succeeded in having the General Assembly pass a resolution creating a UN Temporary Commission on Korea (UNTCOK) which would supervise an election throughout the peninsula. The elected candidates would then form an administration and take over the governmental functions of both occupation authorities. Korea would thus become united and independent, the Department of State would be relieved of a distressing political dilemma and the American army could happily withdraw its troops without leaving an inviting vacuum of power in their wake.

What was significant from the Canadian point of view was that the United States without prior consultation had included Canada among its nominations for UNTCOK membership. The principal historian of the Commission has suggested not only that the Canadians were startled and surprised when the American list of nominations was read out to the Assembly but also that their decision to accept it was governed by a desire "to save the United States from embarrassment."[9] This may or may not be true. What is certain is that the Americans made the nomination because they felt that Canadian membership would strengthen their hand. Indeed almost all the Commission members appear to have been selected with this purpose in mind. Most were closely tied with the United States, and those that were not were firmly committed to the principle of national self-determination and could be expected to support proposals for a united and independent Korea.

But if the Americans really thought UNTCOK would give them little trouble, they were shortly to suffer a rude surprise. The Commission assembled at Seoul in January 1948 only to discover that the Soviets would not allow it to function north of the 38th parallel. In the light of this development the American Commander suggested on behalf of his government that the necessary elections should take place in South Korea alone. It was at this point that conflict appeared for, while the US position was supported by

China, France and the Philippines, it was opposed by Canada, Australia, India and Syria (El Salvador remaining neutral). These four powers insisted that the Commission consult with the Interim Committee of the UN General Assembly in New York before making a decision, clearly expecting that the Committee would advise them not to proceed unless they could operate in both occupation zones.

At the Interim Committee Philip C. Jessup of the United States argued that UNTCOK should be advised "to implement its programme . . . in such parts of Korea as are accessible to the Commission,"[10] and he and other members of his delegation engaged in several days of corridor-to-lounge lobbying for the American position. Leon Gordenker has suggested that the Americans "were especially anxious to convince India, Australia and Canada" to support the US view but in the case of the two Dominions they met with little success. Australia and Canada were the only two countries to persevere in their opposition to the American resolution, and the final vote was 31 to 2 in favour, with 11 abstentions.

In presenting the Canadian case Lester Pearson argued that to hold elections in the South alone would involve changes in the Commission's terms of reference which were beyond the power of the Interim Committee to decide. He appeared to agree with the Australian view that the creation of a separate South Korean regime would tend to harden the 38th parallel into a permanent and therefore disruptive international boundary, and in defence of the Canadian position he commented acidly that it "would at least have the advantage of proving the unwarranted nature of certain allegations to the effect that the Temporary Commission was in the service of the United States of America."[11] More startling still, he warned the Committee that if the advice contained in the American resolution were accepted by the UNTCOK majority, "a new and serious situation would be created which would have to be taken into consideration by the governments who are members of the Commission and who feel that the advice from this committee is unwise and unconstitutional."[12] If this was a threat that Canada would withdraw from UNTCOK if the Americans had their way, then in terms of the usual interpretation of Canadian subservience to Washington it was a bold stroke indeed.

It was also, however, a futile one. When news of the success of the American resolution reached UNTCOK headquarters in Korea, Dr. Patterson was occupied with other business in Tokyo, and on February 28 the seven remaining members met on an informal basis without him. By now the growing impatience of a number of political groups in South Korea had reached alarming proportions, and with a view to forestalling public demonstrations the seven representatives unanimously decided to announce on March 1 that elections would be held in the American zone not later than May 10. The American Commander promptly issued a declaration setting Sunday, May 9, as the precise date.

On instructions from Ottawa Dr. Patterson immediately journeyed to Korea to protest the Commission's decision. A procedural wrangle ensued with Dr. Patterson arguing that the election announcement was not binding and warning, as he had been authorized to do, that unless the Commission changed its mind he "would be compelled to abstain from further participation in the activities of the Commission until he received further instructions from his Government."[13] Finally he withdrew, and when confronted with his departure the Commission decided by a vote of 4 to 3 to issue a press release stating that the Canadian delegation had questioned the March 1 declaration and that the Commissioners were therefore still considering whether it would be confirmed. For the time being Canada had scored a point: UNTCOK had to consider again the "advice" of the Interim Committee, and American plans for a May 9 election were once more placed in jeopardy.

The victory, however, was small and short. When discussions resumed, Dr. Patterson once again reiterated his position and added that he was haunted by "the terrible doubt that the one and only purpose for which the Commission is in Korea will not be furthered one step but rather perhaps disastrously set back if the advice of the Interim Committee is accepted. . . . If elections in South Korea alone contribute nothing to the unifying of Korea, then the United Nations Commission has no right to participate in them."[14] But in spite of his efforts the final vote was 4-2-2 in favour of proceeding with elections in the South alone, with Australia and Canada opposed, and France and Syria abstaining. Dr. Patterson withdrew once more to await instructions from Ottawa but after an absence of 11 days he returned with orders to cooperate in the task of supervising the elections. Canada had at last capitulated.

Three observations can now be made with regard to this lamentable chronicle. The first is the obvious point that, in spite of the fact that Ottawa had used every diplomatic technique at its disposal from simple persuasion to outright boycott, in the final analysis its policy failed in the face of American opposition. The second is that this failure was due almost entirely to the fact that, in a situation in which Canada and the United States were competing for the support of the same foreign powers, the Canadians were bound to lose; indeed while Dr. Patterson was at first supported by a majority of the UNTCOK membership, by the time the dispute had been debated in the General Assembly's Interim Committee his diplomatic allies had been reduced to one. The third is that there is no evidence anywhere that Canada's relations with the United States were seriously or even temporarily jeopardized by the Canadian role in the UNTCOK episode. It is true, of course, that in view of their ultimate success the Americans had no serious motivation for undertaking retaliatory measures. Nevertheless the Canadians had put up a good fight and Washington must have been irritated as well as surprised; yet so far as is publicly known there were no untoward effects on the Ottawa-Washington connection.

Conclusions

Not forgetting that generalizations drawn from specific cases must be regarded with caution and that a rigorous study would require a far greater number of tests and much more intensive analysis than has been provided here, the two instances of post-war Canadian foreign policy discussed seem to suggest four conclusions.

Firstly, as a matter of historical fact the Canadian government occasionally *has* executed foreign policies which have conflicted with those of the United States. A thorough review of Canada's external relations in the postwar period would probably reveal that these occasions have not been so rare as many Canadians assume.

Secondly, it is in turn possible that the frequent appearance of *identical* Canadian and American policies in foreign affairs need not necessarily be due to the success of irresistible American pressures on Ottawa. It may result instead from the fact that Canadian decision-makers tend to reach similar policy conclusions by independent means. To put it differently, those who are dissatisfied with the conduct of Canada's post-war external affairs would do better to blame the objectives and values of the government in Ottawa rather than the hidden machinations of the American Department of State. A Canadian official has suggested privately that one of the reasons for Canada's independent policy in Cuba was the fear that any other course would arouse an outcry from Canadian nationalists. Ottawa is thus not immune to public pressure and its diplomatists are sometimes able to use the opinions of Canadian electors in bargaining with other powers, the United States included. There is therefore no excuse for Canadians who deplore official policy on Vietnam and other issues and yet refrain from speaking out.

Thirdly, when Canadian policies have in fact collided with those of the United States, they apparently have *not* produced serious or permanent ruptures in the important Washington connection. The threat of American retaliation therefore is probably not as effective a restraint upon the options of Canadian policy-makers as some commentators have alleged. Canadians would accordingly do well to view such excuses for governmental inaction with some degree of scepticism, at least in cases where the conflict with the United States is not vital to the American national interest. There are doubtless many theoretical policy options which would indeed invite severe American retaliatory action; the conclusion of a Canadian military alliance with the USSR provides an obvious hypothetical example. But the evidence suggests that within the range of realistic choices Canada enjoys a genuine freedom which she can exercise without fear that her fundamental interests will subsequently be mutilated by Uncle Sam.

Finally, it is probably true to say that the direct influence of Ottawa upon decision-makers in Washington is very slight, and certainly in cases like that of UNTCOK, where Canada and the United States are in competition for the support of other members of the international community, Canada seems destined for defeat. By the same token, however, it is true to say also that an independent Canadian position, as in Cuba, is unlikely to make the Americans more intractable than they already are. The frequently expressed view therefore that Canada should maintain her silence on sensitive issues lest she inflame the emotions of the calculating policy-makers at the Department of State is almost certainly invalid. Canada cannot single-handedly make the world a community of angels, but neither on the other hand is she likely to populate it with demons.

James Steele

CANADA'S · VIETNAM POLICY: THE DIPLOMACY OF ESCALATION

James Steele is Associate Professor of English at Carleton University. He is at present at work on a biography of Edmund Waller, a seventeenth-century English poet, and maintains a continuing interest in the Vietnam situation.

Canada professes to give the highest priority to diplomatic initiatives designed to bring about a peaceful settlement of the war in Vietnam. At least this is the intention declared to the public by the Canadian government. But these statements of best intentions are not just ambiguous, they are also equivocal. Ambiguous, because our leaders' concrete policy statements on Vietnam are meticulously worded so as to placate both the anxious demonstrator on Parliament Hill and the businessman concerned with his American contracts. Equivocal, because our efforts to assume the role of the complaisant mediator are belied by our government's actual record of supporting the United States' hard-line policy in Vietnam. Our government regards the American involvement there as a necessary and justified attempt by the United States to prevent international communist aggression and hence to guard the security of the free world.[1] Accordingly we give general sup-

ANGEL WITH AN ANGLE

port to "American purposes" in Vietnam.[2] Our policy in what must be regarded as an unjustly provoked,[3] clearly illegal[4] and barbarous[5] war raises grave doubts not just about the worth of our policies in themselves but also more general questions about the usefulness of quiet diplomacy in the present circumstances and the reality of our foreign policy independence.*

Posture of Mediator

Our leaders have managed to acquire the image of would-be mediators. They have regularly deplored the fact of the war, occasionally made ambiguous apologies for the American bombing and often stressed the desirability of a negotiated settlement.

This posture is based upon an institutional reality: Canada's membership with India and Poland on the International Control Commission (ICC), which is officially charged with supervising the observance of the 1954 Geneva Agreement. Nevertheless, while the unilateral renunciation of the Geneva Agreement by South Vietnam (with Canadian approval) in 1955[6] and the resumption of the war have made a mockery of the ICC's mandate, our continued presence in this supervisory commission is not considered incompatible with reaping the profits that accrue from selling the United States' military machine $300 million of war materials. Although the ICC's role has been reduced to that of a symbol for the authority of the Geneva Conference of 1954, our official delegates to the ICC see no need to refrain from adopting an open bias in favour of one of the warring parties, the United States of America. The recent allegation by an Associate Editor of *The Montreal Star*, Mr. Gerald Clark, that Canadian officers on the International Control Commission have been "acting as informants for US intelligence agencies" and a similar allegation by CBC newsman Mr. Tim Ralfe, that a Canadian officer on the ICC had passed on to the Americans photographs and tape recordings of a bombing raid carried out against the oil storage dumps near Hanoi last June, do not generate confidence in this regard.[7] "Spying" would undoubtedly be too harsh a word to describe such activities as it connotes duplicity on the part of the Canadians on the ICC. In fact there seems to be little posing by

* Although we write in the present tense, political developments happen so quickly that we would hope this chapter by publication time, will be history, not policy. But as the most alarmist predictions by critics of American escalation have been overtaken by the events themselves, one cannot be overly sanguine.

our diplomats and soldiers there, for one of the extraordinary aspects of our presence in Vietnam is the ideological commitment of our officials to the American position.* A loyal ally does not spy; he simply exchanges information.

Our pretensions to peace-making in Vietnam are buttressed by our government's claims to be actively fostering negotiations between the warring parties. That this activity was going on behind the scenes made sense in terms of the government's public image of quiet mediator. In reply to a question in the House by Mr. Brewin on March 4, 1965 asking if Canada were going to make representations to Washington about the bombing attacks, Mr. Pearson replied that Canada was "in the middle . . . of discussions" to help secure negotiations.[8] The same assurance of effectiveness through diligent diplomatic activity was given two years later by Mr. Martin to a University of Toronto delegation. Apart from the mysterious episodes of Chester Ronning's visits to Hanoi, the significance of Canadian mediation efforts dwindles upon examination of the record, incomplete though the public's information may be.

For one thing Canada has repeatedly supported the American interpretation of what should constitute fair conditions for negotiations. When US bombing resumed after a brief pause on January 31, 1966, Mr. Pearson repeated publicly the distorted, simplistic American position that negotiations had not taken place because Hanoi had failed to respond, although he later stated that Canada had asked the United States to extend the pause "until all reasonable possibilities for negotiations had been exhausted."[9] He implicitly discounted the major reason for Hanoi's refusal to negotiate: the American objection to negotiating with the National Liberation Front (NLF). Dean Rusk actually rejected U Thant's request that the US recognize the NLF's legitimate role in a post-war South Vietnam.[10] The year before, our government had gone through the same performance of supporting the highly questionable American stand on negotiations. On June 10, 1965 Mr. Martin gave the United States full marks for agreeing to negotiate "without reserve" while he thought the other side had not been as responsive during the test pause in American bombing of May 13-18. On the day after the bombing resumed, the State Department announced that it was greatly disappointed because there had been no response from North

* See above, Peyton Lyon, Chapter 3, p. 38.

Vietnam. But the following November the public learned that this was false: the French government had in fact transmitted to the Americans an offer to negotiate from Hanoi. It is possible that Washington did not inform Ottawa of the Hanoi offer. In any event Canada was hardly making good its claim as mediator by so solidly and publicly supporting the version of one of the belligerents.

Nor have we given unequivocal support to various international efforts to achieve meaningful negotiation. In March and April of 1965 there were unsuccessful attempts by the non-aligned nations to bring about negotiations without preconditions. Admittedly Tito's proposal of March 1st was scorned by Peking and Hanoi because it overlooked the Geneva agreements. Washington rejected it on March 14 because Hanoi was still unwilling "to leave its neighbours alone."[11] Mr. Martin certainly did not help in getting unconditional discussions underway by his announcement on March 6 of a three-point settlement plan that contained the preconditions of both a cessation of bombing and a halt to infiltration. As was confirmed by Canada's reply to a new proposal by 17 non-aligned nations, we were in favour of negotiations on the basis of Hanoi's aid to the NLF being considered on the same level as American bombing of North Vietnam. Canada was also reluctant to support U Thant's renewed calls for negotiations such as his appeal on November 17, 1965 for a reconvening of the Geneva Conference:

> Even at this late hour – perhaps ten years too late – I still hold the view the Geneva Agreements can still be implemented. The only alternative to such a course is prolongation and escalation of the conflict resulting in appalling loss of life and tremendous destruction of property . . . the more the conflict is prolonged, the more complex and difficult will be the solution to the problem.[12]

Dean Rusk, in his reply of December 4, "declined in effect to accept 'application' of the 1954 Geneva Agreements, but expressed willingness 'to engage in negotiations on this basis.' "[13] The bombs began to fall around the Haiphong area on December 15. Canada, however, neither publicly nor privately through diplomatic channels assisted U Thant by bringing pressure to bear on the United States to come to such a Conference. Mr. Martin let it be known nine months later that he had in fact "resisted" such a move.[14]

An index of the unreality – not to say hypocrisy – of Canada's posture can be found in Hanoi's reaction to Canadian moves. Mr. Martin's most recent four-point plan of April 16, 1967 suggesting a disengagement of forces and a general cease fire was immediately denounced by Hanoi as a "hoax." Clearly Hanoi's impression is that Canada's role is an extension of US policy in Vietnam. When North Vietnam learned about Canadian military sales to the United States, Hanoi insisted that

> the Canadian Government's action proves that statements to the effect that Canada takes a "neutral" attitude towards the Vietnamese problem and attaches a great importance to the search for a solution for putting an end to the war are false. . . . The Vietnamese people know that the Canadian Government has always supported and tolerated the intensification of the armed aggression of the United States.[15]

Hanoi's interpretation of Canadian policy shows why our government's effort to be a peace-facilitator, if not peace-maker, is less than credible: one of the parties in the eventual negotiations considers us to be an unwavering supporter of its opponents. And it is not obvious that Hanoi's interpretation is wrong. The North Vietnamese could be forgiven for thinking that Canada has given the US strong support if they have studied the record of Canadian reactions to American policy, a problem we must now consider.

Canadian Support of American Policy

The question of interpretation of Canada's relationship to American-Vietnam policy is highly delicate. It depends for one thing on our evaluation of American policy, an issue that is more emotive than usual at a time when "credibility gap" is the polite wording for White House and State Department false statements. While everyone can agree that a war is being fought, it makes a great deal of difference to one's view of Canadian policy whether one agrees that the Americans are really defending the cause of democracy in South Vietnam and freedom in the world, are caught in a senseless and highly dangerous military operation that is out of their political control or are engaged in a struggle to maintain economic and military control over a rapidly expanding American empire in South-East Asia. In addition one would like to be able to come to some judgment about the Canadian involvement in American policy. Is it premeditated complicity in the policy of escalation? Is it freely-willed support for American policy? Is it piecemeal and reluctant loyalty to our major ally? The outsider has little chance of answering definitely for a correct judgment would require inside information on the motivations of our cabinet leaders together with the content of our diplomatists' policy discussions and knowledge of the extent of American pressure exercised on Ottawa in this matter. Though the amount of information provided by the government is deplorably low it is still possible to make some observations about Canada's record.

The most mild statement would be that the Canadian government has continually given the benefit of the doubt to the American official version of its activity in Vietnam. The minority "Statement" contained in the *Special Report* of the ICC (February 1965) was a deliberate dissociation of Canada from India's and Poland's criticism of American actions. In fact, we repeated the American view that their extension of the war and bombing was a warranted response to aggression on the part of North Vietnam. The bias of this minority Statement became evident, however, several weeks later when I. F. Stone obtained further information from the Pentagon which rendered the conclusions of the "Statement" essentially untenable. Indeed the figures in the Canadian minority report, like those in the American white paper *Aggression from the North*, really indicated, in the context of Stone's more comprehensive statistics concerning the over-all capture and loss of weapons, that assistance from the North had been minimal and that the conflict in South Vietnam was primarily a civil war.[16] This interpretation later found confirmation in facts cited in the *Mansfield Report*.[17] That there are close fraternal links between the NLF and Hanoi is obvious. That the guerrilla activities of the NLF are co-ordinated to some extent from centres in the North is indeed a plausible thesis. But, as the late Bernard Fall recently pointed out, fraternal links and some tactical direction from extra-territorial bases do not prevent the NLF from being basically an indigenous South Vietnamese guerrilla movement. It is also important to note that the Canadian and American equating of assistance to such a movement with "aggression" would have little foundation in international law even if national states were involved. The Northern and Southern areas of Vietnam are, however, part of the same nation. The Geneva Agreements recognize explicitly "the sovereignty, the independence, the unity and the territorial integrity" of only *one* Vietnam. In this juridical context there can be only one aggressor in Vietnam. In his minority "Statement" the Canadian delegate was therefore nurturing an American-spawned red herring which has now grown to gigantic proportions.

"Giving the US the benefit of the doubt" is too anaemic a description for our Liberal leaders' repeated declarations of support for American policy developments over the past few years, a policy of continual, inexorable escalation. During his celebrated speech at Temple University in April 1965, our Prime Minister affirmed that "the government and great majority of the people of my country have supported whole-heartedly US peace-keeping and peace-making policies in Vietnam." This was a remarkable assessment of American conduct. Mr. Pearson must have known that the US had resisted the efforts of U Thant and the French to effect a reconciliation among the Vietnamese themselves in the autumn of 1963 and, thereafter, that the United States had spurned a reconvening of the Geneva Conference in July 1964, that the United States had squelched U Thant's plan for secret negotiations in the autumn of 1964 and that the United States had refused to approve of a reconvening of the Geneva Conference in January and February of 1965. Were these the peace-*making* policies that Mr. Pearson had in mind? And by peace-*keeping* policies was Mr. Pearson referring to the first non-retaliatory raids on the North carried out in March of that year, or to the then recent huge Marine landing at DaNang or to the then fresh arrival of South Korean troops in Vietnam – or to what?

It was in this same speech that Mr. Pearson proposed that there should be "a pause in the bombing at the right time," a statement given great publicity as an independent initiative by Canada urging American moderation. But Mr. Pearson did not ask for a complete halt to the bombing (as many countries had done) or even for an extended suspension of the bombing. The mildness of Mr. Pearson's modest proposal for a mere "pause" and that "at the right time" concealed the bellicosity of the assumption upon which it was based: that the United States has the right to bomb or not to bomb just as it sees fit. Mr. Pearson is reported to have been received coolly by President Johnson on the following day. Although the President had reason to be piqued at receiving advice on home ground in public by a foreign Head of State, his annoyance could hardly have been over the substance of Mr. Pearson's proposal, particularly in view of the fact that a pause did come soon afterwards. In the final analysis, Mr.

Pearson's speech at Temple University was hardly a significant attempt to change the US policy of war.

As American involvement in the Vietnam war has increased, Canadian statements after major escalations form a pattern of endorsement of ever-higher levels of American military activity. For instance, in the Gulf of Tonkin incident of August 1964, the official American version is that US warships were attacked without provocation on the high seas by three North Vietnamese patrol boats. South Vietnamese commando units had, however, begun carrying out special raids against key industrial and harbour targets in North Vietnam as early as July 10.[18] American destroyers on patrol had sometimes collaborated with the South Vietnamese. What is more, there had been an increase in these raids during July. On July 27 and again on July 31 North Vietnam complained to the ICC that American and South Vietnamese warships had intruded into its territorial waters carrying away eleven fishermen in the first instance and bombarding two North Vietnamese islands in the second. Furthermore it has since been conceded by the Americans that the US destroyer *Maddox* at the time of the incident of August 2 was violating the twelve-mile territorial waters limit claimed by North Vietnam. A second exchange of fire is alleged to have occurred two days later after American warships had been ordered to return to that same area. President Johnson thus misled the American public in telling them that the attacks were "unprovoked . . . deliberate, wilful, systematic aggression" which had to be answered by retaliatory action.

Canada might have been more circumspect in its assessment of the episode. We had a representative on the International Control Commission which had received the North Vietnamese protests. Moreover, he could have read the *Saigon Post* of July 23 reporting General Ky's boast that raids on North Vietnam were taking place. Mr. Pearson was, however, remarkably precipitate in his reaction to the American "retaliation," the first American bombardment of North Vietnam on August 5, 1965. Within hours he announced that he had been informed by Dean Rusk of President Johnson's intention to take retaliatory action against North Vietnamese bases and went on to note that "the action taken by the United States was a reaction to an attack made on United States ships on the high seas." Moreover, the Prime Minister assured Parliament that the United States "would limit . . . their action in this matter to the requirements of the situation."[19]

77

The statement was an unfortunate and unnecessary declaration of verbal support for this major escalation.

The Canadian government does not hesitate to provide material as well as moral support for the American war effort. Although one of the functions of the ICC is to guard against the inflow of war material to Vietnam in accordance with the Geneva Agreements, our membership in this body does not prevent the government from selling $300 million of weapon components to the United States. In answering those who are critical of these arms sales, Mr. Pearson and Mr. Martin have referred to the Defence Production Sharing Agreements of 1959 and 1963. Although the term "agreement" implies a commitment, these particular accords merely define an arrangement allowing Canadian companies to tender bids for American arms contracts. These companies would be breaking no "agreements" if they declined in the future to place bids. Such restraint, however, would run counter to official *policy*, which is what Mr. Pearson and Mr. Martin really mean when they talk about these "agreements."

When we agree with the American interpretation of their war in Vietnam as defence of the South against Northern aggression, when we provide verbal support even for new phases of American escalation, when we continue to sell the US military material part of which is used in Vietnam, what is there to conclude but that our government has elaborated a conscious policy of actual support of this criminal war? It is impossible to measure precisely the effect of Canadian policy, whether on the moral fibre of our nation or more concretely on American policy itself. It is obvious that we have made no effort to strengthen moderate opinion in the United States. It is probable that our repeated declarations of agreement with official American policy has been a factor in helping to make the policy of escalation appear legitimate to the American people. It is in any case clear that the Canadian government has its own "credibility gap." Our Prime Minister finds no difficulty in ambiguously agreeing with critics that a cessation of the bombing would be "one of the key elements if not the key element". in reaching a settlement of the conflict,[20] and doing nothing effective to bring the conflict to an end.

Dependence or Complicity?

If there is no doubt that Canada's Vietnam policy follows closely if passively American policy, there is room for disagreement over the implications of this unfortunate record for Canada's foreign policy. Is it proof of Canadian diplomatic dependence on American foreign policy, or is it a question of a policy closely supporting the American line but freely chosen by the government? There is certainly little indication in the public record of Canadian initiative, apart from the missions of Mr. Chester Ronning to Hanoi, both of which immediately preceded major escalations in the war.[21] At the private level, the freedom of draft-resisters to find refuge in Canada and the sending of medical supplies impartially to North and South Vietnam by several organizations provide a palliative for our national conscience. Nor has the government shown signs of moral or intellectual independence in this whole story. It would appear that the large size of military contracts has been a significant influence on the government's reluctance to make any critical gestures. Nor has much evidence turned up to indicate inordinate American governmental pressure on Ottawa to keep in step with Washington on Vietnam. A further indication that this unexemplary record is a product of its own free choice is the government's resistance to modification of its stand despite the articulation of much critical opinion in the universities and churches, in the mass media and even within the cabinet itself. This feeling of outrage at American Vietnam policy would have been as easy to mobilize as was economic nationalism in the Mercantile affair. It would seem in other words that the government's Vietnam policy is not entirely the result of external factors, but partly a reflection of the considered judgment of certain dominant members of the government to support the American prosecution of the war regardless of what is involved.

It can be argued that the public has the Vietnam policy it deserves: if it wanted more independence it should have demanded this of the Government; if public opinion was not always clearly expressed, the Government had to make up its own mind. It is of course compatible with our parliamentary system for the elected government to pursue the policy it sees fit and for which it is responsible. But when it practises ambivalence to the point of equivocation with the result of misleading the public as to the real nature of its policy, it is no longer the public that is entirely to blame.

In its almost obsessive subservience to American policy, one can see the strategy of Quiet Diplomacy pushed to its practical absurdity. The official idealization of this technique endows our diplomatists with the felicitous image of mediators. It has proven to be a remarkably successful device for quietly muffling criticism, especially in the House of Commons. But the mere domestic utility of Quiet Diplomacy cannot justify the unfortunate discrepancy between appearance and reality. Hanoi's explanation is that there is no discrepancy, that Canadian diplomatic initiatives have been part of a well co-ordinated programme directed by Washington. The evidence for such a conspiracy theory is lacking even though Canadian policy may appear in retrospect, like American escalation, *as if* it had been part of a carefully worked out plan. Canadian diplomatic behaviour can perhaps be more plausibly explained by the essential congruity of Washington's strategic hard-line goals with the goals as defined by our diplomats who have learned their alphabet in the cold-war environment and absorbed the conventional – but now tragically constricted – wisdom of the Merchant-Heeney Report. To these factors may be added the traditional faith of Ottawa in the general beneficence of the United States which has left us blind to the diplomatic tricks of that country and uncritical of the limitations in its strategic thinking.[22]

It is easy to make constructive suggestions as to how we might assist in bringing about a settlement in Vietnam. We could begin by declaring our intention to respect and uphold the Geneva Agreements and by requesting other nations to do likewise. We could seek ways and means to effect the type of political settlement envisaged in the Final Declaration of the Geneva Conference by insisting that the National Liberation Front be accorded an official role in South Vietnam commensurate with its popular support. Meanwhile, we could support the plea of U Thant for an unconditional cessation of the bombing of the North. We could request Canadian companies to refrain from placing bids for new arms contracts under the Defence Production Sharing Agreements. We could send respectably large amounts of medical and economic aid to all parts of Vietnam.

But the irony in making such mild proposals is that the government seems to feel that the implementation of almost any one of them would be tantamount to an entirely new departure in our foreign policy and might entail a fundamental alteration in our relationship with the United States. The economic cost in terms of loss of exports and possible retaliation might indeed be high depending on how the policy change was implemented and how it was conveyed to the United States. Yet it is equally true to say the cost of our continued collaboration in this irrational and unjust war may be much higher. For what is involved here is our very self-respect. We have always paid dearly for the benefit of our satellite status, but this price is intolerable. It is no exaggeration to say that our dignity as human beings now depends on our collective willingness and ability to act as a sovereign nation by withdrawing our general support for American policy in Vietnam.

THE
DOMESTIC
ENVIRONMENT:
INDEPENDENCE
BEGINS
AT
HOME

If Uncle Sam is a scapegoat, not a reason, for our lack of foreign policy integrity, is the cause of our diplomatic weakness to be found closer to home?

Is our house too divided to have an effective presence abroad? Paul Painchaud feels that an increase of political autonomy for Quebec must necessarily reduce the effectiveness of Canada's foreign policy. In Louis Sabourin's view an expanded international role for Quebec will not detract from the effectiveness of the total Canadian foreign policy effort however much it would change its mechanisms. The difference may be more apparent than real; for Painchaud, in his answer to LaLande, accepts an increased role for Quebec in the international exercise of its provincial prerogatives.

Biculturalism when seen by English Canadians is always the "Quebec problem." As suggested by Gilles LaLande's brief comments, the Anglo-Saxon contribution may also be a causal element in Canada's foreign policy ineffectiveness. Take for instance our élite policy-making structure modelled on British lines. In Franklyn Griffiths' opinion (chapter 9) this "closed circuit" decision-making system excludes both the elected Members of Parliament and the interested public from contributing to the decision-making process, thus depriving our foreign policy of the support that an aware public opinion could give our international bargaining.

In chapter 10 Thomas Hockin looks at another internal restraint. The transposition of our domestic political pragmatism to international affairs has created a view of the external world that exaggerates the importance of international machinery to the detriment of seeking solutions to underlying problems.

Paul Painchaud
(with a reply
by Gilles LaLande)

DIPLOMATIC
BICULTURALISM:
DOCTRINE
OR
DELUSION?*

Paul Painchaud is Professor of Political Science at Laval University.
He teaches international relations and is doing research on interest
groups in Canada as they relate to Canadian foreign policy.

Gilles LaLande is Professor of International Relations at the University
of Montreal. He is the author of L'étude des relations internationales et
de certaines civilisations etrangères au Canada *and the recent* Le
Ministère des Affaires Extérieurs et la dualité de culture au Canada.

To a disquieting extent the tensions caused by Quebec nationalism have compromised the possibility of achieving an independent, creative and effective foreign policy for Canada. This is not
only because internal division diminishes the plausibility of our
international initiatives but especially because the major effect of
this new nationalism leads to a gradual transfer of political legitimacy from Ottawa to Quebec. Thus for a large part of the country's population the primary repository of political authority is
not in the federal government but, on the contrary, the "state of
Quebec."

* Translated by the editor.

This radical transformation of Quebec's political culture, whose nationalism has acted as both cause and effect of the rediscovery of the notion of statehood, has a definite impact on the formation of Canadian foreign policy. Besides the fact that the decline of federal power in Quebec deprives our diplomacy of a major source of the energy and ideas which it urgently needs, the fillip given to nationalism tends to focus on Quebec the already small amount of its population's interest in international affairs. In other words, if Quebec is the prime political structure for French Canada's destiny, there is no reason why this Province's government should not assume international responsibilities to the extent that external factors may affect its destiny. Up to now, Quebec leaders have been content to claim a "special status" in international affairs, i.e. the freedom to act on the world scene within the areas of provincial jurisdiction. Who can say, however, that the next generation will not push this development to its logical conclusion?

The New Doctrine

A recent remedy proposed to solve this problem is what can be called "diplomatic biculturalism." As a fairly well articulated conception of the ends and the means that should constitute our foreign policy on a lasting basis, we have here a real foreign policy doctrine. Biculturalism is proposed as the fundamental basis of Canadian diplomacy whose objectives should be defined in terms of the country's cultural duality and implemented by the two principal ethnic groups as such.

Diplomatic biculturalism is not a completely new idea in Canada. It turns up at least implicitly as a constant element of our international policy decisions from our origins up to the present. Until recently, however, biculturalism has only played an occasional, negative role, defining the "limits" beyond which certain external actions might constitute a danger for the country's stability. But the situation has been changing for several years. Biculturalism is now expressed as a *positive*, long-term element of our foreign policy, and a whole school of thought has attempted to formulate this doctrine as a body of concrete policies. There is little doubt, then, that the first writings will be developed more systematically at the great debate on Canadian identity is pursued. This doctrine strikes me, however, as unacceptable whether as a solution to the problems raised by Quebec's nationalism or as an instrument to make our diplomacy more effective.

Diplomatic biculturalism is implicitly based on four main postulates:

1 French Canada has specific interests in foreign affairs;
2 these interests can be known;
3 only if these interests are granted equality with those of English Canada can a new and independent Canadian foreign policy be formulated;
4 this equality must be implemented by the complete bilingualism of the Department of External Affairs.

The proponents of biculturalism will perhaps find this picture of their views outrageously simplified. But from whatever angle one views their claims, it is difficult to deny these implicit assumptions. Indeed biculturalism would have no sense if it did not recognize the existence of distinct international aspirations in French Canada, if these aspirations were not judged *a priori* to be legitimate, hence able to modify our foreign policy, and lastly if some kind of reorganization of the power structure could not guarantee the representation of these claims and the assurance of their satisfaction. While it is possible to add some complementary and secondary elements to this group of postulates, they are the logical core of the whole doctrine.

The International Interests of French Canadians

Do French Canadians have specific attitudes and interests in foreign affairs due to their culture, history and societal structures? Biculturalism gives an affirmative answer to this question for this is the touchstone of the doctrine. This problem must be studied on various levels. One must distinguish very clearly the more general and theoretical question of the *possibility* of French Canada having its own international interests from the historical problem of how these interests may have been expressed in the past. The first aspect of the question is the more important, for the answer will determine whether biculturalism has any future as a coherent foreign policy doctrine that will outlive the particular circumstances that gave it birth. This is the test that biculturalism must pass if it claims to be a rational criterion for diplomatic policy-making and if it wants to be useful as a viable expression of the new Quebec nationalism.

Whether one thinks there are specific French-Canadian international interests depends in the final analysis on one's definition of what French Canada. Is it an ethnic group comparable to the other minorities in Canada, or is it on the contrary a historical community having an autonomous political destiny?

If the former, the international interests of French Canada are those of any segment of the Canadian population as international events may affect its ideological sympathies or preferences. The cultural traditions of French Canada would give these interests a slightly distinct colour, of course. But are these interests different from those of any other economic or religious group that would be normally reflected in Canadian diplomacy? If not, what justification can one accord a theory like biculturalism which gives an exceptionally privileged position to the ethnic interests of French Canada relative to those of similar, theoretically equal, groups in Canada?

In reality biculturalism is based at least implicitly on the other view of French Canada as a society with such a degree of social self-sufficiency and geo-political organization that it cannot be completely identified with the whole political entity, that is the *federal* state as opposed to the *Quebec* state. Given this interpretation, does such a special Quebec have specific international interests? Here again we must distinguish between the international interests of the *government* of Quebec from those of individuals and private groups who inhabit its territory. These two types of interests do not necessarily coincide. In the case of the Quebec government, the problem is primarily one of its constitutional competence as a province. The only question to resolve on this level is the procedure to follow for it to exercise this competence in international affairs. But this is above all a technical question of law, not a bicultural one for it concerns the other provinces equally. The second case is a question of determining whether Quebec's population has distinct interests in international affairs by virtue of its belonging to the province. To give an affirmative answer to this question would require proving that international affairs affect the province of Quebec in a unique way compared to the other parts of the country. Is this conceivable as long as Quebec is part of Canada? How can one imagine that Quebeckers *qua* Quebeckers could have points of view and interests which would be different from those of their compatriots in Vancouver or Halifax towards the Cuba crisis, the Vietnam war, or the financial difficulties of the United Nations? The error and the danger of biculturalism is to give the impression that these special interests exist or can exist. The truth is quite different. As long as Quebec is not a full and independent member of the international system with the responsibilities appropriate to this title, its international interests will be those of Canada as a whole. In other words, Quebec's international interests are not those that it wishes to have but those that the structure and nature of the international system compel it to accept – like it or not – that is those of the whole Canadian society. The diplomatic particularism that biculturalism artificially stimulates has thus no chance of being realized and so, in the full sense of the word, it is a political delusion.

To this I would add three supplementary remarks. Firstly, if it is true that some international policies of the federal government – especially its defence policies – have impeded Quebec's development by inefficient exploitation of the country's available resources (and this would perhaps be the only possible "French-Canadian" criticism of our diplomacy) the same remark could be made with as much validity about other regions in Canada. Quebec's underdevelopment is not the only one to be affected by the bad administration of federal funds; so bicultural analysis has no precise and constructive contribution to make here either.

Furthermore it is true that Quebec's government thinks it has international responsibilities within its legitimate jurisdiction. This is the theory of "diplomatic federalism" that all Quebec parties have made their official doctrine, but that is not so popular elsewhere in Canada. There are doubtless various possible technical and political solutions for this problem. One that would be completely unacceptable for Quebec but which is implicit in biculturalism would be to have the federal government play a more active internal role in social and cultural affairs so that its international coincided with its domestic competence. It is this approach that the new Quebec "federalists" defend in various ways and in various forms. But at the same time this centralization could lead to the abandonment of strict federalism as the great majority of Quebeckers conceive it and thus more than anything else would lead to the break-up of the country itself.

As for historical claims of French Canada in international affairs, we should note that none of them, except a rapprochement with the French-speaking world, is really unique to Quebec. Diplomatic representation in the Vatican, for instance, concerns Catholics outside Quebec who could have different opinions from French-Canadian Catholics. Concerning our relations with Latin America and the entry of Canada into the OAS, it is not excessive to say that French Canadians' opinions in this matter were once based on the absolutely false idea of what they called Latinity. This has never had any historical substance apart from the dreams of some of the post-war French-Canadian élite seduced for a moment by the lure of Peronism. Their abandonment of these dreams is proof enough.

It is thus rather difficult to detect either the possibility or the *de facto* existence of external objectives that are specific to French Canada, objectives that could be the basis of a special policy in Canadian diplomacy, at least in the post-war period. We can disregard the preceding years when Canada's international position was quite different. To sum up: French Canadians will only have specific international interests when Quebec is an independent state.

The French-Speaking World

The theme of rapprochement with the French-speaking world has become the chief battle cry of biculturalism. It is indeed the only policy area unique to French Canada that could generate new policies in our diplomacy and that could genuinely be justified by biculturalism. The problem is complex and has not been studied systematically, but my feeling is that this interpretation of biculturalism in foreign policy is unconvincing and ambiguous.

We must look at the problem on several levels. To start with, is it a question of political or cultural rapprochement? The answer to this question is not clear. In fact, and this is the danger of biculturalism, it never seems possible to distinguish these two forms of rapprochement clearly one from the other. The political-cultural complication itself may have various sources. First, the pressure for solidarity with the French-speaking world cannot only be cultural once this participation is considered as an indispensable condition for French Canada's survival. Sooner or later the close links between Quebec and the other French-speaking countries, especially France, would create the need for a more advanced integration in which the cultural and the political could not easily be disentangled. The emotional attitudes that would develop towards these countries would certainly complicate the formation of our external policy. The best example of this imbroglio is Canada's attitude to foreign aid. By choosing a cultural criterion rather than a strictly political measure for distributing its largesse, our foreign policy is put in a doubly weak position. For one thing, these cultural considerations are totally irrelevant for the under-developed countries as a whole who expect aid only because of their under-development. In addition, Canada might have better political reasons at a given moment to invest its already limited resources in more strategic areas such as Latin America than in the French-speaking countries where France in any case already invests a great deal. Only the internal pressure of French Canada can explain such an artificial external aid policy. The federal government's position on biculturalism in foreign policy has other political consequences.

How could one, for instance, refuse to sell uranium to France or not accept its strategic conceptions without running up against French-Canadian public opinion which has been told by such leaders as Jean-Luc Pepin, that France is one of the pillars of our foreign policy? A choice must be made: either biculturalism is proclaimed purely for electoral consumption which guarantees the federal government some difficult moments in Quebec, or it is an integral part of our foreign policy and must be pursued consistently. It is precisely the confusion that obscures at present the practical meaning of biculturalism that confronts our foreign policy with the most dangerous political implications, neither intended nor clearly worked out.

Moreover, even if it is strictly a cultural rapprochement with the French-speaking world, the problem is far from settled. The notion of culture is highly ambiguous. If Quebec wants to develop its cultural relations with the French-speaking world it does not intend to do this uniquely in the area of the humanities, the arts or education. Such a narrow conception of culture would be unacceptable in French Canada since the whole of societal life is understood by the term, economic institutions, technical developments and scientific research included. Does diplomatic biculturalism intend to be as explicit and vast in its ambitions? If this is the case, federalism has lost its *raison d'être* in French Canada.

Furthermore Quebec does not have common cultural interests exclusively with the French-speaking world. Quebec's culture needs contact with everything that is happening in all dynamic civilizations – those of the Soviet Union, America and the other European countries. The danger of biculturalism in practical terms is to shackle Quebec's prospects of advancement to developments in the French world.

Finally the responsibility for culture does not belong entirely to the federal government and so to *Canadian* foreign policy. Biculturalism foresees no means whereby the division of powers could be made between Quebec and Ottawa. This is serious and would provoke useless conflicts as we have already seen.

For this whole group of reasons biculturalism as a doctrine raises considerable difficulties. This does not, of course, exclude the possibility of intensified relations with the French-speaking world on the same basis as these can exist with countries of different culture.

The Last Postulate

Biculturalism also is based as we have seen on certain extremely important theoretical postulates that should be analysed more extensively than the following brief considerations allow.

Even if one could admit the existence of international interests unique to French Canada, the problem of the representation of these interests in the federal system remains without apparent solution. In addition to the fact that the French Canadian federal Members of Parliament are elected on the basis of a vast and diversified mandate, there is no procedure and no structure that, at the present moment, would allow these international French-Canadian interests to be identified, formulated and converted into policy. Only a new constitutional revision would permit this on the basis of an associate status.

Furthermore, whether they like it or not, the biculturalists are led to postulate the equality of the two principal ethnic groups in the elaboration of Canadian foreign policy. Indeed, what is the usefulness of the identification of specific international French-Canadian interests if French Canada has no effective means for expressing them? The theory of "democratic pluralism" invoked to resolve this difficulty is utopian: the majority would never cease to be a majority as long as foreign policy finds its inspiration in "corporate" interests.

Not only, then, is the principle of equality absolutely impracticable but it is not even certain that the envisaged result for our diplomacy, a renovated foreign policy safe from continentalism, could be achieved. In fact, international problems can only be dealt with in a strictly political perspective and not in the light of some vague "cultural" criterion whether it be French or English. As for English Canada, it will not be saved from the temptations of continentalism by the injection of a little more French culture but only by a clear comprehension of its own destiny as a distinct social and cultural community.

As for bilingualism, however noble and ideal it might be, one can doubt whether it will of itself lead to a transformation of the real structure of power in Ottawa and even whether it can be achieved in the near future in foreign policy. For one thing, foreign policy is no longer the exclusive responsibility of the Department of External Affairs but depends on a large network of administrative institutions that maintain very complex links with the outside world.

Conclusion

On the whole diplomatic biculturalism appears to be an artificial doctrine. It tends to create an ambiguous dualism in Canada's foreign policy that no diplomacy could implement. It is in danger of giving French Canada a partial and folkloric view of international life. It does not appease Quebec nationalism, which has much deeper sources than the way our diplomatic affairs are conducted in Ottawa. In fact, nothing indicates that fundamental disagreements exist between Quebec and the rest of the country on the objectives and methods of our diplomacy.

Consequently, there can only be one and the same foreign policy for the whole country. It is possible that one day a third foreign policy may appear in North America. But until that time the only possible path is that French Canadians agree to participate on the same basis as other Canadians in the formation of the foreign policy of their country without trying to define special interests. Biculturalism is an escape that solves nothing.

Gilles LaLande: *A Reply to "Diplomatic Biculturalism"*

The word "biculturalism" may be new, but the phenomenon it describes is not. It is only the latest term in Canada's political vocabulary for the reality which politicians have been describing since the Act of Union (1840) with expressions such as the two "peoples," the two "nationalities," the two "nations" or the two "founding races" of Canada. Biculturalism is not synonymous with bilingualism. Moreover, it has never been a doctrine or a system. Biculturalism is a plain and straightforward situation which needs no qualification.

Biculturalism has come to be described appropriately as the cultural duality of Canada. As such, it does not deny the pluralism of the ethnic origins of the Canadian population. What it does register, however, is no less than a fundamental condition for the continued existence of Canada as we know it.

93

By denying the need for a Canadian foreign policy based on biculturalism, while at the same time acknowledging the existence of the French fact in Canada, M. Painchaud embraces two absolute and mutually exclusive points of view and then offers the following alternative: either a Canadian foreign policy or a Quebec foreign policy. By forcing this choice upon the reader, M. Painchaud first implies that as long as Quebec remains within the confines of Confederation, she can play no international role whatever. And, second, that as long as Quebec is denied any international role, Canadian foreign policy can be formulated and executed without really considering the distinct cultural personality of the French Canadians.

Much has been made of the fact that there can hardly be such a thing as an English-Canadian or a French-Canadian view of our foreign policy. For instance it is only common sense that in questions of war and peace, French Canada and English Canada have genuine common interests. It is also obvious that the federal system of government imposes obligations on both French-speaking and English-speaking Canadians. Still, it is very difficult to comprehend how biculturalism can be regarded as not being the very foundation and an essential source of inspiration in formulating and executing Canada's foreign policy.

Of course this is not to say that cultural factors should be the predominant consideration in determining Canadian foreign policy. It does not mean that biculturalism necessarily threatens the unity of Canada's international personality. Nor does it imply that biculturalism requires a strict equality in the pursuit of the foreign policy interests of the two main cultural groups of Canada, any more than it requires the integral bilingualism in the federal departments and agencies most active in the field of foreign relations.

Biculturalism does call for a willingness to accept ways of doing things which are not exclusively Anglo-American in the field of foreign policy. More specifically, biculturalism requires that the all-too-British type of organization and set of policies of the Department of External Affairs be questioned and that the exclusive pragmatic approach in our foreign policy be reappraised. Biculturalism also involves a more recognizable and authentically French-Canadian voice in the process of defining a foreign policy for the Canadian nation. It means opening the way for a greater number of French Canadians into the power élites in the Department of External Affairs and other related agencies. Above all, biculturalism demands the recognition and acceptance that is long overdue of the vital need for Quebec to draw much closer to France and to the French-speaking community of nations.

Paul Painchaud: Replies to the Reply

Either Canada *or* Quebec foreign policy? I did not intend to say that Quebeckers would not have a position rather different from that of other Canadian opinion-groups on a particular international problem. On the contrary this is perfectly possible – just as it is possible that the Jews can have distinct reactions at a given moment to certain world problems, as we have seen just recently. But this is different from the doctrine of biculturalism which postulates that our foreign policy should be based in a permanent fashion on the specific interests of French Canada. In this case, yes, it is an absolute "either Canada or Quebec." But nothing stops Quebec (or any other group or section of opinion) from articulating its interests in Ottawa: this is the normal game of democracy. But to say that Quebec has an *equal* and *constant* interest in our diplomacy is not only "unacceptable" but also impossible – and moreover is in no way desired by Quebec, as the current discussions in Quebec demonstrate.

No international role for Quebec? I did not mean to imply that. For the moment I am quite happy with the theory of 'diplomatic federalism" which confers certain international responsibilities on the Quebec *government*.

To the extent that *diplomatic* biculturalism tends to create specific interests for French Canada in international affairs, I maintain that it leads Quebeckers to become conscious of the need for an independent state. The international system is evolving in such a way these days that one can very well imagine new ways of organizing the mechanisms of foreign policy. But, once again, in my view this has nothing to do with the application of biculturalism to the foreign policy *made by Ottawa*.

Irrelevance of cultural criteria for foreign policy making? We still lack a major empirical study on the role of cultural factors in foreign policy. Possibly they will become one of the future accepted facts of diplomacy. Up to now I would guess that their role has been negligible, even in the policy of countries like Great Britain and the United States. But it is another thing entirely to advocate in a normative sense that cultural considerations should be the criterion of *Canadian* foreign policy in the current circumstances. For in my view if this criterion is used for French Canada, there is no reason why it would not become a "conscious" criterion for English Canada. Then how far will we go? On what new paths will our diplomacy be launched when there are so many other much more important problems in the world that our diplomats should attack?

I do not wish to maintain that we should not have a foreign policy in the cultural domain, which is different from using a cultural *criterion* of behaviour. But this cultural policy could be *implemented* in various ways. Why, for example, could the main responsibility for cultural relations with the French-speaking world not be given to the Quebec government? Under such an arrangement, Ottawa would remain free to carry out a much more supple foreign policy, one that would be free of these artificial cultural considerations and free too of the political-cultural imbroglio.

Louis Sabourin

SPECIAL INTERNATIONAL STATUS FOR QUEBEC?

Louis Sabourin is Director of the Centre for International Cooperation at the University of Ottawa. Former Dean of Social Sciences and President of the Societé canadienne de Science Politique, Me. Sabourin has published many articles on the dual role of a bicultural Canada in international affairs. He is the editor of the recent Canadian Political Institutions.

If many Canadians were not yet aware of Quebec's intentions to look for a distinctive international role, President de Gaulle's 1967 trip to Canada has certainly wakened them up to that new reality. For most of them, it was shocking to realize in such a way – especially in a decade when there hardly exists a single fundamental disagreement between English and French Canadians on problems confronting the world and at a time when the Federal Government is seeking and establishing closer ties with French-speaking countries – that Quebec was determined to establish official international activities.

"What Does Quebec Want?"

Too few people – including too few French Canadians – have yet understood that this is not a new caprice but a desire on the part of the Province of Quebec to use fully its legislative pre-

97

CHARLIE'S AUNT

rogatives which have many international implications nowadays in order to assure the continued progress of a French-Canadian society that is open to the world.

Besides, French Canadians have finally realized that, in about thirty years, they will represent less than 20 per cent of the Canadian population; and unless the Government of Quebec undertakes more positive steps in order to assert their identity, the role of the French-speaking Canadians will then become very marginal in almost evry field of life in Canada. If French Canadians have survived, it is mainly because it was possible to live (and because they wished to live) in a closed society *en marge du monde*. But in the era of mass media and the new technology, this is not possible any more. Besides, every small society which refuses to welcome foreign know-how is bound to remain mediocre. French Canada must obviously look for such know-how in countries with a close cultural affinity if it wants to create many more *mileux de travail* where French-speaking people will be able to work in their own language.

In the past, the term "culture" was interpreted in a narrow sense. But sociologists recognize today that a culture is not simply an intellectual, spiritual, artistic phenomenon, but also a set of material phenomena which condition and characterize a society. French Canadians have also a right to a culture of their own which is defined not only in terms of language, art and literature but also in terms of their institutions, their administrative methods and a socio-economic environment which will reflect their particular heritage. It is therefore necessary for French-Canadians to import from France not only literature and songs but French science, technology, research and administrative methods which will allow them to progress materially and collectively.

Many people will ask why French Canadians – at least those living in Quebec – are not ready to leave such a task to the federal government or to private institutions as it is being done in English-speaking provinces.

The reason is that French Canadians control very few important institutions besides the government of the province of Quebec. And, now that they have set aside their traditional anti-state views, they have realized that they must exploit much more this one institution which can effectively influence and impose norms on the whole society within the province.

Secondly, even if Ottawa has established closer ties with French-speaking states, most *Québecois*, rightly or wrongly, have second thoughts about these new federal activities and are not ready to forget the past record of neglect. Besides, the narrow conception which most English-speaking civil servants hold about French culture is not reassuring. In such circumstances, whatever Ottawa does in order to develop its relations with the French-speaking world, Quebec will not back down for it is not only a question of seeing something being undertaken "for Quebec" but of deciding if it can be done "by Quebec."

If Quebec's international activities stem, on the one hand, from a new self-awareness and a better knowledge of the rest of the world, it is undeniable, on the other hand, that foreign countries are now discovering the French-Canadian people. Expo 67 and de Gaulle's controversial visit have been the most important factors in that regard. Besides, there is no doubt that France and the other French-speaking States have been taking a greater interest in French Canada in the last few years.

But above all these factors, two main reasons have conditioned the behaviour of the government of Quebec. First is its determination to assume all its legislative and administrative responsibilities. In concrete terms this means that the government must make sure that the million and a half young people who will look for jobs in the next fifteen years will be able to work in their language. Most private corporations are not yet able to create a French-speaking *milieu de travail* for they import most of their scientific know-how from the United States and English Canada. It is then up to the government of Quebec to try to counter-balance such a trend. The only way to do so is to establish more exchanges with French-speaking countries which can provide such scientific and technical knowledge.

Finally, French Canadians are determined to put an end to their traditional isolation and to make tangible steps in its search for collective equality with English-speaking Canadians in Canada.

In a speech delivered on June 25 (Quebec's day) at Expo 67's Place des Nations, the Premier of the Province, Mr. Johnson, addressed an urgent plea to the federal government to recognize that Quebec must have freedom to negotiate international agreement as a condition of equality and cultural survival:

There is no possible equality in Canada for the French cultural community if Quebec cannot negotiate the necessary agreements for the preservation of its particular heritage.

Speaking on the same subject, Mr. Marcel Masse, a young but authoritative voice in the Quebec cabinet, revealed that Quebec did not want to continue playing "hide and seek" with the federal government and proposed that "mechanisms for a discussion with Ottawa on this matter be set up."

What She Already Has

Three points strike the observer. First, the considerable progress that Quebec has achieved in its search for a distinctive voice in the concert of nations in less than six years (1961-1967). Secondly, the determination of the Quebec government to go further in this area. Thirdly, the general consensus existing among all provincial political parties that such a policy is highly beneficial to the interests of French Canadians.

As soon as it came to power in June 1966, the Union Nationale adopted the policy outlined a few years before by the former Minister of Education in the Liberal Government. Mr. Gérin Lajoie had stated that Quebec should have these rights.

1 to conclude international agreements in the fields of its jurisdiction while taking into consideration Canada's foreign policy;
2 to participate – probably as an observer or as an associate member – in a few international agencies like UNESCO, ILO, WHO and FAO whose objectives are closely related to provincial domains;
3 Quebec's international activities should be clearly recognized and defined in the Canadian constitution;
4 Mechanisms of consultation and cooperation between Ottawa and Quebec should be institutionalized to regulate these activities;
5 a constitutional tribunal, whose members should be appointed not only by the federal government but also by Quebec, should be set up to determine the "legality" of international agreements.

Mr. Gérin Lajoie repeated that such an international activity was constitutionally feasible, politically desirable and culturally essential for Quebec.

At the beginning, Ottawa was quite surprised but not astonished by Quebec's desire to seek closer ties with French-speaking countries. Many other Canadian provinces in the past, especially Ontario, which has signed pacts with a dozen foreign states, had had several dealings with foreign authorities and nobody had protested too loudly. But as more and more initiatives were taken by the government of Quebec and more and more statements of principle were handed out by its leaders, making it clearer every day that the province was truly looking for some sort of "international personality" of its own, the federal government became more suspicious of the province's stands and actions in this field; for a time Ottawa seemed very hesitant in taking a strong stand itself. In 1965, the federal government took a conciliatory attitude and a solution was found when Ottawa and Paris concluded an *accord-cadre*, a framework agreement which allowed any province to sign a cultural entente with France. But at the end of 1966 Ottawa stated in unmistakable terms that the federal government was the sole authority in the conduct of Canada's international relations and that there was no room for the theory of the dual international personality in Canada.

For a fairly large group of people, Quebec's international activities have been overemphasized and exaggerated. They contend that the press is largely responsible for the misleading of public opinion. They hold the view that Quebec is speaking a lot but not doing much in the field. They assert that Quebec's position is very weak on the world scene and that even if paragraph 132 of the BNA Act is obsolete, the constitutional practice has clearly shown that Ottawa is the only level of government in Canada which is competent to deal with foreign powers. According to them, no country besides France is ready to enter into official relations with Quebec. Ottawa's position is one of strength and as long as the federal government does not wish to "bow" to Quebec's demands in that field, Quebec will not be able to expand its "official external relations" very much: besides Quebec cannot financially afford to compete with Ottawa in the field of international cooperation.

Others maintain that Canada is facing here a political problem only. According to them, it is quite useless to attempt to circumscribe, from a legal standpoint only, a question which has such far-reaching economic and social consequences on all levels of life in Canada. They argue that fundamentally the problem is related to the various ways of looking at the role and the place of Quebec vis-à-vis the whole French-Canadian society in Canada. They conclude that the only important question is to discover if the government of Quebec can really pretend to be a better interpreter of French-Canadian views on the world scene than the federal government. They state that as long as Quebec has not proved such a point, Ottawa has no reason to make any major concession.

In reality, the main issue should not be to decide whether it is a legal or a political problem (in fact it is both) or to decide if Ottawa is right and Quebec is wrong or vice versa.

Objective analysis shows that both Quebec and Ottawa have a strong case.

There is also no doubt that a lot is at stake in this dispute: the image of Canada on the world scene and the very existence of a strong French-Canadian society in North America. It is then unfortunate that the debate has been launched so badly. Quebec has stated its goals on political rostrums but has not yet presented to Ottawa any specific plan on how the necessary mechanisms for coordinating these international activities would function. On the other side, Ottawa's refusal to recognize official-ly Quebec's unusual situation in the field of international rela-tions will eventually lead to a real confrontation of power. Ot-tawa may have every *legal right* to "short circuit" Quebec's international programmes but it would be a grave *political mistake* to try to do so. Unless there is a change of moods in the near future, it is easy to foresee that many people in Quebec will react with impatience, will tend to forget the real issue and will speak only in terms of self-assertion and prestige. In reality, the whole question is so complex and so important that it will take a few years before it can be solved, if indeed it is ever solved!

Even if Quebec's first official international activities of some significant importance in the twentieth century was the opening of an *Agence du Québec* in New York in 1940, it was not until the coming of the Lesage Government that any serious steps were undertaken by the Province on the world scene.

October 1961: Quebec opened an office in Paris. Such a gesture did not create a problem *per se*. Ontario has offices in London, New York, Dusseldorf and Milan. A problem arose when Quebec wished to obtain for its representatives rights and priv-ileges ordinarily given to consular officers. After some discus-sions, the question was resolved to Quebec's advantage when Paris agreed to give full immunities to the *La Délégation générale du Québec*.

During the same year, the government adopted an order-in-council which almost passed unnoticed but will prove to be quite important in the years ahead: Quebec gave fiscal privileges to members of the Consular officers working in the Province.

1962: Quebec opened a new *Délégation générale* in London and appointed Mr. Lapointe, the present Lieutenant-Governor, as its representative.

1964: The provincial government established a "Division for *délégations étrangères*" within the Department of Trade and Commerce. During the same years an agreement was reached between the Department of Youth in Quebec and a subsidiary organization of the French Government, *l'Association pour l'organisation des stages en France* (ASTEF), establishing a programme of exchanges of young civil servants and technicians.

February, 1965: The debate between Ottawa and Quebec gained considerable momentum when Quebec sought and succeeded in concluding a cultural *entente* with France. There was surprise and anger in the English-speaking press at the news of this "new federal concession to Quebec." The *Globe and Mail* of April 20, 1965 warned Ottawa that it should go no further in satisfying Quebec's demands and stated that external affairs were solely and exclusively a prerogative of the central government. In May, the first meeting of the permanent commission responsible for implementing the "entente" between Quebec and France took place in Quebec.

August 25, 1965: Quebec announced that the Deputy Minister of Federal-Provincial Affairs was to chair a new committee composed of deputy ministers of departments "likely to have close knowledge of relations with foreign countries and groups." Involved were the Departments of Federal-Provincial Affairs, Education, Cultural Affairs, Health, and Commerce. This committee was to coordinate departmental relations with foreign governments and organizations. Although Mr. Lesage said that the committee would stick to provincial jurisdiction, many looked at this move as a first step towards the creation of a Department of External Relations.

November 17: Canada and France signed an *accord-cadre* or master agreement enabling all Canadian provinces to conclude "ententes" with France. On November 24, Quebec and France concluded their second cultural "entente" under the master agreement.

104

During the same year, an office was opened in Milan and the second meeting of the permanent commission of cooperation between France and Quebec took place in Paris.

November 1965: A *Direction des programmes internationaux* was established within the Department of Cultural Affairs and was given a budget of more than $3,000,000 per year. Of this, $2,000,000 were attributed to programmes of external cooperation and especially to the carrying out of the cultural ententes between Quebec and France. The rest was to be attributed to the *Délégations générales* and agencies abroad.

June 1966: A third meeting of the Franco-Quebec permanent cooperation committee took place in Paris.

January 1967: Quebec's *Délégations générales* and agencies were transferred from the jurisdiction of the Department of Trade and Commerce to the Office of the Premier.

April, 1967: But without any doubt, it is the adoption of Bill 33 establishing a "Department of Inter-Governmental Affairs" that must be regarded as the most important initiative that Quebec has taken in this regard. From then on, all the *Délégations générales* and agencies abroad and the province's international activities were to come under one central authority. While the main purpose of the Department is to coordinate the various existing international programmes, Bill 33 contains an article which created quite an uproar in Ottawa. It foresees that the Department of Intergovernmental Affairs is responsible for "all relations that can exist between the government of Quebec, its departments and organisms and all other organisms or governments outside Quebec, as well as for the negotiation of 'ententes' that can be concluded between Quebec and these organizations or governments."

May, 1967: The Franco-Quebec permanent cooperation committee met for the fourth time in Paris. As a result of two private meetings with General de Gaulle, Premier Johnson laid the basis for extending cultural, technical and economic projects of cooperation between France and Quebec.

July, 1967: De Gaulle made Quebec "enter history."

September, 1967: While a few Ministers of de Gaulle's Government came to Quebec to consolidate the new direct relationship with Paris, René Lévesque proclaimed his manifesto for a "sovereign" Quebec.

November 1967: De Gaulle's press conference confirmed his support for a *Québec libre*.

How Far Will She Go?

What lies ahead in this field? It is certain that Quebec, while developing ties with France in numerous fields, will pursue its present policy in order to obtain the formal constitutional recognition of its international competence. In concrete terms, Quebec will do everything it can to

conclude certain types of international agreements;

play a distinctive role in a few specialized agencies;

play a part in the setting up of a *Communauté des peuples francophones*;

look for a role in most non-governmental international organizations (like *l'Association des parlementaires francophones*) dedicated to the promotion of the interests of and to foster the cooperation between French-speaking nations;

adopt a general law concerning consular immunities and privileges applicable to consular officers living in the Province, so that Quebec officers working abroad could eventually get reciprocal treatment;

open a *Délégation générale* somewhere in French-speaking Africa and a few other offices around the world for the promotion of its economic and cultural interests and to attract prospective immigrants;

institutionalize some sort of cooperation with the Office of Foreign Aid in the field of educational and technical assistance to French-speaking countries. It would not be surprising if Quebec might even go as far as assisting directly a few African countries;

set up a permanent provincial parliamentary committee of external affairs;

undertake numerous projects – like participating in international exhibitions, developing its own programme of cultural exchanges, in order to assert Quebec's personality abroad;

join with other French-speaking countries in the settting up of a telecommunication satellite system to make sure that French-speaking programmes will be directly televised over Quebec.

Naturally, such a list is not exhaustive and by the time this book is published, other projects may be put forward by the Quebec government.

Many Quebeckers seem to believe though that the provincial government should act with caution and should assert its stand without too much noise. They think that the province simply cannot afford itself financially to go ahead on a large scale. They think that Quebec will gain much more in establishing a *de facto* international identity through gradual steps rather than asking for a *de jure* recognition of a certain international competence.

Another school believes that, if the "gradual approach" has succeeded between 1960 and 1966, Ottawa is now determined and is capable of "blocking" almost every new international activity which Quebec wishes to undertake. According to them, the only method left to Quebec, if it is to make some progress in this field, is to provoke a new debate with Ottawa which will lead to a formal amendment of the constitution recognizing Quebec's right to act in specific areas on the world scene. Such a view was expressed very clearly by Mr. Gérin Lajoie in a special interview published in *Le Devoir* of June 29, 1967. The Premier of Quebec, Mr. Johnson, expressed a similar idea in *La Presse* of July 1, 1967:

> Our aim is not to pick quarrels but to end them by making with the English-Canadian community a new alliance that corresponds to the needs of the situation in 1967. This is why Quebec intends:
>
> 1 to exercise to the full powers that the current constitution gives it, in other words assume them fully both internally and externally without reducing the constitutional rights of the central government;
> 2 at the same time prepare for a few constitutional order that can assure Canada's general progress and harmony while encouraging the full development of its two constituent nationalities.

René Lévesque's sovereign Quebec in a Canadian Union with foreign policy determined cooperatively is yet another proposal short of complete separation. Evidently, Quebeckers know that a new constitutional order will not come tomorrow but they are determined to strive for major change. Even if Ottawa is now determined to treat Quebec like any other province in this field – in fact the central government will probably set up a mechanism of permanent consultation with all provinces for the carrying out of international agreements which cannot be implemented in Canada without the approval of the provinces – it will probably have to look for some sort of a compromise. Political factors, especially at the eve of a new election, will be determinant. Besides, more and more people seem ready to accept the idea of Quebec's particular status within the Canadian federation.

A Test Case of Mutual Trust

In any case a solution to this dispute will be found only if Quebec recognizes Ottawa's right to speak for all Canadians on the world scene even if, as Premier Johnson put it "no-one will ever convince anyone that the Canadian government is a French-speaking government" and if Quebec agrees not to undertake any international activity which could be contradictory to Canada's foreign policy or would reduce Ottawa's bargaining power in international negotiations or transactions.

For their part English-speaking Canadians must recognize that it is vital for Quebec – if it is to remain the *point d'appui* of French-Canadian society – to assert its identity and to take advantage of everything abroad which can help its search for progress according to its cultural heritage and to its cultural aspirations. Besides, nobody should deny that in the technological age, almost every provincial program has some sort of international extension. All provinces will have to create machinery to supervise their external activities. Ontario set up such a committee in 1967.

Quebec's role in international affairs represents both a challenge and an asset to Canada's foreign policy. It will force Ottawa to look for more imaginative programmes, while it will oblige the central government to think *a priori* about French Canada rather than *a posteriori* as it did before in devising its international policies.

Quebec's international role represents also a definite challenge to Canada's foreign policy and to Canada as such. It is a test case of mutual trust. It all depends on Quebec's restraint in its attitude toward Ottawa and on English-speaking Canadians' sincerity toward Quebec. If Quebec demands too much in the field of international affairs, this cannot but lead to the establishment of a dual image of the country on the world scene which is an inevitable step towards breaking up Canada.

On the other hand, if English-speaking Canadians do not recognize that Quebec has every right to develop international activities which will favor the self-fulfilment of French-Canadian society, this will give ample proof that they do not wish to accept French Canadians as equal partners in Canada. This also may lead to separatism.

Restraint and sincerity are certainly not qualities which all Canadians share but one can hope that a sufficient number of leaders who possess them will be around the negotiation table in the coming years.

Franklyn Griffiths

OPENING
UP
THE
POLICY
PROCESS

Franklyn Griffiths is Assistant Professor of Political Science at the University of Toronto. He teaches Soviet politics and has worked for the Canadian Peace Research Institute.

In Canada, as in most democratic societies, foreign policy questions do not normally receive wide public discussion. But Canada is notable for the extent to which a small group of politicians and civil servants dominates the foreign policy making process. Closed-circuit decision-making on external affairs, combined with the cautious temperament of the dominant policy-makers and the federalist style discussed by Hockin below,* produces a characteristic diplomatic style – a preference for "quiet diplomacy," a smoothing-over of differences among allies and a patient elaboration of the middle way in the United Nations and Commonwealth. Often substituting style for the substance of policy, our political leaders are inclined more to work within existing situations than to attempt their transformation to suit Canadian needs and the needs of others as we perceive them. Indeed, a systematic determination of such needs and of the means of satisfying them

* See Chapter 10, pp. 119-30.

would probably be alien to most of our foreign policy decision-makers. On the other hand, their preoccupation with the continuing situations in which Canada finds itself has led to the acquisition of a considerable, if not widely-shared, expertise in achieving marginal change for the better. Despite the inevitable exceptions, a flexible and discreet pursuit of the possible has long been the order of the day in Canadian external relations. Is this good enough?

There is no brief answer to this question. Nor can a proper one be given without reference to the way we make our foreign policy. Canadians may accomplish many new things in international affairs, but unless we begin at home, the system of closed-circuit policy-making and our exaggerated preference for private diplomacy will assure a continued muddling through in our foreign relations. Beginning at home means above all an expansion of the range of groups and individuals taking part in the making of foreign policy. This enlarged participation is necessary both for a fuller realization of the parliamentary democracy to which we are committed and for a better integration of the Canadian political community. It is also vital to the effectiveness of foreign policy. The key to an improved foreign policy process would seem to lie in more intense public discussion of the issues. Yet we are faced with decision-makers who suffer from political laryngitis, so far as raising and explaining foreign policy problems are concerned. How then are we to achieve a more democratic and efficient system of foreign policy making?

The Role of "Intermediate Groups"

The ideal of full democratic control over foreign policy by a concerned and enlightened citizenry is practically, if not technically, impossible. But opportunities do exist in Canada to increase popular participation in foreign policy making and to broaden the role of interested groups at the intermediate level between the general population and the federal leadership. In domestic and external affairs alike there is a common problem: federal politics are largely an élite affair in which the decision-makers are inadequately linked to the people for whom decisions are being made. The political parties clearly have a role to play in expressing the public interest and in providing for communication between foreign policy leaders and popular constituencies. At the same time, the diverse interests represented in Canadian parties, seem to be only remotely concerned with external affairs. In addi-

111

tion to parties then, more specialized and coherent groups are needed to perform the linking function between the political leadership and the public at large. Let us look at the role of these "intermediate groups," and at possibilities they offer for improving the discussion of external policy in Canada.

In this country we do have church and professional associations, trade union, business, ethnic and expatriate organizations. We also have, although in much smaller numbers, associational groups specifically concerned with external affairs, such as the United Nations Association or the National Zimbabwe Committee (which is seeking to mobilize public opinion on the Rhodesian question). But the overall effectiveness of such groups remains limited. On important issues such as the renewal of North American Air Defence arrangements (Norad), or the Canadian position on anti-missile defence, we have heard little from groups interested in foreign policy. Nor are there intimations of significant behind-the-scenes group activity on these issues. It must be granted, as many in Ottawa will point out, that few Canadians are equipped to discuss this kind of technical problem.[1] Moreover, it is the rare "intermediate group" which is willing and able to secure the services of research staff to work out policy positions on a continuing basis. The result is that unless something happens to fix the attention of the public, Ottawa will decide even far-reaching questions primarily on its evaluation of the technical factors and of the general state of public opinion.

The presentation of intelligible foreign policy demands and alternatives by the Canadian public to its authorized decision-makers is hampered by the lack of more strongly developed "intermediate group" activity. The Prime Minister, the Secretary of State for External Affairs and their subordinates are, of course, able to scan the newspapers for signs of public opinion; they may receive polls conducted by their party; and they may also address a good many associational groups each year, and in doing so receive indications of public sentiment on current foreign policy questions. But this is as far as it goes. Such consultation does not offer our decision-makers reasoned choice between specific ends; nor is it likely to provide them with recommendations as to how a specific end may best be achieved. How in fact are we to have a more positive influence on the Vietnam situation? And at what acceptable costs? How, further, may we best influence American policy-making on the problem of European security? And so on.

Given only the general preferences expressed by public opinion and the few associational groups concerning themselves with foreign affairs, our decision-makers find themselves working in something of a political vacuum. They would seem to have an extraordinarily free hand; but in fact they are reluctant to exercise this freedom lest they agitate the public to which they are already exposed in the absence of effective intermediate bodies. Conversely, Ottawa is vulnerable to unspecific demands to "do more" in international affairs. An example of this sort of unspecific demand occurred during the Middle East crisis of 1967: the perception of accumulated public demands to act more firmly in foreign relations helped to push Ottawa into a line of action that prematurely destroyed its potential for mediation. Denied the possibility of choosing between discriminating and politically significant proposals for foreign policy action (such as might accompany stronger "intermediate group" activity), the federal leadership must rely largely on its own limited political and bureaucratic resources in devising responses to international events. In its dealings abroad, it lacks the confidence and capacity to influence which would come with clear public support for its objectives. But given more intense participation by "intermediate groups" in the Canadian foreign policy process, the responsibility and effectiveness of our decision-makers and diplomats could well be increased.

In addition to associational groups, Canadian foreign policy making would benefit greatly from the development, outside the Government service, of a stratum of well-informed observers of external affairs. The elements of this particularly attentive and specialized public do exist in the press and universities, and perhaps at the higher levels of business and other organizations concerned with foreign policy. But communication among its members is weak, and there is as yet little continuing discussion of alternate policies. Accordingly, Ottawa is not obliged to conduct policy before a discriminating audience which not only has ideas of its own about external affairs, but also has access to the general public through the mass media. In turn, the government is denied the intellectual and political resources which these expert observers could bring to the foreign policy process.

The problem, then, is not simply one of increasing the number of associational and expert "intermediate groups" as such. Instead, it is one of restructuring the communications network of Canadian foreign policy making – of opening up many of the closed circuits to public scrutiny, and of "wiring in" whole new sections of the population across the country. In this way the foreign policy process may become more democratic and effective, and conducive to a greater sense of popular involvement in the Canadian community. This applies particularly to the people of Quebec, who more than most have felt the lack of rapport between the federal government and the governed of Canada. Moreover, should there be changes in the nature of Confederation reducing the constitutional powers of the federal élite, it would become all the more important to further a participatory foreign policy process.

From Closed-Circuit to Open Policy-Making

The essential precondition for the appearance of greater intermediate activity is political action in favour of a more open discussion of foreign policy problems. This action may ultimately be taken for the reason that Canadian politicians will find public discussions necessary in order to profit from certain changes in the popular attitude toward external affairs.

Looking first at the question of a more open discussion of external affairs, we may take note of Lester Pearson's observation that the "formulation, expression and dramatic confrontation of major viewpoints" improve the workings of government by encouraging more care and responsibility by administrative authorities."[2] A continuous and open airing of the issues in foreign policy stimulates activity by individuals and groups who otherwise would be inhibted from participating in the policy process by the lack of debate and authoritative information on sensitive questions. Among the Canadian political élite, however, feeling runs deep that open discussion of the issues and public intervention into policy-making are hazards which must be avoided. Canadian politicians have usually been anxious to avert any "dramatic confrontation of viewpoints," and have often sought to prevent public debate and to play down politically important information about current affairs. Indeed, for most Canadian leaders, a "political" issue is an undesirable one, one to be eliminated. They prefer that the public accept quietly the ministrations of its elected servants.

If no great encouragement is to be expected from this quarter, how is a broader public discussion of foreign affairs to be encouraged? Members of parliament certainly have something to contribute here, and parliament could itself become a focal point of improved public deliberation on foreign policy. As is the case with other parliamentary democracies.[3] Canada needs an invigorated parliament to take over some of the powers accumulated by the executive branch in external as well as domestic affairs. Already there is discussion of the need to revitalize parliament and its handling of business; to remove issues from the chaos of uninformed debate; and to reduced the privileged control which the prime minister and civil service technicians have over public policy.

If the political will were present to further an expanded discussion of external affairs in parliament, the relevant committees could well assume a more prominent role. While modest steps are now being taken in this direction, substantial progress will require the provision of permanent research staff for committee members, and also an understanding that it is proper for ministers and senior civil servants to be less guarded in their responses before committee than is now the case. The committee could undertake to solicit briefs on specific foreign policy problems from interested groups. Furthermore, committee-proceedings could on occasion be made available for television broadcasting, in the interests of wider public involvement in the foreign policy process.

Parliament and the public could also benefit from more intensive consideration of foreign and defence affairs within the political parties. After all, there is only so much that can be done to open up foreign policy making through the development of "intermediate group" activity if the parties continue to offer unsatisfactory discussion and comment on external affairs. If permanent staff were available within the parties to provide expert information and analysis on a broad basis, the quality of parliamentary debate on external affairs might be expected to improve. A more favourable setting might then be produced for transactions between interested groups and parties, and for the consideration of foreign policy matters by the general public.

Ultimately, however, the development of a more representative system of foreign policy making will depend upon creative leadership by federal politicians.

Political Style and the Available Public

During recent years there appear to have been significant changes in the availability of the Canadian public for participation in the making of foreign policy. For generations Canadians have made a practice of leaving external affairs very largely to Ottawa while focusing their attention on the private benefits made possible by order and good government. It is, of course, still true that Canadians have little time for the consideration of foreign affairs and even less for political action. Yet, as a result of post-war revolution in communications technology and of changes in social structure, more people have been exposed to a growing volume of images and information concerning foreign affairs. The level of their attentiveness to such matters would seem to have risen slightly but significantly. Television in particular communicates a sense of involvement as well as information – a dual function particularly evident during the recent United Nations debates on the Middle East crisis. And, although the individual will rarely feel a need to become involved in the making of external policies, his enhanced *attention* to foreign relations makes him potentially responsive to novel political appeals.

Federal politicians of a new type may well find it profitable to convert this increased popular attention into political power. These politicians may be expected to differ markedly from our traditional foreign policy decision-makers in their mastery of the communications media and in their willingness to engage in controversial public discussion of foreign policy at home and also at times in relations with other governments. On occasion they will be ready to emphasize rather than to smooth over political conflicts in Canada, and to seek out new constituencies for foreign policy proposals even at the cost of more intense political and social – as opposed to regional – divisions across the country. Rather than trying primarily to keep the ship of state on an even keel, they will attempt to get in touch with the passengers to see where the ship should be going. Whether "independence," anticommunism, a political assault on the monarchy or a combination of these and other appeals will provide the formula to mobilize the general public and create a more favourable setting for "intermediate group" activity remains to be seen. But given sufficient skill in raising issues and fashioning coalitions, the practical possibility of building a better way of making foreign policy is present in Canada.

Open and Effective Diplomacy

Up to this point I have been discussing policy-making in the stages of the process that precede and accompany the taking of decisions by authorized officials. But foreign policy making does not stop with formal decisions. The manner in which decisions are implemented diplomatically affects and reflects the character of decision-making. This raises the question of effectiveness in Canadian external affairs.

A willingness to engage in more open discussion of international issues would increase the diplomatic effectiveness of Canadian policies by stimulating influential non-government groups abroad to make claims on their governments that would assist in the achievement of our own purposes. In the same way that a more frank and detailed discussion of our external affairs would catch the attention and promote the intervention of the public and of "intermediate groups" in Canada, so also a similar effect might occur in foreign countries. Open discussion is particularly important in influencing the debate among officials and semi-official groups abroad who otherwise may be denied access to important information. What Canadian officials have to say about the Vietnam situation, for example, increases the relevance of certain views among American policy-makers and reduces the salience of other recommendations. Whether we like it or not, our actions or inaction, our statements or silence, affect to a varying degree the influence of the Fulbrights and Dirksens in the American policy-making process. It is important to be systematic in our public discussion of and comments on current international problems, so as consciously to influence the role of foreign policy groups and publics abroad, as well as to encourage such group activity within Canada.

Obviously there are many occasions when private negotiation, the customary mode of diplomacy, is indispensable to foreign policy implementation. The operational question is one of the proportion in which public discussion and private diplomacy are combined over a period of time. We should be aware that a foreign policy that is served chiefly by "quiet diplomacy" – by private communication only with the authorized decision-makers and diplomats of other states – surrenders important potential sources of strength. In domestic affairs, the effect of prolonged diplomatic activity carried out privately, by statesmen or by diplomats acting with large discretionary powers, is to negate any extensive public role in the making of policy. Democratic deliberation and decision-making are made difficult, if not impossible, and the political leadership also denies its actions maximum public support. In external affairs, a predominantly private diplomacy is pursued at the price of influencing important publics and groups which might be affected by what Canadian statesmen and their representatives have to say. "Quiet diplomacy" helps to minimize participation in policy-making abroad. The "quiet diplomatist" in effect accepts the political situation in other countries as given, and seeks to influence the conduct of the official decision-makers by force of ideas alone. A creative and effective foreign policy is one that also is concerned to increase support for the purposes of the Canadian government among non-governmental and semi-official groups in other countries as well as in Canada.

As our society is increasingly a complex and diverse one, so also are many of those with which we have dealings. Our relations with other powers are not the relations of nation-states conceived of as self-contained "billiard balls" each acting independently. Rather we are caught up in a multitude of processes in which the foreign policy discussions and actions of other countries influence the individuals and groups engaged in our policy-making. Simultaneously the intended and unintended communication of our views and actions influence to some extent the participants in the policy-making of other states. In this interlocking relationship we have the very real interdependence which both confines and gives scope to the Canadian will in external affairs. While there are limits to what we can do to affect the decisions of others, much can be done to shape our own political system to give Canada a true sense of purpose and a more effective role in world affairs.

Thomas Hockin

FEDERALIST
STYLE
IN
INTERNATIONAL
POLITICS

Thomas Hockin is Assistant Professor and Senior Tutor at Winters College, York University. He has published articles and essays on Parliamentary reform and foreign and defence policy.

Most Canadians would agree that Canada does not pursue one of the world's most exciting foreign policies. Is our lack of concern caused by our awareness that we are not a major power and by our vision of the compelling, at times tyrannical, pressures of the international system which leave Canada little elbow room for imaginative, constructive action? Time after time we hear our opinion-leaders justify our monotonous and incoherent foreign policy by pointing to our status as a middle power.

I would argue however, that our infirmity in international affairs comes not from our limited power compared with other nations, but because of our *domestic* habits of mind, our Canadian political style. We tend to project into the international arena techniques and ideas that make sense domestically but which are useless internationally. The policy pronouncements of our politicians and the actions of diplomats who represent us abroad reflect the influence of national behaviour patterns.

WALTER GORDON NOT ONLY PINCH HITS FOR THE MINISTER OF FINANCE BUT SOMETIMES GOES TO BAT FOR EXTERNAL AFFAIRS.

The most familiar ingredient in the Canadian political tradition practised by almost all Canadian political leaders from Macdonald through King to Pearson is our preoccupation with federalism. To be sure, most Canadians could not cite a clear definition of federalism, but the diversity of the federal system's components may impel its political leaders to avoid ultimate questions of purpose in order to maintain a minimal common denominator of consensus. This demands only a basic agreement on the rules of the power game. A procedural consensus may be necessary but a substantive one is not. The international situation is hardly similar. There is as yet no consensus on the fundamental questions. The Canadian genius for compromise and temporary solutions bears little fruit in the international arena where the more basic conflicts have yet to be solved.

Organization Before Purposes

When our "federalist" impulse is appropriate, Canadians have not pursued its implications very far. We rely too much on the compromising tactics and thought-saving clichés of this approach rather than force ourselves to generate the deeper reforms that may be needed. Our preoccupation with holding the nation together has made the organization itself, not its purposes, our fundamental concern. We tinker so often with our own political system, continually adjusting the mechanism of Federal-Provincial relations, that mere survival after each shock seems a cause for relief and celebration. As John Robarts exulted after the 1964 Premiers' Conference "tough old Canada still hangs together." Royal Commissions, parliamentary committees and Federal-Provincial conferences have frequently produced positive results by giving a crisis time to cool down. To de-fuse political timebombs by calling another meeting is a device that has often worked inside Canada. It is not surprising then that we believe that these techniques will work in the world arena.

It is this century-old preoccupation with keeping Canada together that we transpose to international affairs. We hear far more Canadian speeches about the need to maintain the Commonwealth, Nato, Norad and the UN – to keep the grand old organization going – than we do about where these organizations should be going or what they should be accomplishing. It is often urged, for example, that if Canada can help hold Nato or Norad or the Commonwealth or the UN together she therefore keeps a forum for exercising her diplomatic influence and that this somehow enhances our independence. Perhaps it is time to inquire if, in fact, the organization itself may divert our energies from more independent action. There is no obviously direct correlation between independence or influence and membership in bickering, sometimes purposeless organizations. The Americans in Seato and, of course, the French in Nato did not hesitate to jettison or to ignore an organization once they felt it had outlived its usefulness. The classic Canadian position was Mr. Pearson's on the first day of the Lagos Conference over Rhodesia: "I have come to listen . . . and help if I can."[1] Canada's External Affairs Minister verbalized the Canadian style when he praised Prime Minister Pearson's participation in this meeting called to decide what to do about Rhodesia's Unilateral Declaration of Independence.

> Canada took an important part in the Conference as you know. At the suggestion of our Prime Minister, consultations will continue in two committees. . . . These committees provide an interesting example of new Commonwealth machinery devised to help deal with a particularly awkward problem. . . . No country has left the Commonwealth on this issue.

"Committees," "new machinery," no one "has left" the association – all these phrases are eerily reminiscent of Federal-Provincial relations. How useful was this transposition? The commonwealth committees did not prevent Rhodesia from surviving the sanctions. The "new machinery" did not prevent several African nations from refusing to participate in the ensuing Commonwealth deliberations. And finally the irrelevance and failure of the "new machinery" impulse became obvious when the Rhodesian issue was turned over to the UN at the end of the year.[2]

The answer to "awkward problems" is not always "new machinery" but more likely a new policy or decision. We Canadians too often assume that the mere readiness of antagonists to meet, to talk or to reconstitute themselves in a new forum is in itself a major step forward. In fact, it is frequently a postponement, or worse, a device to divert our attention from the root of the problem at hand. More importantly, our willingness to expend tireless efforts in getting organizations to meet again and to talk can deflect us from working out a concrete programme which alone would make the new meetings and new committees meaningful. Countries with a reputation for constructive ideas rarely need to clamour for new or renewed machinery for the right to be consulted, or to make an impact with a new policy.

This point should not be misunderstood. There is nothing intrinsically wrong in Canada's effort to keep multi-national organizations together or to formulate new machinery for consultation and decision. These steps, however, should not be substitutes for thought about what these groupings are supposed to do once they meet. Mr. Martin has spoken with pride of the "10,000 votes" Canada cast in "international conferences in 1963."[3] He might better have spoken of the ten relevant ones.

Our Defence Ministers talk the same way. Paul Hellyer admitted March 1, 1966 to the Canadian Club of Ottawa that Nato needs to be revised:

What is needed is a look at the real strategic situation in the world today. A look at the change in the balance of power since the treaty was signed. A look at the restored and increasingly powerful Europe and the part it should play in relation to its North American partners.

His suggestions for revision however, soon degenerated into the familiar plea for better organization and administration: ". . . the organization is becoming top-heavy with headquarters and their bureaucratic machinery."

To call for better machinery is not irrelevant. Nato seriously needs it, but there are compelling reasons for basic and fundamental changes also. Defence Minister Hellyer's *White Paper on Defence* provides further evidence: "flexibility is the key to our new defence policy." We should not forget that "flexibility" can be another word for "indecision" or even worse, for leaving all decisions to others. An independent foreign policy is not always a mediatory and flexible policy; it must also be a declaratory one.

The propensity to substitute pleas for the establishment, continuance or reconstitution of multi-national conclaves, in place of discovering a new policy or consensus for these conclaves can be seen throughout our international activity. Expending great diplomatic effort as international organization man seriously diminishes our ability to act and sound independent. Our position is seldom heard. Our style can also lead to a kind of intellectual inertia, because we tend to regard our success in setting up a new forum or reactivating an old one, as if this were almost a solution in itself. (How often, for example, does our Federal Government praise the establishment of a Royal Commission as if this were almost a solution in itself?) We often project this domestic style into the world scene when we grope for "détentes," "relaxations of tensions" or "new hopes." The complexities of international politics unfortunately are not amenable to this type of solution.

Patience and compromise have sometimes worked in Canada. This trait is interesting because it is so distinct from American attitudes. Public opinion in the US has shown, and continues to show (especially during the Vietnam conflict in 1966) alarming signs of impatience and omnipotence. Here Canada is quite different. Canadians are quite familiar with apparently insoluble problems. Onr English-French split makes us so. Nor have we ever been accused of harbouring visions of omnipotence. Our patience and sensitivity to obstacles is an important diplomatic resource.[4] For example we do enjoy the goodwill and even the ear of Americans. However our patience and sense of obstacles will not, of themselves, impress Americans. We must combine these Canadian traits with positions that clearly point to the contours of a positive new solution.

If we do not exhibit the more heady enthusiasms and feverish impatience so evident in the United States, and so dangerous for the world, our patience has its disadvantages as well. Aside from Howard Green's more optimistic and moralistic speeches ("This is no day for a pessimist in world affairs."),[5] we are so deeply impressed with the complications in international society that we seldom propose any independent or clear policy positions for the multitude of organizations of which we are members. We are afraid to lest we look ridiculous not only to others, but more importantly to ourselves. We retreat into banal generalities. Witness Mr. Green in the House of Commons:

> What is Canada's role in this world? As a people we have traditions of courage, of commonsense and of religious faith . . . we must then take our full part in world affairs and do it with a spirit of optimism.[6]

Compare Mr. Martin's reply to this homily accusing the then Minister of External Affairs of vagueness and calling for his own brand of clarity instead:

> We urge him now to appreciate . . . the urgency that attends us and to indicate in bold and clear terms something that represents the character and wishes of our people along the lines spoken by people like C. P. Snow, Barbara Ward, and other strong protagonists of the Western position. This is the kind of leadership we need at this time, not only here at home but throughout the West and throughout the world.[7]

This reluctance to formulate clear policy positions produces two consequences: first, our disinclination to be frank; secondly, our almost pavlovian peace-keeping response to international conflagrations. We seem to insist on speaking ambiguously and on carrying a peace-keeping baton.

We prevent ourselves from raising issues of possible embarrassment to the Soviet Union or the United States, for example, because (we tell ourselves) we must not destroy the climate of confidence by making "unacceptable" proposals. We are careful not to confront various absurdities of the Soviet or Chinese positions, because we don't want to "poison the air". We believe that the mere readiness of our adversaries to talk is considered encouraging. An aura of unintended cynicism then surrounds our policies with Communist countries. It could well be that the Soviet Union, or Poland (in its role on the ICC) would prefer us to be frank. As Henry Kissinger has explained, evidence of goodwill or reliance on friendly personalities is a frivolous, ultimately irrelevant, way to negotiate with any nation that understands negotiations to be tests of power.[8] It may be true that federal-provincial relations are as much a test of goodwill as of power. For Ottawa to be brutally frank publicly about a Provincial Premier's ideas might break up the federation. It is by no means evident that the same kind of public ambiguity ought to surround our relations with Communist countries. They would probably prefer us to be frank so they could know our attitude before bothering to meet with us.

Mr. Martin's circumlocutions in attempting to explain how Canada and Poland had "moved closer together" on Vietnam left his Polish audience "visibly amused" according to the *Toronto Star* reporter, November 10, 1966. The major loser, however, is the Canadian public. We are told that we are flexible, mediatory and of good will so are disconcerted to hear our action in Vietnam denounced as being solidly pro-American.

The organizational imperative of Canadian domestic politics has led to the tendency to see in peace-keeping, not so much the need for basic social reform, but the necessity to prevent or at least postpone violence. In the post-Suez litany of objectives for Canadian foreign and defence policy, peace-keeping has almost unreserved approval. We are careful not to be clear about the various kinds of peace-keeping we engage in because the very word has emotive, moralistic appeal. We assume so readily that peace-keeping is positive that we fail to address ourselves to the original conflict. In our naïveté, we were willing to believe that the UNEF had solved the Egypt-Israel war not just postponed its next battle. And again we fool ourselves thinking that by peace-keeping we are being the neutral, international Good Guy. We fail to see that the intervention of UN Emergency Forces in the Congo, Cyprus or (if necessary in the future) Kashmir is not neutral in its effect. There is always a bias. To prevent violence in Cyprus or Kashmir has meant the entrenchment of the status quo, the artificial freezing of a naturally untenable social and political situation. It is not necessarily "just" and "right" to race into these conflagrations without first demanding that a "just" and "right" political solution follow these interventions.

This is inordinately difficult for Canadians to grasp. We are proud of our non-violent history. Whatever may be questionable about W. L. Morton's thesis on the stability and conservatism of the Canadian identity, we do have something of a consensus on the proposition that "peace and order" are as vital as "good government."

This Canadian insistence on "law and order" and therefore peacekeeping forces should not be disparaged in an age when small violences could erupt into nuclear ones. But our unthinking belief in peace-keeping as an end in itself, the romance of being a sort of "international RCMP," blots out thought of how to achieve lasting solutions. The mere stationing of interpositioning, de-fusing or disarming forces in an untenable political status quo is neither glorious nor despicable. It is merely a postponement of the major task. We should not think our duty is done when we go only this far.

The Limitations of Pragmatism

Another ingredient in the Canadian political style is faith in pragmatism. It is related to (in fact may underpin) all the rest. The Aberharts, Bucks and a few other ideologues may rant at the extreme Right and Left of national policies but the huge middle ground is pragmatic. The pragmatists, not the ideologues, take the credit for holding Canada together, for preventing internal explosions. Our federal-provincial relations are conducted by pragmatists confronting each other over basically commercial problems. We know that the instrument for settling disputes in international politics during periods of peace is piece-meal diplomacy. But we too easily conceive this as being analogous to commercial negotiations and this attaches disproportionate emphasis on bargaining technique and sometimes on personalities. This makes Canadian tactics almost continually inappropriate when we try to negotiate with an ideologically inclined government.

Communists, for instance, look for what they call "objective" factors. Objective reality here consists not in what a country's diplomats or statesmen say, but in its social and economic structure.

A good example of our failure to recognize objective factors is this statement on Vietnam by Mr. Martin:

> We did not think it profitable at this stage to enter a controversy with President Ho Chi Minh over the interpretation of events in Vietnam. . . . Rather [in our reply to him] we availed ourselves of this opportunity to re-state the Canadian view that there could be no lasting solution of the present conflict other than through negotiations.[9]

To say this is to put faith in technique over objectives: that the momentum of negotiation will somehow overcome all brutal realities.

Our position on disarmament is based on the same mistake. Howard Green, in explaining why the 1960 autumn session of the UN failed to produce results on disarmament (and why the spring 1961 session might succeed), never once mentioned structural, political, or military factors. The key, he argued, was the atmosphere of the UN:

> The atmosphere at the United Nations last fall was very tense. . . . It was very difficult to have agreement reached on many questions, let alone . . . disarmament. . . . Fortunately, during the session which ended last Saturday morning, there was far less tension. I cannot say whether this was because there had been a change of administration in the United States, or because everyone was tired of that quarrelsome attitude just as we in the House get tired of such an atmosphere after a few hours and decide it might be better to be less pugnacious.[10]

The UN debate on the Arab-Israel conflict should surely have shown that the mere process of negotiation does not generate solutions on its own. We ought to be less reluctant to face the structural cases of "ill will," "bad atmosphere" or "hard line" positions. Our pragmatic dependence on personalities is understandable domestically. The personalities of provincial premiers explain a good deal of the positions their governments take vis-à-vis Ottawa. But in our efforts to defrost the cold war we must not rely on this alone. If we do so we run the risk, not of being dishonest, but of being irrelevant. A nation that bases its policies and attitudes on what it sees as the "objective forces" in international society cannot concede to another nation or personality but only to the reality of these forces.

This point is especially difficult for Canadians to grasp, for Canadian public policy and constitutional evolution have not been based on a clear recognition of, let alone agreement on, a systematic set of ideas. Our federal politicians have survived by acting as brokers and pragmatists. They have proof in the Canadian setting at least, that negotiations often generate enough momentum in themselves to permit solutions to be found. But we cannot assume the same about relations between armed and ideologically inclined sovereign states. Canadian pragmatism, compromise and our concomitant faith in negotiations have their place in international politics when sovereign states are not arguing ideology or are agreed on interpretations of events and potentialities. Otherwise our pragmatism can be irrelevant, escapist and therefore a liability. It was useful to be pragmatic and to act as a broker during the 1956 Suez crisis. All the antagonists were agreed that their interests would not be gravely undermined if there was a compromise. But now in the Middle East or in Vietnam pragmatic negotiations are impossible while both sides believe that their objective must be almost total victory. Negotiations will succeed once the objectives change. And to say that negotiations or the conference table *alone* will somehow miraculously change objectives is a faith with little confirmation in history. Canadian diplomacy must work on changing the objectives of antagonists, not simply on urging negotiations. An independent foreign policy position must be based upon assessments of the causes of conflicts not simply on the forums where they might be resolved. The latter question is for nations with no opinions to concentrate on. The former is for nations which honestly want to help resolve the world's basic conflicts.

Canadian foreign policy since the Second World War has shown a remarkable capacity to escape into tactical postures so that our strategic positions become clouded or forgotten. It is true, that we are participating in the world in ways remarkably varied and demanding compared to three decades ago. Mr. Martin speaks with pride of the 118 International Conferences we participated in in 1965. This does point out the extent of our international responsibilities but we must not forget that the huge effort that these conferences imply for Canada can sometimes dilute our capacity to make bold and useful contributions.[11] We have not marshalled enough independent thought to make all this business as useful as it could be. Immersion in detail can be a substitute for thought.

It would be unfair to say that our foreign policy-makers have been wilfully trying to escape from reality. What is closer to the truth, and very debilitating for an independent foreign policy, is that these policy-makers are not aware of the extent to which they are escaping.

But the proof of this flight from reality is becoming all too clear. Our tendency to put organizational viability before purposes of organizations, our penchant to put ambiguity and peacekeeping in the place of clear declaratory policy, our naïve faith in the magic of negotiations: all these behaviour patterns flow genuinely from our domestic experience. When Howard Green claimed that the great Canadian virtue of common sense will work internationally because it has worked domestically, we are hearing honest but irrelevant attempts to articulate a view of Canada's international role.

Perhaps these tendencies are the best our domestic attitudes can produce for international attention. In some cases they are salutory. But we must recognize that they do not add up to a vivid picture of an independent power. They do not prompt other nations to say, "Here is a nation that knows what is to be accomplished through international organizations, through negotiations or after the peace-keeping forces have pacified the populace."

This identification has been difficult to make because we have prided ourselves on not taking public positions. We seem to believe that ambivalence, far from being a vice, is a virtue. We are saved from pursuing a more declaratory policy in Vietnam because we are on the International Control Commission. We have been saved from declaring how the Congo, or Cyprus or Kashmir should be ruled lest we not be invited to take part in peace-keeping forces in these areas. We have discovered a dozen ways to avoid speaking firmly and creatively. In short, we have found dozens of ways to avoid controversy.

However, the measure of a nation's independence is not found in its ability to avoid controversy. The price of progress internationally is often argument. If Canada is to remain independent with a voice in world affairs that emphasizes it, it is inevitable that we will create some controversy.

We have, nonetheless, through our federalist view of world affairs an outlook that could generate ideas of real relevance for the international system. We have relied too much on the expedient tactics this outlook sometimes implies instead of pressing the strategies and structural reforms that outlook could produce. By concentrating on finding solutions to particular conflicts lies both the hope for a useful independent foreign policy and one of the justifications for our independence in the first place.

PART B:

THE
PURPOSES
OF
INDEPENDENCE

SECTION III:

TOGETHERNESS
IN
ATLANTIC
PATTERNS

If the special American relationship is no excuse for Canada's diplomatic sins of omission or commission (section I) and if the real constraints on our international dynamism are internal – and remediable – problems of attitude, style and political structure (section II), then independence is realizable. Yet what should this foreign policy autonomy be used for?

If, as Hockin has just argued, our preoccupation with organization is a major cause of international irrelevance, should the main centre of our policies continue to be the supranational organizations and alliances of the Atlantic world? Whether alliancemanship is compatible with new policies is the question underlying Jack Granatstein's examination of the foreign policy effects of tri-service unification (chapter 11). While this military reorganization creates a force particularly well-equipped to act as a peacekeeper on a more independent basis, in fact it is taking place so as to maintain our Nato commitments and, more alarmingly, fit into the next generation of Norad's weaponry.

In terms of effectiveness at the multinational level, Michael Sherman explores the difficult question of controlling proliferation. His conclusion in chapter 12 is that Canada, as a non-nuclear middle power, can still contribute by unspectacularly continuing *not* to succumb to the nuclear status race. Harald von Riekhoff also argues we should keep steadily on course by participating in Nato which, he maintains in chapter 13, gives Canada more influence in the Atlantic Community than we would have as a non-aligned power.

Kenneth McNaught, however, emphatically repudiates this apologia for alliancemanship. For him both Nato and Norad symbolize Canada's satellite incorporation in the American foreign policy grid. It is only by withdrawing from these alliances that independent, internationally effective action can be undertaken along the lines of serious commitments to disarmament and United Nations activity for international equality.

Jack Granatstein

ALL
THINGS
TO
ALL
MEN:
TRISERVICE
UNIFICATION

*Jack Granatstein is Assistant Professor of History at York University.
He is the author of* The Politics of Survival: The Conservative Party of
Canada 1939-1945.

A persistent complaint of Canadian servicemen is that they are
scorned in time of peace. They are a "waste of money" or
"obsolete," useful only to pose for the tourists on Parliament
Hill or to tour the nation with a Centennial Tattoo. And yet for a
nation that is allegedly uninterested in defence matters, Canadians have spent an inordinate amount of time in recent years
arguing about such matters as Bomarc missiles and the unification of the three services. Too often this debate has focussed on
inconsequential issues, and the right questions have rarely been
raised.

For example, does Canada really need armed forces? Most
Canadians do not feel threatened by external enemies, and the
few who do usually recognize the nation's powerlessness in the
face of the ICBM. In fact Canada gets such protection as there is
by virtue of our geographical propinquity to the United States.
Canada, therefore, maintains military forces not for protection,

135

but because they provide certain political and diplomatic advantages. Since the Second World War, to cite two specific cases, we have contributed to continental air defence so that we could share in determining North American strategy and to Nato so that we could exercise some influence in the North Atlantic area. Inevitably, however, we have become a technological and military dependency of the United States. The effect of this dependency on our influence in the world is in dispute, but clearly there is a growing interest in Canada in developing and strengthening our independence from the United States. The armed forces can be used to work toward this end. If this is so, there is a rationale for maintaining Canadian armed forces. The Canadian government, however, has not seen the situation in these terms to date.

"The objectives of Canadian defence policy," Paul Hellyer, the Minister of National Defence, said in his *White Paper* in 1964, "are to preserve the peace by supporting collective defence measures to deter military aggression; to support Canadian foreign policy including that arising out of our participation in international organizations, and to provide for the protection and surveillance of our territory, our airspace and our coastal waters." And, the Minister went on, "there have developed four parallel methods by which the objectives of Canadian defence policy have been pursued. . . ."

1 *Collective Measures* for maintenance of peace and security as embodied in the Charter of the United Nations, including the search for balanced and controlled disarmament;
2 *Collective Defence* as embodied in the North Atlantic Treaty;
3 *Partnership with the United States* in the defence of North America;
4 *National Measures* to discharge responsibility for the security and protection of Canada.[1]

There was little of this assessment of national objectives that differed from statements by previous Ministers of National Defence. In 1960, for example, Conservative Defence Minister George R. Pearkes, V.C., had listed Canada's defence commitments as being the defence of the Canada-United States region, contributions to Nato, and the provision of forces to support the United Nations.[2] What was new in Mr. Hellyer's listing was that he had placed the support of the United Nations at the top of his list. In itself this was not startling, but when it was examined in conjunction with the Minister's proposed unification of the armed

136

forces, certain understandable fears were aroused. With a unified force, critics like Air Marshal W. A. Curtis charged, Canada would be unable to fulfill her commitments to Nato and Norad and would be unable to cooperate with her allies.[3] And after the United Nations blocked Canadian initiatives on peace-keeping in December, 1966, John Diefenbaker jeered that Hellyer's force would be all dressed up with no place to go.[4] Rear Admiral William Landymore echoed this charge in his testimony to the House of Commons Standing Committee on National Defence. Unification, he claimed, could only make sense if the government intended to concentrate upon one role such as Cyprus-type peace-keeping operations.[5] Robert Hendy, Vice-President of the Tri-Services Identities Organization, made similar statements before the Defence Committee, and he added that the roles of the armed forces should be settled before reorganization was undertaken. "The defence tail," he said, "should not wag the external affairs dog."[6]

Is the tail really wagging the dog? Is the unification of the armed forces, as Mr. Hellyer's many critics have proclaimed, merely the prelude to the complete abandonment of our alliances? To this observer, unification regrettably does not seem to imply Canadian withdrawal from Nato. In fact, unless both Mr. Hellyer and Secretary of State for External Affairs Paul Martin are unmitigated liars, the restructuring of the armed forces seems predicated on the assumption that Canada will maintain its ties with the alliance. The only area in which change is likely – well-nigh inevitable, indeed – is in the form the Canadian contribution will take.

Clearly the Canadian penchant for impossible compromises is still very much alive: unify the armed forces, yes; but adapt our military commitments to fit the realities of the world, never. Mr. Hellyer is evidently cast in the classic Mackenzie King pattern (but without the boyish charm of the master). He straddles the middle of the road, offering something – but not much – for everyone. This brief essay will attempt to examine the effects that Mr. Hellyer's policy is likely to have on the implementation of Canada's foreign policy.

I

When Paul Hellyer took office as Minister of National Defence in late April, 1963, the armed forces numbered more than 120,000 officers and men. In Europe, the army brigade deployed with Nato was well-trained but poorly equipped. There were no armoured personnel carriers, the brigade had no air support and the Honest John missiles, that had been foisted on the troops so that they could play their part in a limited nuclear war, had no warheads. The RCAF air division of eight squadrons of CF-104 strike-reconnaissance aircraft was in even worse straits. The House of Commons Special Committee on Defence of 1963 noted that the air division "has at this time no weapons whatsoever, either conventional or nuclear, for use with its CF-104s."[7] In Canada, the air force contribution to Norad – two squadrons of Bomarc B missiles and five squadrons of Voodoo interceptors – also lacked a nuclear capability. Canada's remaining defence commitments in 1963 included an anti-submarine role in the Pacific and in the North Atlantic, capably performed by the RCN's destroyer escorts and the RCAF's Maritime Air Command, and the provision of forces for UN peace-keeping operations. Canadian soldiers and airmen on UN service were stationed in the Congo, in Suez, in Palestine, in Kashmir, in New Guinea and in the Yemen. The remaining forces in Canada were engaged in training, although two army brigades were allotted to Nato in the event of an emergency and an army battalion group was on stand-by for United Nations peace-keeping duties.

With the exception of the troops employed on UN missions, the Canadian forces in 1963 were preparing to fight a nuclear war. The fighters and missiles assigned to Norad contributed to the credibility of the deterrent, the brigade and the air division attached to Nato were geared for limited nuclear war, and the RCN's anti-submarine warfare training was designed to counter the undersea capability of the Soviet Union.

Four years later the Canadian armed forces are still filling the same roles. The brigade in Nato is much better equipped now, its Honest Johns are armed, and it is ready at last to fight the limited nuclear war that strategists have been declaring an impossibility for six or seven years. The CF-104 squadrons have been reduced in number, but they now have the capability to carry both nuclear and conventional weapons. Their Nato missions remain unchanged. The Bomarcs and Voodoos assigned to Norad are still poised to ward off a manned bomber attack from the Soviet Union, and the navy continues its anti-submarine patrols off Canada's coasts. Until Mr. Hellyer began to restructure the forces, all that had changed was the world situation.

Certainly Nato has felt the effects of the Soviet-American

détente. France has severed almost all links with the alliance, the United Kingdom has reluctantly agreed to limit its troop withdrawals from Germany to one brigade of infantry and some aircraft and the Germans themselves are apparently looking toward a rapprochement with the countries of Eastern Europe. In the United States, the demands of the Vietnam war have resulted in a decision to withdraw up to 35,000 soldiers and 100 supersonic aircraft from German bases. But thus far Canada has shown no signs of any desire to further rock the boat. External Affairs Minister Martin told the Senate External Affairs Committee on March 15, 1967 that Canada would damage its good name by pulling its troops out of Nato:

> It could start a chain reaction by exerting pressure for similar action on the governments of the other members of the alliance, which are just as concerned with the cost of providing defence forces. . . . It could damage the fabric of co-operation that has been established for twenty years. It could do harm to Canada's good name with its allies. It could cause our allies to ask themselves whether we are making a respectable contribution to maintaining security in the world.[8]

Mr. Hellyer was probably more forthright in May, 1966 when he answered a question relating to the possibility of American or Canadian withdrawals from Europe. "I have no doubt," the Minister said, "that what one country decided to do might have some influence on what the other would eventually do or be under pressure to do."[9] Until such time as the Americans finally decide to remain or depart from Europe, in other words, Canada will do nothing other than to "engage in serious examination of the state of the alliance."[10]

And certainly there are few signs of a military nature that would indicate that Canada is planning to pull out of Nato. The brigade in Germany is being re-equipped with self-propelled 155 mm. howitzers, new armoured reconnaissance vehicles and armoured personnel carriers. The Centurion tank is said to be good for five more years, and the air division has enough CF-104s to continue the strike-reconnaissance role until 1972.[11] The navy's anti-submarine capability, the bulk of which is committed to Nato in event of an emergency involving the alliance, is also being increased. The destroyer escorts and the aircraft carrier "HMCS Bonaventure" are being modernized, two additional submarines are being purchased and four modern helicopter-equipped destroyers with the best available anti-submarine weapons will be constructed by 1970.[12] In addition the government has seized with some eagerness the chance to participate in the Allied Command Europe Mobile Force, Nato's attempt to deal with brushfire war situations on its northern and southern flanks. Canada has committed two battalion groups to this force and is providing the force commander. Judging by the emphasis the Minister of National Defence placed on this role in his 1966 testimony before the Defence Committee, the government feels that this is an important contribution.[13]

The prospects for an immediate change in policy are no more hopeful with respect to Norad. The manned bomber threat to North America has virtually disappeared, but the Pearson government shows few signs of any willingness to recognize this fact. The Bomarcs and Voodoos apparently are to be maintained until they slide into obsolescence in the 1970s, or so Mr. Hellyer has indicated.[14] And although John Diefenbaker, Walter Gordon and Tommy Douglas have all urged a reconsideration of our Norad commitment, if Mr. Hellyer is to be believed, the government will probably renew the air defence arrangement with the United States in 1968.

The possibility that the joint efforts of the American aerospace industry and the United States Air Force might soon force the United States to build and deploy an anti-ICBM system makes the Canadian position very uncomfortable indeed. ABMs will cost billions, they will create a need for extensive and expensive shelter systems, and they will not prevent the slaughter of at least five million Canadians and fifty million Americans even if they function as planned (something that is not certain) in the face of an all-out nuclear attack. The terrible wastefulness of this should be evident. But if the United States chooses to take this new step in the arms race there is probably nothing we can do to dissuade them. A clear statement that Canada has no intention of playing this particular game might strengthen the hand of the Pentagon moderates, but clear statements do not seem to be a Canadian vogue (and there are precious few Pentagon moderates). Certainly, however, there is no reason for Canada to squander any of her limited resources on ABMs. We will be devastated if we have the anti-missile missiles or not, so why waste the money? Whether the Canadian government would be able to resist American diplomatic pressures and the probable demands of the Canadian public to be as well "protected" as their neighbours to the south, however, is highly uncertain.

The third of our four defence roles, the defence of Canada, is a chimera. The active defence of our territory is not now and never has been either practicable or necessary, for any attack on Canada would inevitably involve the United States from the outset. The commitment of any of our limited defence resources to this role – with the possible exception of naval forces – for anything more than the barest of surveillance purposes would be a grotesque waste.

II

Peace-keeping, the last of our defence objectives, is the only one with any growth potential. Although we will likely continue to participate in Nato and Norad, there can be little doubt that our commitments to these alliances will decrease both absolutely and relatively. On the other hand, the probability of an increase in the number and variety of peace-keeping missions is good. To be sure, Canada's recent efforts to improve the United Nations capability to respond to crises have not met with success, and the withdrawal of the United Nations Emergency Force and the subsequent third Arab-Israeli War have severely shaken confidence in the UN and in the entire concept of peace-keeping. But certainly crises will continue to arise in every corner of the globe. The need for peace-keepers of some variety or other can only increase, and it seems probable that UN appeals for troops will continue to go to those nations that are prepared. Canada is. And peace-keeping carries with it additional benefits. This is one area in international affairs where Canada can play a role independent of the United States, and there is a real national necessity for an external focus of attention on some such activity. Participation in peace-keeping operations generally has united Canadians, and there are few enough issues that do. The ACE Mobile Force, it may be suggested, is an attempt to create a new kind of peace-keeping force, and the Canadian government's enthusiasm for this task is almost certainly related to this very fact.

Indeed, the force structure that Mr. Hellyer is in the process of creating is geared for just this sort of role. In its broadest sense, peace-keeping is to be the *raison d'être* of the Canadian Armed Forces. With its equipment and capabilities carefully tailored, the unified force will be capable of intervening in a wide variety of situations ranging from the suppression of terrorism to participation in conventional wars. Training is being shifted in emphasis from preparation for the impossible condition of limited nuclear war to a more realistic concentration on the methods of controlling conflicts of any size short of nuclear war. To accomplish this spectrum of tasks, the Canadian forces have been organized into six major commands on a functional basis. Maritime Command has as its primary responsibility defence against the submarine and embraces all the sea and maritime air forces. In addition Maritime Command is to provide sealift and support to the forces of Mobile Command. Air Transport Command's mission is to provide the strategic airlift capability for the mobile force and plans are afoot to acquire huge C-5 transports by 1972. As its name implies, Air Defence Command is to provide for the defence of North America. The Command embraces the Canadian contribution to Norad, and its task will presumably cease with the phase-out of the Bomarcs and Voodoos. Training Command is responsible for individual training, including flying and trades training, for all military personnel. Material Command supplies all logistic support to the unified force.[15]

The key to the reorganized force structure is clearly Mobile Command. As the Minister of National Defence said, "Mobile Command . . . is a completely new formation and depicts more than any other the new concept of Canadian defence policy."

Mobile Command has the responsibility for providing operationally trained and combat-ready land and tactical air forces, capable of rapid deployment in circumstances ranging from service in the European theatre as part of Canada's contribution to Nato, to United Nations and other peace-keeping or peace restoring operations. . . .

In addition to providing the rotational brigade for our European-based Nato contribution, mobile command will train the other two brigades in Canada to be air-transportable under the expanded concept of mobility.

This command will also produce an air-portable-air-droppable Canadian Airborne Regiment for even quicker response to special situations.

Among the tactical air elements of Mobile command will be a tactical aviation group of CF-5 tactical ground support aircraft, Buffalo short take-off and landing (STOL) transports and a variety of light and heavy helicopters.[16]

142

Air Transport Command and Maritime Command, to a lesser extent, are designed to support the ground forces of Mobile Command.

So for the first time, Canada will have forces in being capable of responding to a wide range of potential crises. When this system is in operation a force ranging in size from a few men to an airborne regiment to three brigades could be despatched with its equipment anywhere in the world within a period of two to thirty days. Never again will regiments have to be cannibalized to prepare a battalion for peace-keeping service (as was the case when the Queen's Own Rifles were prepared for UNEF service in 1956); never again will technicians be pulled out of training (as was the case when the ONUC signal squadron was formed in 1960). If Mr. Hellyer and his planners are correct in their assumptions, Canada's forces-in-being will be sufficient to meet any demands likely to be made upon them.

This new mobility is certain to affect our Nato position. In his testimony to the Senate Committee on External Affairs on March 15, 1967, Paul Martin was franker than is his custom when he conceded that Canada's military commitments to the alliance may change. "The Government," he said, "is not insensitive to the argument that Canada's contribution be made from bases in Canada. . . . The day may come with changes in technology and strategy when it would be feasible and satisfactory to ourselves and our allies to make our entire contribution from Canada."[17] By 1972, the Canadian Armed Forces should have sufficient airlift and sealift capability to deploy the entire mobile force with some speed. What better time could there be for the government to change its commitments to Nato? The brigade and the air division could be brought home to be replaced by a Canadian pledge – and a realizable pledge – to commit the mobile force to the alliance in case of an emergency. This surmise, and it is of course nothing more, becomes credible when Mr. Hellyer's paeans of praise for the ACE Mobile Force are recalled. The Canadian battalion group was airlifted to Norway in just five days in 1966, and the new concept of mobility had passed its first test. Who can doubt that by 1972 virtually the entire mobile force could not be similarly deployed? Certainly not Mr. Hellyer; and probably not our Nato partners. Conceivably, too, the withdrawal of Canadian (and American) troops from the continent could be undertaken in conjunction with reductions in the forces of the Warsaw Pact powers.[18]

Mr. Hellyer's opposition might be prepared to accept this sort of reasoning, but the critics are almost certain to maintain their attacks on the Minister's destruction of the traditions of the three services. Did the uniforms and hallowed customs of the forces have to be scrapped in order to secure additional mobility? (The credibility of the critics, I suspect, has suffered from the popular belief that they would prefer the traditions to the mobility any day of the week.) The answer to this not entirely unreasonable lament is probably yes and no. In the first place the Minister has explicitly stated that ship-regimental-squadron traditions will not be sacrificed. Under pressure, he has also granted permission for the old uniforms to be worn in certain, very broad circumstances, and he has apparently agreed that present rank titles may be preserved for the time being.[19]

What then is to be gained from unification? The most important result of combining the services is that unification will create a larger pool of trained specialists.[20] In 1960, for example, signallers needed for the Congo could be taken only from army units, despite a severe shortage of trained men. At that same time, apparently, the RCAF had ample signallers who could not be cross-posted to the army. Similarly in the late 1950s the air force was in the process of disbanding its heavy helicopter teams and reconverting pilots to jets, while the navy was launching a crash programme to train helicopter pilots.[21] Once again there was no coordination between services. With unification, however, specialists will fill vacancies regardless of the environment in which they began their service. This should result in eventual savings of men and money and in increased flexibility. Unification will have at least one other major effect. The very act of giving the force a single uniform and a functional organization will mark a break with the past. This psychological impetus will make training for the new tasks of the 1970s easier. Peace-keeping requires a different breed of soldier from war-making, and the duties of the Canadian Armed Forces are certain to involve heavy emphasis on the peace-keeping role. The inability or unwillingness of many senior officers to accept this change in emphasis is presumably one reason for the large number of resignations from the services.

The officers have left for other reasons, of course. Some senior officers are frustrated by their inability to practise "military mastery of ministers" on the stubborn Mr. Hellyer. Others see the unified force as symbolizing the death of their particular service. The RCAF sees itself reduced to flying transports for the army, its fighter role soon to disappear.[22] The navy apparently believes that its anti-submarine role has been placed in jeopardy by Mr. Hellyer (although why this should be so is difficult to comprehend in view of the new submarines and destroyers soon to come into service). Both RCAF and RCN officers see the army emerging as top dog in the new unified structure. Some or all of these fears may be valid, and the officers and men who have spent their lives in the services are entitled to a measure of sympathy.

Many Canadians, however, do not agree with the government's apparent willingness to continue membership in Nato and Norad. But certainly we can all applaud the government's efforts to rationalize these roles and to carry them out in the most efficient manner possible – and moreover to carry them out in a fashion that maximizes the possibility of a major effort in peace-keeping operations. Unification has laid the groundwork for a military force capable of carrying out coherent, realizable roles. What is more, unification will produce a force that is unique, a situation that should give a healthy fillip to Canadian nationalism. For all his arrogance and air of overwhelming rectitude, for all his unwillingness to be explicit about his plans, Mr. Hellyer has produced the first meaningful defence force in Canada's peacetime history. Whether or not the government will have the strength to use its handy, multi-purpose tool to serve Canadian national interests effectively, however, is most unclear.

Michael Sherman

CONTROLLING NUCLEAR PROLIFERATION: CANADA'S OPTIONS

Michael Sherman is on the staff of the Hudson Institute doing research on nuclear proliferation.

Some Canadian Attitudes

There is no consensus on the nature or extent of the dangers posed by a further spread of nuclear weapons. Indeed, some analysts argue that extensive proliferation would enhance rather than diminish international stability. These observers maintain that nuclear spread should be welcomed and perhaps even encouraged. Canada has traditionally taken a more pessimistic view, and an important part of our effort in foreign policy has been devoted to restraining nuclear proliferation. This is a correct policy, but it would be well to acknowledge some of the reasons why it comes naturally to us.

The main explanation lies in a Canadian perspective which is certainly peculiar and perhaps unique. All nations recognize that nuclear weapons are potentially dangerous items but many feel

---

*   This article is condensed from a volume to be published by the Canadian Institute of International Affairs.

that the dangers which arise from having these weapons are smaller than the dangers of not having them. Canada finds it difficult to share that view. As detailed below, this nation perceives few dangers in the present world which would be reduced or offset by possession of an Independent Canadian nuclear arsenal. Our intuitive sense that nuclear weapons are dangerous does not have to compete with a calculation of the national interest which cuts the other way. And this sense of danger leads quite naturally to (a) a pessimistic view of what would happen if atomic arms spread widely, (b) a partial inability to appreciate the incentives which other nations may have to acquire nuclear weapons and (c) a low tolerance for the behaviour of nations which regard those incentives as decisive.

On the military side, these attitudes flow from our strategic situation and our close ties to one of the superpowers. First, we are sitting under the American nuclear umbrella, and we do not feel the need of an independent capability to deter direct strategic attack upon us. China, for example, rightly or wrongly does feel such a need. Secondly, for over a century and a half we have not had to fight a war on our own soil, and we do not feel a need for nuclear weapons to deter conventional ground attack or avoid local conventional defeat. Thirdly, perhaps because of their geographic proximity to the United States, Canadian observers are especially alarmed by the prospect that lesser nuclear powers might somehow drag the superpowers into a general war. This is true even where those observers acknowledge that they may not be able to write a plausible "scenario" to portray how it might happen.

On the political side as well, our interests and perspectives lead us to a pessimistic view of the implications of proliferation. Despite Beaufre's reassurances, Canadian leaders fear that proliferation within an alliance weakens, rather than strengthens, the alliance. They fear that small nuclear nations may want to go it alone, while their protector becomes wary of involvement where his clients are waging or threatening nuclear war. (Although this view is partly inconsistent with the fear that small nuclear powers will drag large ones into a general war, some observers nonetheless hold both positions simultaneously.) Insofar as her planners hold these views, it is not surprising that Canada has pereceived a political incentive for opposing proliferation. For twenty years the nation's foreign policy has been based on alliance; until that changes, Canadian governments will regard with dismay any development which threatens the alliance structure.

In related areas of diplomacy, Canada finds it difficult to share the nuclear incentives of others. For example, to some nations nuclear weapons promise (paradoxically) a greater influence in arms control. Canada has never had this problem. From the earliest days of the atomic age, we were charter members of the diplomatic club which dealt with the implications and control of the bomb. This was true both at the allied level, from the wartime Combined Policy Committee to the present Nato Nuclear Planning Committee, and at the international level, from the UN AEC to the present Geneva Eighteen Nations' Disarmament Conference (ENDC). Our lack of an independent nuclear capability has never been a diplomatic handicap. On the contrary, it has usually been regarded as one of our stronger cards.

Nor can we sympathize fully with the feelings of those who hope proliferation will bring a sweeping equalization among nations. This is another case where the Canadians' perspective makes it hard for them to see or respect the motives of nations which do seek national nuclear arsenals. For those countries at or aspiring to the second tier of the international social scale – "great" but not "super" – nuclear weapons appear to be, and probably are, a great leveler. This may be a dangerous way to go about it, but the recent experience of both China and France seems to suggest that it works. To Canada, decidedly moored at either the third or fourth level – "middle or "small," depending upon how chauvinistic one is feeling that day – the efforts of the more recent nuclear powers seem ludicrous. They will never match the superpowers, it is felt in Canada, and why can't they realize it? Well, in the first place, they do not have to match the US or Soviet arsenals in order to become equal for many practical deterrence purposes. Secondly, they may have many good non-deterrence reasons for going part way. If the mark of a major power is a nuclear capability, and certainly both the US and Soviets have done a great deal to foster that impression, then those who are seeking major power social status will do what society indirectly requires of them. Canada cannot aspire to such status, and has little patience with those who not only can but do.

It must be said, however, that there is a contradictory tendency in Canada's attitudes on this point. The natural resentment of the small for the big, and the specifically anti-American bias of some elements in this nation, combine to give many Canadians mixed feelings about the partial levelling which may accompany pro-liferation. On the one hand, Canadians regard the attempt to keep up with the superpowers, in nuclear weapons or otherwise, as wrong-headed. On the other hand, they feel that in some ways the world might be more stable and less violent if the predominance of the superpowers were not so marked. Some Canadians (as well as, incidentally, some Americans) feel that too much power leads, in Senator Fulbright's words, to the arrogance of power. And some of them, secretly or even subconsciously, welcome with half a heart the prospect that nuclear diffusion might induce a prudence which restrains this arrogance.

We have seen, however, that this last is very much a minority opinion. Overall, Canadians are no more in a position to share the political motives of those who welcome proliferation than they were to support the military arguments in favor of it. This is natural, but it may also be a handicap. For one effect on our anti-proliferation policy has been to make it too little analysis and too much cant. We have spoken as if our own nuclear restraint comes from a happy combination of high moral tone and acute aware-ness of the dangers of nuclear weapons. In so doing, we may have obscured our understanding of the ways in which the present international system has been conducive to past proliferation and the ways in which that system must be changed in order to fore-stall more proliferation. By saying there are no good reasons for acquiring nuclear weapons, do we hope to make others believe it is true? Or do we really doubt that for many nations in today's world, there *are* good reasons? We can, and should, remain pes-simists about what further proliferation might mean for interna-tional stability. But we should give more attention to the motives others have for being optimists. And we should recognize that not everyone places as high a premium on stability as we do. Not everyone is as satisfied as we are with the present world, or as little afraid of it. We must convince those nations which seek changes that even if they want some instability, they do not want the kind that proliferation will bring. Secondly, we must contrib-ute to creating a world in which they can accept that conclusion, one in which they can pursue their search for instability without a felt need for nuclear weapons. Neither goal will be much served by the repeated insistence on the contrast between Canada's ab-stention from nuclear weapons and the policies of the purportedly evil, vain or stupid nations which seek them.

Some Canadian Options

Against this background, let us consider some of the practical options open to Canada in the area of nuclear policy. In the pages which follow, three arbitrary categories have been used to organize the ways in which Canada might affect the pace or direction of nuclear proliferation. These are (a) options "on her own," (b) options within her alliances and (c) options beyond her alliances in the broader diplomatic context. It is acknowledged that these categories cannot be mutually exclusive – clearly, independent decisions affect alliance policy, etc. – but they do have some utility in separating out the various options open to the government.

(a) *Options "On Her Own"*

The most obvious aspect of this policy area concerns the possibility of obtaining our own nuclear weapons arsenal. Official statements since 1946 have repeated the stand that Canada is not interested in either the manufacture or acquisition in any other way of an independent nuclear capability. In fact, the issue is not quite that simple. In the nineteen forties the decision might have gone the other way if American policy had been different – specifically, if the United States had pressed Canada to get into the weapons game rather than to stay out of it. In the nineteen fifties and early sixties the nation seemed at times in danger of backing into possession of an independent capability. And one cannot know what new strains may be placed on this fundamental principle of policy by altered circumstances in the future. Nonetheless, it remains true that Canada's most direct contribution to restraining nuclear spread continues to be her own abstention. She has an option on a military capability. She has not taken it up. If she were to do so, especially in the face of American opposition, this would certainly have an effect on the way nuclear weapons are regarded by others. Partly because Canada has so long opposed the spread of nuclear weapons, partly because she has no apparent security incentive for acquiring them, the impact of a Canadian decision to go nuclear might be quite dramatic. In particular, the absence of a security incentive would create the impression that Canada had sought atomic arms as tools of diplomatic independence or international prestige. This in turn might encourage others to regard them in this way, and most observers feel that it would have this effect.

150

Thus in our search for novel things Canada can do in the cause of anti-proliferation, it is easy to take for granted familiar and correct things she is already doing – or in this case, not doing. It may be objected that other non-nuclear nations regard Canada's situation and experience as unique, and as irrelevant to their own. To a great extent, that is true. But by now Canada's capacity for ill in this area may exceed her capacity for good. That is, while continued Canadian abstention from nuclear capability may not perceptibly encourage others to abstain, a positive Canadian decision to acquire nuclear weapons would at any point in the future encourage others to follow suit.

A second, related area in which Canada may affect proliferation by decision "on her own" is that of others' capacity for atomic arsenals. There are three branches here.

Weapons export: Even if Canada had no use for a nuclear capability of her own, she could be in the business of making them and selling them to others. If the product were good, there would certainly be a market in all the current nuclear powers and possibly in many currently non-nuclear states. But happily, there has thus far been no Canadian interest in this particular export industry.

Reactor technology: Having been in the military atomic research field since 1942, Canada had a long technological lead over most countries. Inevitably, Canada has been asked and will continue to be asked to share the benefits of that lead. The extent to which she ensures the peaceful purpose of her aid has a direct effect on proliferation. Some observers have noted, for example, that we once built a largely "uninspected" reactor for India. In more recent arrangements, the Canadian government has insisted on tighter safeguards, but two difficulties remain. First, the safeguards are necessarily weak on enforcement of sanctions against violators. Furthermore, there are other nations willing to share reactor technology without bilateral or IAEA safeguards. Canada can do little more than help establish a principle in the hope that others apply it.

Uranium sales: The focus of recent interest has been on this question, and Canada has several options here. She might simply sell uranium to any paying customer and let it go at that. She might refuse to sell to anyone at all, on the grounds that in the absence of enforceable, universal controls there could be no certainty that a "peaceful uses" pledge would be honoured. Or, Canada might sell only to those countries which give such pledges and allow inspections to confirm them.

This policy area has presented a real dilemma for the Canadian government. The recent Franco-Canadian uranium negotiation is an example. Here the French government wanted to buy something we wanted very much to sell. On the one hand, Canada was uneasy about appearing to aid – even indirectly, by freeing other material for military purposes – a French programme of which she heartily disapproves. On the other hand, she recognized that the French programme is a fact, and would continue with materials gained from other sources if the Canadian deal fell through.

Of the alternatives listed above, Canada chose – what else? – the middle way. Assurances were sought that the materials obtained from Canada would be used only for peaceful purposes. To meet French objections that previous uranium sales to Britain and the United States were free of such restrictions, Mr. Pearson told the Commons in 1965 that for any new contracts to export Canadian uranium to any destination, "the Government will require an agreement with the government of the importing country to ensure, with appropriate verification and control, that the uranium is to be used for peaceful purpose only."[1]

Nonetheless, the deal does seem to have fallen through. This may be for reasons other than those just described, with which the author is not familiar. But Canada has apparently shown herself willing to take a considerable financial loss in the name of a worthwhile principle. This is a praiseworthy policy, but its limited effect may be typical of our predicament in formulating an anti-proliferation policy. In one of the few areas over which she can exert direct control, Canada's influence is at best marginal. Uranium and thorium are available in large if spotty deposits in several areas of the world. But more important, in the 1970's the spread of fast-breeder reactors will mean a spread of plutonium as well. Whatever international controls may be sought to prevent the diversion of these materials to military purposes, it is fruitless to hope that unilateral restraints by Canada can prevents a determined country from going nuclear. About the best Canada can hope for is a policy which satisfies her own principles and sets the right example for others. That is no mean achievement; but if the example is not followed, there is very little Canada can do about it by decisions taken on her own.

It is unfortunate but true that so far as decision on her own is concerned, Canada is strongest in the areas where the problem of proliferation is least amenable to control. Our areas of direct decision are primarily technical, and the problem of weapons spread is increasingly one of political will. We should avoid technical policies which abet or encourage weapons programmes, but the key which locks the Pandora's box of nuclear spread is not to be found here.

(b) *Options Within Her Alliances*

Let us now turn to another area in which, it is often argued, Canada can by her own national decision help control nuclear spread. This concerns the nuclear aspect of our roles in Nato and Norad. In general, the debate has been confused by a failure to isolate the dangers which might arise out of nuclear sharing. Some Canadians are worried about our view of ourselves: If we accept nuclear weapons under joint control, it is felt, the line in our own national consciousness between nuclear and non-nuclear is blurred. Once that happens, runs the argument, it is but a short step to an independent capability. It is this fear, though not always made explicit, which has led many to argue that weapons held under 'two-key' control with the US are just as bad for proliferation as if Canada controlled them independently. Another group maintains that by refusing to accept nuclear weapons even under joint control, we may set an example for other Nato members and lead them in the direction of a more conventional, less automatic nuclear strategy. It is felt that this in turn reduces the general premium on nuclear weapons and thereby retards proliferation. To still others, Canadian rejection of jointly controlled nuclear weapons promises to improve our credentials outside the alliance in urging nuclear restraint upon others.

In the opinion of this writer, all three arguments have some force. We did seem to lose our non-nuclear balance in the debates of the fifties and early sixties, and an early study of proliferation explicitly noted the possibility that Canada's sharing plans might lead to a desire to acquire Canadian nuclear weapons under national control. In the context of a search for what Kahn has called anti-nuclear traditions and fashions, it would ideally be desirable if Canada did not have even a derivative military nuclear capability. And on the third point, the following judgement might apply to Canadian diplomacy as well: "If a Dutch pilot is training to drop an atomic bomb (even though it is kept in American hands in peacetime) on a target in Eastern Europe, it is not easy for the Netherlands to sustain the proposition that she is not a nuclear power."[2]

Nonetheless, my own view is that these arguments are not strong enough to conclude that the best policy for Canada is an immediate, unilateral rejection of our present roles and a ceremonious declaration of non-nuclear virtue. On the contrary, for two reasons, our next steps should be from within the alliances we seek to change. First, the proliferation issue cannot be isolated from the broad diplomatic requirements of a nation which hopes to play a continuing role on the world scene. As a general principle, we should try wherever possible to renegotiate rather than to renege: to revise commitments cooperatively rather than unilaterally. But even if the question of continuing diplomatic credit could be ignored, I would still maintain that the proper area for consideration of our present nuclear roles is within the alliance. This is especially true of our European roles. A unilateral rejection of our jointly controlled nuclear weapons in Europe might assuage some Canadian consciences, but it would have far less impact on the overall proliferation issue than a formal, convincing solution to Nato's nuclear woes would have. If Canada wants to help move European nations in an anti-nuclear direction, this is a task for skilled and informed diplomacy, not to be served by public renunciation of Canadian commitments already accepted. Such diplomacy, however, is an area of real opportunity for Canada: Nato's collective nuclear future is bound up with the general proliferation problem in a way which Canada's individual posture is not. We may be able to affect that future by intelligent persuasion of others; we cannot do it by a purely Canadian national decision. It we want to change or drop our European nuclear roles, it should be as part of a cooperative revision, not as part of a strained search for independence.

A word should also be said about continental defence and its ostensible link to nuclear spread: If the United States decides to deploy a ballistic missile defence (BMD) system, Canada may — although this is by no means certain — be asked, or may even consider initiating her own request, for siting of some of these weapons on Canadian soil. Almost certainly, such a development would prompt opposition from those who believe of BMD as they did of Bomarc that jointly controlled weapons placed in Canada are inconsistent with our anti-proliferation policy. This is a complicated question, and a full analysis of it would carry beyond this short paper. But in can be said here that insofar as there is an inconsistency, it is a marginal one and should not outweigh such considerations as the possible prudential case in favor of deployment in Canada, or the possible damage to US-Canadian relations of a refusal to participate if asked. There may be many policy issues on which we should be willing to pay the price of damaged relations with the US. But it would be unfortunate if we paid it out of a mistaken belief that our termination of cooperation in continental defence would be a major contribution to checking the spread of nuclear weapons.

(c) *Options Beyond Her Alliances*

This brings us to the wider diplomatic framework, beyond the alliances of Nato and Norad. To a Canadian reader, the remarks which follow may be even more unpopular than those in the preceding section. For here as in the area of alliance policy, there is a real danger that Canadians will prefer measures because they are independent rather than (although the two are not necessarily exclusive) because they are sound anti-proliferation initiatives. There may be a real tension between two Canadian goals, independence and anti-proliferation. On the one hand, one finds in Canada a recognition that the superpowers – especially the United States – hold an important key to the proliferation problem. On the other hand, one finds an intense Canadian desire to be independent of the superpowers – especially of the United States. And when the second element predominates, the result is all too often a barrage of arms control proposals which are at bottom irrelevant to arms control.

For example, consider the Eighteen Nations Disarmament Conference (ENDC) negotiations at Geneva and the deadlock in 1966 over nuclear sharing. Although the principals were agreed on the desirability of a non-proliferation treaty, they had run aground on the issue of how much freedom nuclear nations should have to share nuclear benefits with their allies. The Soviets insisted that the treaty must be designed to preclude non-nuclear allies gaining access to nuclear weapons. Specifically, the Soviet position was directed at preventing the American sharing of nuclear hardware with Germany through such schemes as the Multilateral Force. Now although the American position throughout the year was moving away from the MLF plan, many Canadians were impatient with the pace of this revision. They considered the sacrifice of this sharing option a reasonable price for Soviet signature, and had little patience with a Canadian Government which failed to attack the supposed stubbornness of the American negotiators. Now it cannot be denied that Canada could have taken a startling, independent initiative in supporting the Soviets at Geneva. But would this materially have altered the American reaction to the sharing issue? It hardly seems so. And if not, then this type of initiative would have promised potential diplomatic costs but no gains in the cause of non-proliferation. The expression of an independent spirit might be a positive feature, but we should not confuse such expressions with genuine contributions to arms control.

Underlying suggestions for Canadian independence of the superpower disarmament positions, there is often the assumption that Canada can thereby win her way into the confidence of the potential nuclear powers. Presumably the idea is that once our objectivity in nuclear matters is certified, we may then convince others that a disinterested Canadian calculation of their interests dictates that they remain non-nuclear. This somewhat strained variation of the Minifie thesis rests on two subsidiary assumptions. First, it assumes that for professional diplomatic purposes, Canadians are now regarded around the world as known smugglers of the American policy line and that our anti-proliferation counsel will not be heeded unless we abandon any policies which resemble that line. Secondly, it assumes that once we have shown our distinctiveness from US positions, other non-nuclear nations will then regard us as especially competent to assess their national interests.

Both these assumptions are controversial. On the first point, the charge is partly right and partly wrong, and that there isn't much we can or ought to do about it. To some extent we do smuggle the Americans' line, in that our own view of the proliferation problem is so similar (though not identical) to theirs. There is no sense in abandoning a position we believe to be correct, just because it resembles one held by the United States. Canada will continue to be a Western, status quo nation, a fact that potential nuclear nations will continue to recognize in assessing our anti-proliferation arguments. More important, however, they will weigh those arguments against their own national interests. Our context will not be much altered, nor will their calculations, by whether we are in or out of Norad or Nato. Even if we could isolate our anti-proliferation policy from all other diplomatic requirements, it would not be essential, and in some cases would be self-defeating, for that policy to be pursued in place of the present alliance obligations. It would be self-defeating in cases where, as we saw above, Canada can serve anti-proliferation better through an alliance than on her own. Elsewhere, though any nuclear roles within the alliances may hinder her anti-proliferation effort, her simple membership in them will be largely irrelevant to it. In these areas it is enough that Canadian anti-proliferation policy be pursued beyond (as distinct from 'in place of') her present alliances.

In that area beyond our alliances, what sort of initiatives should we be taking? Concerning conference diplomacy, consider in contrast to the Geneva tactic criticized above a Canadian approach which seems more in keeping both with our international goals and our national interests. We saw that during the second part of the 1966 ENDC session, the super-powers had apparently reached an impasse in their efforts to reconcile their respective drafts of the proposed non-proliferation treaty. In an effort to break the log jam, Canada prepared a special paper (a) giving an article-by-article comparison of the Soviet and American drafts, which dramatized the number of important points on which the super-powers were already agreed and (b) suggesting language which might be acceptable to both on the central issue where disagreement still existed. For example, Canada proposed a proviso that a non-nuclear State party to the treaty should not take any other action which would encourage or result in the acquisition of control of nuclear weapons by itself or any other non-nuclear-weapon State in any way, through units of its armed forces or its military personnel, even if such limits or personnel were under the command of a military alliance.

Such initiatives do not make noisy headlines, precisely because diplomacy of this kind is, or ought to be, a rather quiet business. The great powers disagree, and a small power essays a contribution toward a compromise. The power of decision rests with the powerful; the not-so-powerful can only cajole. The noise comes only if and when the powerful decide to agree, and even then it it unlikely that the mediator's contribution was decisive. But to the extent that mediation by a nation such as Canada can be successful, it depends heavily on the acuity of our understanding of the arguments and motives which divide opposing parties, and on our skill at devising new arguments which meet the concerns of both. Sometimes this may take as modest a form as formulating a position which allows someone to crawl more or less gracefully back along an embarrassing limb. And we do have some credentials in the field. Bernhard Bechhoefer, for example, a former US State Department expert on arms control, has written that from the earliest days of postwar disarmament efforts, we have sent to international conferences "a long line of brilliant Canadian representatives who, because of their ability and knowledgeability, wielded an influence out of proportion to the military strength of Canada."[3]

This American emphasis on Canadian expertise should set this whole section in the proper perspective. For it makes clear that any and all of the general policy proposals which analysis of the broad problem casts up, may be the subject of Canadian initiatives. They are general principles, characterizing the outline of an antiproliferation policy open to elaboration by any nation. If we can find practical applications for some of these principles, surely this is a useful contribution. We might search for ways to make a "no-first-use of nuclear weapons" pledge palatable to our allies. If we think the guarantee concept is a fruitful one, perhaps we can be instrumental in overcoming the difficulties which keep the nuclear powers from participating in the recent effort to de-nuclearize Latin America. Another area, diplomatically well charted for us, might be a combined effort by Canada-Australia-New Zealand, perhaps with others in the Commonwealth, to negotiate a non-nuclear pledge in return for a formal US-British commitment. Australia in particular, worried about China and already talking about keeping options open, might be especially interested.

Similarly, if we feel that the non-nuclear club concept has merit we might press it pending the conclusion of a binding treaty. If our efforts have been at all successful in rebutting the "equality of sacrifice" theory once popular among smaller powers, we might find a surprisingly large number of nations willing to sign a declaration of abstention for some fixed period of time, without any guarantees or corresponding move by the nuclear powers. The virtue of such a declaration would be simply that some achievement, some progress, would have been made. In addition, Canada might seek to institutionalize the notion of a non-nuclear group. It has been said that Canada is a charter member of this group, but perhaps the club could use a clubhouse. We might take the lead in pressing for an organization which would be not an antiproliferation forum like ENDC, but rather an anti-proliferation lobby active both inside and outside such forums.

Let me conclude by repeating two qualifications for any Canadian initiatives we do pursue. First, they should not be chosen simply because they are distinctively Canadian or simply because they differ from American views. That may do a lot for national dignity but will not do much for arms control. Secondly, they must be bolstered by strong strategic (in the largest sense) arguments. This emphasis on analyzing the conditions of stability should balance the tinge of self-righteousness which sometimes characterizes Canadian statements on these matters. We are not, presumably, arguing that nations should abstain from nuclear capabilities so that they can be as virtuous as we, but rather because it is not in their interests to have nuclear weapons. In the present world many nations may perceive many good short run reasons for ignoring our pleas. Our task is to attempt, in whatever necessarily marginal ways we can, to change the system and the attitudes which dominate it – not to elevate wayward nations to the moral standard we sometimes seem so sure to have attained.

Harald von Riekhoff

NATO:
TO STAY
OR
NOT TO STAY

Harald von Riekhoff is Assistant Professor of Political Science at Carleton University. He is author of a recent book on Canada's role in Nato.

Only a few years ago the cold war seemed to represent a permanent state in international affairs. Similarly, the alliance which emerged under cold-war conditions seemed designed for perpetuity. Meanwhile the cold war has given way to a nuclear stalemate and partial superpower détente, and the international system has moved from bipolarity to one which, at least with respect to non-military capabilities and political behaviour, displays characteristics of multipolarity. With the waning of the unmitigated and pure conflict situation that existed under cold-war conditions, the future of the principal alliances, a product of those conditions, has been put to question.

Whatever the future outlook for the North Atlantic Alliance, it would be difficult to challenge its past record as an organization which helped deter aggression in Europe, which provided a protective umbrella under which Europe's political and economic recovery could proceed without physical or psychological interruption, which facilitated the incorporation of West Germany within the Atlantic community of nations and which assisted in the reconciliation of former enemies.

In relation to her power status, Canada's contribution to Nato has been impressive. Apart from the active role played by Canada in the conception and realization of a defensive alliance among Atlantic nations – in the words of Lord Ismay, Canada turned "a general reflection into a practical possibility" – one can list her military contribution to the creation and maintenance of an integrated system of defence in Europe and her promotion of the gradually emerging practice of continuous consultation among allies, thereby emphasizing the political and communitarian aspects of alliance membership rather than purely military preoccupations. The establishment of the physical apparatus for continuous consultation in 1952 proceeded largely from a proposal made by the Canadian Government after the outbreak of the Korean War.[1] In his capacity as Canadian Secretary of State for External Affairs, Mr. Pearson played a major role in producing, what still stands as the principal guideline on consultation in Nato, the 1956 Report of the "Three Wise Men." In addition to these more tangible contributions, the Canadian "Boy Scout" approach in maintaining high standards has assisted in raising the standards of military performance for the rest of the alliance. The influence that can be gained by means of example, and especially the example of a smaller ally, is necessarily limited. But in an alliance atmosphere of continuous mutual exposure, influence through good performances cannot be disregarded altogether.

Given the absence of a Canadian tradition of military alliances and the isolationist foreign policy of the preceding generation, the decision to join was taken with remarkable ease and little controversy. But under the altered circumstances of today's military and political situation, the question whether Canada should continue her membership in the North Atlantic Alliance cannot be answered with the erstwhile automatic affirmation but involves a very real policy choice. After 1969, withdrawal will become "legal," that is to say, it would be in strict conformity with undertaken international commitments. And even before the 1969 target date, the existing international situation would make it possible to pursue a Gaullist strategy which combines formal membership with minimum participation in the practical operation and management of the alliance.

161

The Strategic Argument

But in reappraising Canadian foreign policy goals and commitments, one should not lose sight of the very compelling arguments in favour of a continued association with the West European powers through the framework of Nato or any successor organization. The decision about Canada's future membership in Nato will have to address itself to the principal issues of Canada's strategic interdependence with West Europe and the nature of the present military situation in Europe.

As to the first issue, the argument that Canada receives adequate protection from the US nuclear deterrent and therefore is in no need to participate in other security arrangements is, in my opinion, not entirely convincing. This argument equates security with safety from the threat of an immediate attack on Canadian territory and ignores the much more likely contingency of security threats that arise from extraneous developments which, at the outset, would not involve the North American continent in any direct physical sense. In a world of increasing interdependence almost any form of aggression or military conflict confronts the entire international community with a security risk because of the threat of escalation. Canada's involvement in preventive paramilitary operations, which have become known under the label of peace-keeping, testifies to this global interdependence. However, a military conflict situation in Africa or Asia presents a different calibre of threat to Canadian security than aggression in the West European area. This arises, firstly, from the closer degree of interdependence that exists in relation to West Europe and, secondly, from the unique strategic importance of West Europe.

The situation therefore seems to have justified Canada's adherence to a forward defence concept with respect to Europe and its implementation through the collective defence system under Nato. It is necessary to bear in mind that this forward defence strategy was undertaken in response to what was regarded as a military threat to Canadian national security and not just for the purpose of lending additional weight to Canadian foreign policy. One might therefore take issue with Professor Eayrs' assertion that "the major function of the Canadian military establishment has had practically nothing to do with our national security, and practically everything to do with supporting and sustaining our national diplomacy."[2]

From the military point of view, what has changed is not

Canada's continuing security involvement in Western Europe but, first of all, the over-all military situation in Europe, due to technological changes and the rearmament and reconstruction of her European allies, and secondly, the nature of the military threat which now confronts Europe. Canada's present allied military commitments in Europe are a reflection of the political and strategic conditions which prevailed in the early and middle 1950's. In view of the changes which have occurred since then, consideration must now be given to the problem of converting this role to one which would be in greater harmony with these new conditions.

Initially the European allies suffered from gross deficiencies of forces, armaments, equipment and the means of producing these. Under those circumstances the presence of Canada's relatively highly trained and well-equipped army and air units in Europe and her participation in the Nato mutual aid programme constituted a very tangible material asset in the defence of Europe.[3] But the rearmament of the European allies, and especially of Germany, and their economic reconstruction have enabled these allies to provide and train efficient European conventional defence forces and to produce most of the necessary equipment. In addition, the bulk of the costly infrastructure programme has been completed, even though some relocation is now required as the result of the French decision to leave Nato's integrated defence system in Europe. Consequently, the importance of any Canadian contribution in the form of forces, infrastructure payments, mutual aid and training facilities has sharply declined.

Furthermore, certain doubts have been raised over the past few years about the wisdom of continuing Canada's association with nuclear weapons as part of her Nato commitments. This particular commitment was accepted almost a decade ago under strategic conditions and considerations which are in need of serious revision in the light of the present situation. The original commitment was undertaken shortly after Suez, Hungary and the launching of Sputnik, when East-West tensions were high and the possibility of a détente seemed remote. During that period it was fashionable to treat tactical nuclear weapons as a replacement for conventional weapons. But in the meantime a more accurate realization of the devastating effect of these weapons and their impact on escalation, in conjunction with an improved conventional defence of Europe, has reduced the emphasis on tactical nuclear weapons.

163

Apart from these more fundamental strategic considerations, other developments would also tend to devalue the importance or even value of a continued Canadian participation in this particular defence role. In 1957 the Canadian air division was particularly suited to undertake the professionally demanding task of a strike role because of its high performance level. But in the interim period the professional competence of the forces of the European allies has been upgraded considerably, with the result that the purely military value of the Canadian presence has declined. Also developments in weapons technology have terminated the exclusive reliance on manned aircraft for strike roles, as this task can now be performed by a variety or combination of systems: land-based Medium Range Ballistic Missiles (MRBM's), mobile sea-based MRBM's and aircraft with intercontinental range, such as the F-111, which can be based on the North American continent or other rear areas instead of the more vulnerable forward sector of West Europe. All of these factors would argue in favour of the earliest possible conversion of this particular Canadian military commitment.

As a demonstrative assertion of her sovereign status, Canada could imitate Gaullist procedure and unilaterally disengage herself from those Nato commitments which involve her in a direct association with nuclear weapons. But apart from any psychological satisfaction that might be derived from such independent assertion, a smaller ally stands to gain little influence over alliance policy or the policy of its major members by such unilateral protest action. If Canadian policy is concerned with creating something other than a purely demonstrative effect, it would be advisable to utilize the present commitments in order to make their negotiated conversion part of the desired policy changes in Nato.

Finally, there remains the option between complete disassociation from or active participation in the newly founded Nato nuclear planning group.

The present Canadian government has clearly expressed itself in favour of the "committee" approach and has accepted the position as one of the three rotating members of the planning group. This behaviour contrasts sharply with Canada's previous refusal to be associated with the MLF proposal, which was largely regarded as an additional nuclear commitment and, furthermore, one that created the appearance, if not the reality, of promoting proliferation.

Even a positive evaluation of the potential role of the nuclear

164

planning group does not in itself settle the argument in favour of Canada's participation in this form of activity. But it must be realized that as long as nuclear weapons exist within the Atlantic Alliance, questions of nuclear planning and strategy will remain a key concern of members. It is thus unlikely that any Canadian Government should willingly let the US act as the only spokesman for the strategic views of the North American continent. Mutual exposure and strategic interdependence doubtlessly produce close affinity of strategic thinking between the two countries. But differences in power and in international commitments are responsible for fostering divergent strategic opinions. The United States for example, as the guarantor of German security, has a very particular interest in preventing Germany from becoming an independent nuclear power. But as the leader of the alliance, the US is also highly dependent on German co-operation in the defence of Europe and is thus more vulnerable to German pressure and consequently more likely to accept a nuclear solution which other allies would regard as a case of proliferation.

A country such as Canada, which has taken an active interest in issues such as the prevention of proliferation within Nato, the negotiation of an international non-proliferation treaty, the revision of the strategic concepts that govern the use of tactical nuclear weapons in Europe and the balanced revision of forces, including nuclear forces, in Europe, would not maximize its bargaining position on these matters by a policy of absenteeism from the forum that is likely going to be of great importance in affecting policy changes on these issues.

In addition, it will be necessary to reappraise the present Canadian military role in Nato in the light of the diminished military, threat against Western Europe. The source of this military relaxation is the global strategic balance of nuclear weapons between the US and the USSR, not a regional adjustment of the unequal force levels between West Europe, on the one hand, and East Europe and the Soviet Union, on the other.

This strategic development has not altogether eliminated the threat to West Europe, or at least the perception of such threat, insofar as the discrepancy of forces continues to exist in the European area. In order to eliminate the threat, it would be necessary to redress this military imbalance and to create the basis for a genuine political settlement in Europe. Such a settlement would be based on the reunification of Germany, on the acceptance of the existing European boundaries by all parties concerned, and to some extent also on a greater tolerance and mutual compatability, in actual practice if not in theory, between the two major social and political systems in Europe.

Before these conditions have been met, the great majority of allies may be expected to want to rely on a common security framework that links West Europe to North America. A common North Atlantic security system is the basis from which the European allies derive their regained political manoeuvrability. In the same way, the prospect for a reduction of military forces in the European area would be enhanced if the European allies found themselves militarily reinsured against any risks that might arise from the disengagement experiment. While Nato itself has until recently demonstrated a rather rigid status quo orientation in military affairs, the security benefits which members derive from the existence of the alliance have indirectly promoted flexibility in behaviour and political change.

It would be counterproductive to try to involve Nato more directly in the process of inter-European economic, and perhaps eventually also political, integration, for as a military alliance Nato tends to reveal a natural predilection for the status quo rather than for experiments with political innovation. It also has a "bad press" in East Europe where it is regarded as a remnant of cold-war days.

But, as indicated above, during the initial period of a policy of engagement towards East Europe, the continued existence of a security system which links the two parts of Europe to their respective super-power would act as a stabilization agent and a means of reinsurance, and thereby alleviate the uncertainties and risks of the experiment. In addition, Nato provides a forum where allies can exchange information about their individual approaches and experiences with East Europe, and thus help co-ordinate these. In certain cases the alliance might be involved more directly by assisting in the preparation of joint proposals for negotiations with East Europe.

The Political Argument

The foregoing points clearly demonstrate Nato's Janus relationship between military and political activities. A functional preoccupation with the former activity automatically creates some involvement with the latter. Canada's participation in the alliance provides good evidence of the intimate interrelation between the political and military sphere.

From the outset, Nato was regarded not only as an organization designed to satisfy Canadian security concerns, but also as one which might fulfill some fundamental Canadian political needs. From a strictly Canadian point of view, the alliance had the advantage of combining within one single framework the power on which she depended most strongly with the two European nations with whom she maintained special historical, cultural and, in the case of Britain, also economic ties. Nato thus offered some assurance against the eventuality of conflict or estrangement between her principal partners. The multinational association, furthermore, served to satisfy an instinctive Canadian desire to secure a balancing mechanism against her preponderant US neighbour, since Britain was no longer in a position to continue her historical role of providing an adequate counterweight.

But recent developments have raised various political questions which did not exist originally or had to be repressed when other issues laid undisputable claims to precedence. Consequently, a re-appraisal of the political implications of our membership in Nato will have to be undertaken.

It is not without historical irony that precisely at a time when internal political needs in Canada and the mesmeric influence of Gaullist policy have placed an unprecedented premium on intimate and friendly relations between Paris and Ottawa, Nato has become a less successful instrument, and in some cases perhaps even an obstruction, in reconciling the diverging interests of Canada's three principal partners.

The situation in the UN also differs substantially from the one which existed at the inception of Nato. The UN has neither evolved into a global collective security system, as envisaged in the Charter, nor into a permanent grand coalition against the Soviet Union and her allies that it seemed to become in the immediate post-war years. Instead, in the security field the UN has organized several para-military or policing actions, the so-called peacekeeping operations, in order to insulate and pacify potential and actual conflict situations. Canada's active involvement in peacekeeping has raised the question whether this particular role could suffer as the result of her alliance commitments.

The past record of active participation in every UN peacekeeping mission does not tend to verify the claim of incompatibility of the two roles. If in future Canadian participation in peace-keeping efforts should be undesired or unacceptable, it would be either because the newly emerging nations would them-

167

selves be able to supply all the expertise and equipment for which in the past they have had to rely very strongly on countries like Canada, or because Canada would simply be unacceptable to these nations as the result of her racial composition, Western cultural status and intimacy with the United States. But these inherent liabilities would apply regardless of Canada's membership in Nato.

The original Canadian aim of creating a system of multilateral political relations under a common alliance framework has not been brought about by any physical juggling act of unequal weights. If the concept has been realized in any way, it has been by the more subtle and less tangible means of exerting influence within a common alliance forum. While the influence which may be acquired in one particular sphere of political activities may occasionally penetrate another area of involvement, political influence within Nato is largely retentive; that is, credits gained from participation in the common alliance system are generally also devoted to the promotion of issues which directly concern the alliance. It would thus be unrealistic to expect that membership in the alliance would give a country like Canada any measurable increase of influence over such issues as US economic policy in Latin America or American military operations in Southeast Asia, which lie outside the more immediate area of Nato's preoccupations.

In the net effect, if one were to summarize the relation between the alliance membership and a country's international political influence, it may be said that participation in an organization such as the North Atlantic Alliance enhances a member's influence with respect to those issues which form the primary focus of alliance activities, that it has little bearing on peripheral matters and that it may impose some, though now gradually diminishing, inhibitions on the choices and policies which are available to members.

Non-alignment does, indeed, offer a greater freedom of verbally assertive independence. However, the free use of verbal assertion to register dissent or consensus on every international issue can hardly be regarded as an adequate criterion for measuring the degree of independence in national foreign policy.

The real measure of independence in foreign policy should be evaluated in a more pragmatic manner which focuses on results and content rather than on status. National independence in foreign policy lies in the ability to shape the international environment in the direction of perceived interests and aims through one's own initiative and efforts. A small or middle power finds that it enjoys only a limited capacity to influence the international decisions and developments to which it is subjected. One method to preserve its independence would be by resorting to retaliatory measures in order to deter violations of its particular interests. But a small power's capacity to act in this manner is severely restricted. Another method for a smaller power would be to move into the orbit of a super-power and thus, as its client state, rely on the protection of the latter. However, this is a position that brings with it certain risks to manoeuvrability and the danger of not being protected against one's own protector. Finally, a smaller nation may try to capitalize its independence through multinational operations as part of an alliance or community.

The relevance of Nato to the latter option stems from the fact that in addition to fulfilling strictly military functions, Nato has evolved into a political clearinghouse for the conduct and adjustment of intra-alliance relations and to some measure also for the planning and co-ordination of the relations of the Atlantic region with other parts of the world, at least insofar as these significantly affect East-West relations. The political functions of the alliance which rest on the triple concept of information exchange, joint planning, and consultation, a process in which the smaller allies are involved as a matter of practice rather than by the rare grace of a super-power, give them an unprecedented opportunity to influence international decisions in accordance with their own national interests.[4]

This opportunity is enhanced both by the increased amount of intelligence and information on world issues that is made available to the smaller powers as the result of participation in alliance functions and by the numerical composition of the alliance which allows for multiple bargaining positions and internal alliance coalitions on specific issues. Smaller allies are not necessarily drawn together into the same pressure groups, but similarity or middle-power status creates a certain complementarity of thinking and "class consciousness."

What Military Contribution?

Given the limited resources of a smaller power, the choice of the best form of military contribution, which would at the same time preserve that power's military utility to an alliance and maximize its political influence in the joint forum, presents a very complicated task. A Canadian military contribution to the defence of Europe should, first of all, serve to assist in fulfilling Nato's principal role, which is to provide a stable deterrent for an area which continues to be marked by a highly imbalanced regional distribution of military forces. But under present circumstances increasing emphasis should also be given to use this military commitment to help bring about a mutual downward revision of force levels in order to facilitate the process of East-West accommodation.

Canada could conceivably support both of these goals without engaging in any military commitment under Nato. A military contribution constitutes no absolute requirement for alliance membership. Iceland provides no more than a passive contribution by making bases and facilities available on her territory.

Other smaller allies, such as Norway, make their military contribution in the form of maintaining a military establishment purely for home defence purposes. Theoretically Canada could adopt the same restrictive practice. But since it would be strategically irrational to contemplate any other form of direct aggression against Canadian territory than a massive nuclear attack, an eventuality for which all domestic measures would be entirely inadequate, a Canadian defence force that was exclusively centred on a home defence mission would have very little military value for the rest of the alliance.

The decision whether or not to continue with an altered military commitment for the defence of Europe will have to consider the following factors. In the first place, a collective defence effort ultimately rests on the ability of members to agree on some equitable sharing formula in proportion to ability. It would be detrimental to the practical implementation of the collective defence concept if a country of Canada's power status and resources should make no appreciable alliance contribution through home defence efforts or to the forward area of Nato.

Secondly, the ability to provide mobile support from the less vulnerable rear areas of North America would not only enhance the strategy of flexible response but would also provide an inducement to the reduction of military forces in the central sector of Europe. A mobile reserve commitment by Canada might thus be regarded as an instrument for political change in Europe.

Thirdly, a commitment of this nature should assist to some degree in upholding the credibility of the US deterrent in relation to Europe after a reduction of American forces from that area. While it would be an obvious exaggeration to represent Canada as the guarantor of the US guarantee to Europe, a continued Canadian commitment to European security serves as a counter-signature to the American guarantee, precisely because it underlines the intercontinental solidarity between North America and Europe.

Finally, a military commitment to the defence of Europe provides Canada with a bargaining lever and a direct role in the process of force-reductions in the European area. Much of the European, and especially German, reluctance to agree to a numerical reduction of "visiting" forces in the European area might be overcome if at least some of the withdrawn units were to be redeployed as part of an air-mobile reserve force based primarily in North America. This air-mobile intercontinental intervention force could either be earmarked for service on Europe's central front or for allied mobile flank duties. The former entails a more intensive and large-scale military role that would involve considerable overhead costs and advance preparations. This would argue against a smaller country like Canada undertaking the commitment to support an air-mobile intercontinental intervention force for duties in the central sector of the European front. It would therefore seem more realistic if, after a general allied agreement on the reduction of forces in the European area and their redeployment, Canada were to convert its present military commitments to the European core area to active participation in the Allied Mobile Force (AMF).

Following General Norstad's recommendation in 1960, the AMF was set up with the aim of providing a capacity for allied mobile support to Nato's exposed and weakly defended flanks of northern Norway, northern Greece, and north-eastern Turkey. The size of the force is small and its role is not to conduct major military operations but to provide a "presence" in periods of tension and to deal with minor probing actions or local disturbances.

The Canadian commitment to the AMF has now been increased to two earmarked battalions. In the 1966 winter manoeuvres Canada participated with one battalion, 18 heavy transport aircraft, and one operational support ship which existed in the deployment and redeployment phase of the exercise.[5] The AMF is of particular interest to a country with a power base like Canada's. It makes only limited demands on manpower and heavy equipment, and Canada's contribution to it could be maintained in the form of an air-transportable reserve force stationed in Canada, except during manoeuvres or emergency conditions. In a small assignment of the AMF type the smaller powers of the alliance can play a proportionately more important role than in more massive defence efforts, where the direction will primarily be a function of the principal contributors, i.e., the major allies. Secondly,

171

the AMF has the particular advantage of providing Canada with a role that shows distinct forms of complementarity with her UN peace-keeping functions with respect to the nature of the task, equipment, and training. Finally, AMF duties which rely on a close interaction between ground forces, air and naval support functions, and air transportability would harmoniously blend with the present Canadian defence policy of bringing about a functional unification of its armed services.

A military commitment which concentrates exclusively on AMF flank functions raises two questions, one strategic and the other political. In the first place, since the inception of the AMF, the bilateral relations between the Nato flank states and their Soviet neighbour have improved considerably, especially in the case of Norway and Turkey. The contingency of Soviet probing actions on the Nato flank has consequently declined substantially, and with it the whole emphasis on the AMF. Secondly, both the strategic nature of the task and the multinational composition of the AMF impose inherent restrictions on the size of any Canadian contribution to this form of allied military activity. A Canadian contribution which was oriented exclusively to Nato flank duties would therefore constitute a reduction of her military spending on the Nato sector of her commitments. This may not be an unwelcome development, even apart from the taxpayer's perspective, provided it does not constitute a solitary move by Canada but is accompanied by at least a partially proportional reduction of the Nato defence costs of other allies, as part of an over-all revision of East-West force levels in Europe.

A cut-back of this kind would be in harmony with the diminishing security threat in Europe and Nato's original goal of transferring an increasing share of defence responsibilities to its European allies.

In the context of gradually evolving East-West relations, Canada's contribution to the AMF, or to a task of similar dimensions, would seem more rational than the long-term continuation of her existing Nato commitments to Europe and more advantageous than a total military disengagement from Europe before the aims of a force reduction in that area had been met. It seems more rational because it is in harmony with Canada's resources and other commitments, and more advantageous, as it helps underline the interdependence between North America and Europe and maintains an active Canadian involvement in the political evolution of Europe.

Kenneth McNaught

FROM
COLONY
TO
SATELLITE

Kenneth McNaught is Professor of History at the University of Toronto. He has published several books, among them A Prophet in Politics *and* Manifest Destiny: A Short History of the United States. *He is a contributing editor of* Saturday Night.

Survival by Balance

The most consistent theme running through the sometimes tenuous tale of Canada's relations with the outside world has been a concern for survival. It was the dominant theme in the Old Province of Quebec and was strongly reinforced in all of British North America by the Loyalist migrations. The War of 1812, the nuisances of border raids in the 1830's and 1860's, the complicated pressures of American expansionism in the 1880's and 1900's produced strong reiterations of the survival theme. These were marked by successive decisions against political union with the United States. Canadians generally, both French- and English-speaking, agreed that the surest safeguard of independent Canadian survival was maintenance of the British connection. While we accepted this necessity (with varying enthusiasm,) we did so with considerable care. If ultimate military protection against the only imminent threats, those posed by American expansionism, required "loyalty" to Britain, super-heated Britishism in such manifestations as the Imperial Federation League was rejected even by that most notable of British-born subjects, Sir John A. Macdonald.

Nineteenth-century Canadian foreign policy was thus based on a consciously-formulated concept of balance. The principal counterweight to dependence on Britain was encouragement of trade with the United States. Of almost equal significance was the steady Canadian refusal to give military support to British policies elsewhere in the world. And when unpleasant side-effects resulted from dependence upon British diplomacy Canadians exhibited some very positive counteracting nationalism.

The imperial basis of Canada's world view came into question with the mounting insistence that overseas dominions contribute substantially to the maintenance of Britain's world position. As long as the demands were not too great we accepted a cautious growth of commitment, although Canadian control of the forces involved became increasingly a criterion.

Unity through Isolation

After 1918 Canadians began to redefine their external relations. Borden and Meighen failed notably to salvage a Britain-centred world view. Under British leaders like Curzon and Amery equal partnership in formulating common imperial policies meant about the same as "consultation with allies" does now to men like McNamara and Rusk. And in these circumstances Mackenzie King reacted more decisively than he ever did in domestic affairs.

King's concept of national interest, which was his sole touchstone in any consideration of external objectives, was summed up in the one word "unity." Knowing well that French Canada was, to a man, opposed to the Borden-Smuts Commonwealth, King dismantled it between 1922 and 1939. In so doing he had, undoubtedly, the support of a majority of Canadians – French Canada plus a wide range of native-born English-speaking Canadians. Ostensibly King was returning to that concept of balance which had been distorted in the twenty years preceding 1918. Yet, in practice, King and Lapointe emasculated the revived strategy of balancing of external influences by failing to use our independence to any real purpose. Their total disinterest in the League of Nations symbolized their policy of ignoring international issues lest, as Lapointe put it, "we divide the country right away."

While the government defended its virtual silence on foreign policy by saying it left us free to decide our own course, in fact we were not free. In the guise of independence, we went to war in 1939, just as we had 25 years before, in defence of policies in whose formation we had refused to participate. The government went through the motions of a separate declaration, seconded with sombre lack of enthusiasm by J. A. Blanchette:

> "It cannot be reasonably contended, after due reflection, that it would not be wise to co-operate to a reasonable extent with France and England in the present conflict, taking into account, however, our resources and our capacity, and without sacrificing our vital interests. . . ."

The tragedy of the 1930's was that those "vital interests" were not defined. In 1939 the unresolved question was, like the depression, simply swept under the rug. And, as with the depression, the drift of affairs, rather than any mastery of purpose, "resolved" the foreign policy problem.

Our American Century

> In 1940 we passed from the British century of our history to the American century. We became dependent upon the United States for our security. We have, therefore, no choice but to follow American leadership.

Do we, as Frank Underhill maintains above, have no choice but to follow American leadership? A Yes to this question could come only from an unrepentant Calvinist.

In the 1940's as well as in the 1950's our external objectives were defined almost by default because governmental actions were hardly debated and only superficially explained. The Canadian-American defence agreements of 1947 set the pattern. As the undeclared "policy" of drifting into the American orbit continued unabated it produced the retroactively debated and documented North American Air Defence Command (Norad.) The government veiled the real assumptions of defence integration in a manner startlingly similar to its ceremonial renunciation of prior commitments in the 1930's. Mr. King described the northern radar plans as civilian in character and announced that the armed forces of the United States and Canada would merely make contributions to the system. Even Mr. Diefenbaker had the courage of his illusions to declare that Norad did not place the RCAF in

North America under American control because a Canadian officer was named deputy commander. Because the opening of the cold war made the political course of commitment to the United States the easiest path to follow, no efforts to maintain a balance were seriously considered. As a result we ended up more subservient to American than we ever were to British direction since our commitments are, for the first time in our history, supported in advance by military pacts and establishments – as well as by unimpeded economic integration.

Two potential countervailing forces were the Commonwealth of Nations and the United Nations. With respect to the Commonwealth, we simply carried on the artificial game of independence – by vastly exaggerating the importance of formalizing our freedom from British influence. At the very time when Britain ceased to be even an imaginary restraint upon our independence we made a great to-do about terminating the "colonial relationship." No one would argue that these things should not have been done; they should have been done more completely and cleanly than they were. But they should never have been billed as the completion of our independence at the very time when our actual policy was to enter a web of unprecedented dependence upon the United States. And closely related to all this was Ottawa's reluctance to take any serious initiative or to seek a real leadership role in the emergent multi-racial Commonwealth, one of the most usable North-South bridges in a perilously divided world.

In the United Nations, Canada seemed to wish to use her independence to advance the international rule of law. But there too our role was closely circumscribed by the same political timidity which had hobbled us in the inter-war years. We allowed ourselves to be dominated by fear of domestic division and by a curiously outdated assessment of the nature of national power in the post-1945 world. King and St. Laurent used the shibboleths of "midle power status" and "functionalism" to cover what was in fact a nervous retreat from independent initiative. Initiative and influence, they proclaimed, must always be strictly proportional to military power, even if "middle powers" such as Canada should have slightly greater influence than small powers.

Despite Canada's participation in all agencies and peace-keeping operations she was reluctant to give leads in basic policy matters. Middle power functionalism remained a synonym for big power and, increasingly, for American decisions. Mackenzie King, as Bruce Hutchison remarked, wrote off the UN as "a failure" within a week of its founding. In 1947 Mr. St. Laurent added his interpretation of functionalism: "There is little point in a country of our stature recommending international action, if those who must carry the burden of whatever action is taken are not in sympathy." The doctrine was plausible as long as "stature" was seen exclusively in terms of military power and, indeed, in terms of nuclear power. Functionalism thus led inexorably away from serious UN commitment and towards subservience to the larger powers. It was a highly convenient rationalization for our political decision to accept a re-clothed world-order of regional military alliances. Once it was accepted we found ourselves under the alleged necessity of playing ball with the power which lay at the centre of all the freshly constructed western regional alliances. Thus, although we are not members of Seato and although both our material and ideological interests are at variance with American policy in Southeast Asia, our spokesman felt compelled to justify the American invasion of Vietnam, to subvert our position on the ICC and to furnish hospitals to Saigon because to do otherwise would make our general position of commitment to the United States too uneasy.

Satellite Status Confessed

The most recent version of King-St.Laurent functionalism goes under the name of "quiet diplomacy." The doctrine that only quiet, behind-the-scenes, confidential methods should be applied by Canada-size powers was succinctly stated by Prime Minister Pearson in March, 1967. In a public letter replying to an appeal by 360 University of Toronto professors to dissociate Canada from the American war in Vietnam, he wrote:

> Confidential and quiet arguments by a responsible government are usually more effective than public ones. . . . Too many public declarations and disclosures run the risk of complicating matters for those concerned. . . . The more complex and dangerous the problem, the greater is the need for calm and deliberate diplomacy.

But Mr. Pearson in the same letter went behind the reasons of diplomatic method to other, more profound reasons for his unwillingness to rock the North American boat. He, like Professor Underhill, pointed to the World War II origins of our entanglement in continental defense. He reviewed the extent to which defence production has been integrated, the technological and mass production advantages we receive and then declared that because of these developments we could not, in fact, refuse to contribute to the American war effort in Vietnam:

> For a broad range of reasons, therefore, it is clear that the imposition of an embargo on the export of military equipment to the USA, and concomitant termination of the Production Sharing Agreements, would have far-reaching consequences which no Canadian government could contemplate with equanimity. It would be interpreted as a notice of withdrawal on our part from continental defence and even from the collective defence arrangements of the Atlantic Alliance.

No more concise or authoritative statement has been made on the subject. After his letter no one can maintain that acceptance of continental integration in defence production and planning leaves us free in general foreign policy – leaves us free to accept one part of the American alliance structure while rejecting other parts of it. Nor can anyone seriously doubt that it is this integration that has produced, as James Eayrs has put it, the smooth Canadians who haunt the corridors of Washington with their confidential, ineffective briefs.

The process by which we accepted the bipolarization of the world was both curious and facile. During the second half of 1947 and through 1948 Canada did appear to define an external objective. It was the objective described by Senator Vandenburg, George Kennan and Harry S. Truman – the objective of crippling communist power by encirclement of Russia. For the Canadian government this essentially American objective was overwhelmingly attractive and Canada leapt with agility to its support. The concept of a deeply divided world within which the West was imminently threatened by aggresive communist imperialism and which required a unified military response was attractive because it settled the Canadian foreign policy question automatically. Moreover, it settled that question along lines which could and did eliminate any serious internal political division.

But, most people say, it is all very well after the crisis is past to discourse upon the other side of the case; in fact the real danger was so great that we only saved Europe and ourselves from having to cower under the Kremlin's knout by building the Nato shield. While one may agree that a genuine dilemma existed in 1949, one should be quite equally aware that a crucial commitment was made to an increasingly military assessment of the situation –

and that this emphasis remained while any justification for it grew steadily less credible as the Communist military threat declined. While the original case for Nato may or may not be convincing, the case for maintaining the alliance as the centre of our foreign policy is entirely without substance.

From the Canadian point of view the case for disbanding Nato (or for simply withdrawing from it) seems virtually unanswerable – except from the abashedly continentalist premises put forward by the Prime Minister and which imply acquiescence in Washington's ideological anti-communism. The case for leaving Nato depends upon one's interpretation of its present and likely future role as well as upon an assessment of its impact upon Canadian foreign policy.

The impact of Canada's membership in Nato has determined our other external policies. The basic premises of the alliance's dominant member have governed our position on all major questions – recognition of China, disengagement in Europe, nuclear disarmament, the creation of a genuine UN police force. While it can be argued that we have been able to play honest broker on occasion (e.g. Suez) the initiatives of this sort that we have taken have always been either in conformity with US policy or they have been such as to cause the US minimum discomfort. Whenever basic questions affecting the US position arise, our commitment to "nuclear security" and production agreements has been decisive. The effects of total loyalty are sometimes veiled, as in the case of Cuba – where we do not formally toe the line but where we are excruciatingly careful not to mount any trade campaign or to facilitate Russian-Cuban air communications. Loyalty is unveiled in hotter situations such as Vietnam where the government defends openly the legal and moral position of the United States and concedes that our position on the ICC is not that of an independent but that of a representative of "the West." One does not envy Mr. Chester Ronning, who no doubt found it difficult explaining in Hanoi why we send aid only to Saigon – an aid policy which enabled General Westmoreland and the State Department to list Canada as one of the "supporting" allies in Vietnam. Indeed this automatic loyalty in situations deemed crucial by Washington is taken absolutely for granted.

But it is not just by choice that we forego within the alliance system the rights and opportunities of independent initiative in major matters. Despite the rhetoric of equal partnership and consultation, Nato remains a military alliance dependent upon United

States decisions and it is now abundantly clear that real influence will not be shared by the power that controls the essential nuclear component of the system. As long as Canada accepts the alliance basis of security she will accept the shackles of nuclear loyalty and the stigma of total commitment. Thus we violate our liberal traditions by refusing entry to deserters from the US army under a "Nato commitment." As Melvin Conant put it somewhat harshly a few years ago: "Fifteen years of effort to meet the security requirements of the air age have concluded with the prospect that the Canadian role from now on will be marginal and certainly not consequential."

Even apart from the question of hobbling ourselves by accepting the nuclear measuring rod, there is the question of the general effect of Nato upon the most dangerous of the world's outstanding problems. Clearly, Nato stands as the principal obstacle in the path to a German settlement. (To argue as von Riekhoff does, that Nato has achieved "the incorporation of West Germany within the Atlantic community of nations" makes light of the fact that we do not even recognize the existence of East Germany!)* Nato stands also as the symbol, in an image-minded age, of western commitment to a cold-war interpretation of international affairs. On these grounds alone Canada should withdraw her Nato contributions and should give notice that she will exercise her right under Article 13 of the Treaty to withdraw from the alliance in 1969. Just as our acceptance of Nato was an implicit definition of external objectives, so our withdrawal from it should be the occasion for redefinition of such objectives.

A Return to "Balance"?

If we cannot return to the simple formulae of earlier times, we *can* define from the frustrations of our alliance experience a more fruitful set of policies.

What we lost in the Nato period should be our chief guide in the future. We abandoned any serious concern for our national independence and based policy upon considerations that are wholly archaic – especially in the light of American predominance, nuclear weaponry and the rise of Afro-Asia from imperialist control; and we have almost wholly ignored the glaring inequality of welfare and opportunities amongst the world's peoples. In "defence" matters we have ignored the obvious reality that the only serious threat to our own territory stems from our proximity

* See above, chapter 13, p. 161.

to the centres of US nuclear power – and the presence of Bomarcs which have been described by Mr. McNamara as bait for Russian missiles. The "nuclear umbrella" is for us a nuclear lightning rod. New definitions of foreign policy should aim at rectifying such crippling inadequacies of assessment and they should take into account changes within Canada as well as changes abroad.

Since Canada's security, prosperity and any hope she may have of exercising a beneficent influence abroad all depend upon the maintainance of peace and are hindered by continuance of cold war divisions it should follow that her principal external objectives should be to achieve: 1) enhancement of the United Nations at the expense of regional alliances; 2) absolute priority for nuclear disarmament; and 3) top spending priority for foreign aid.

These three objectives are obviously interrelated and rest upon certain assumptions about the post-1945 world which are implicit in the foregoing discussion, but which deserve explanation.

The most important assumption is that after the nuclear revolution in the nature of military power Canada can no longer seek to measure her influence in terms of the dominant military weaponry. She cannot hope to build a nuclear weapons system and therefore cannot be completely Gaullist; she is therefore, if she continues as a committed party to the arms race, completely dependent upon American decisions. Moreover, the evidence of the past twenty-two years leads irresistibly to the conclusion that no one can help to moderate the arms-race tensions simply by pious participation in disarmament conferences while wearing prominently the US arm-band. Yet, while nuclear disarmament is already a subject to produce yawns it is, nevertheless, one which must lie at the heart of our international objectives. Few people now doubt that the *gravest* danger facing the world is unlimited nuclear war and that limited nuclear war is, at the very least, unlikely. While we remain committed to Nato we are also committed to the use of nuclear weapons on our behalf, and in some cases by our own forces – that is, committed to risking the destruction of civilization. Although we have learned to live with the bomb, we do not have to love it. If our foreign and defence policies are to be founded on morality and realism they must exclude membership in alliances which depend upon nuclear power. Even in terms of seeking to persuade others to deny themselves the bomb (i.e. the limited goal of non-proliferation) our present position is hypocritical.

A militarily non-aligned Canada could do more than a committed Canada to mobilize a growing pressure within the United Nations for acceptance of the most advanced disarmament offers that have been made by both the United States and Russia during the ebb and flow of past disarmament talks. While the history of the arms race is not such as to encourage ill-considered optimism neither is the present instability of terror something to induce lethargy and a failure of nerve. Surely the most striking facts ignored by advocates of cautious debate, quiet diplomacy and iron-clad guarantees is that twenty-two years of such methods have succeeded only in producing the most dangerous arms-race in history – whose most recent peak is the edgy debate about anti-missile systems and the development of Chinese nuclear capacity. It is clear that in this field words are no substitute for actions. Our most significant action would be immediate renunciation of nuclear weapons and withdrawal from nuclear alliances. The cries of hypocrisy that would be raised in some quarters would have much less base than those which can now be *legitimately* raised.

Much of what I have been suggesting by way of redefining our international objectives has already been canvassed by our government. But in each case the extent of the tentative moves has been minimized by the facts and psychology of commitment to the American military alliance. We do not, for example, really wish to keep any military force in Germany and it is evident that in terms of power our presence there is ridiculous. Thus we have elected a kind of equipment-erosion method of withdrawing from the scene – a method that impresses no one, but which is required in order not to offend American political-strategists openly. We have expanded our aid to the West Indies and Afro-Asian states but on a scale that should make us blush. Many people hope that Norad will be phased out in the face of new air-screen devices developed in the US, but we retain in Canada the useless and dangerous Bomarc missiles. We are rearranging our own military forces so that their essential role will be that of mobile emergency forces for peace-keeping operations. But we have made no real progress toward the establishment of a full-fledged UN police force. The concept of do-it-yourself stand-by forces clearly falls far short of the police project proposed by Tryggvi Lie as early as 1949. Since it is not possible, save in the case of individual or collective mania, to use nuclear power, the roles of economics, diplomacy and minor specialist military force have all been remarkably enhanced. Our role in peace-keeping must be complemented by a serious commitment to the concept of international equality. In our own country we have decided that, on grounds both of justice and utility, we must establish basic minimum standards of welfare and that we must work for the realization of equality of opportunity. The same grounds should be the basis of our approach to international affairs. Utilitarian reasons also require the effort to establish international equality of opportunity – for the seeds of conflict and of extremist nationalism find favourable ground in the desperate inequalities that divide the affluent from the underprivileged world. Without entering the debate about the most efficacious methods of raising welfare and opportunity levels in Latin America and Afro-Asia* it is more than apparent that we now devote to the problem only a tiny proportion of the manpower and resources that we consider appropriate in other fields. Here again, as in the area of nuclearism, our intentions and policies will be convincing and have influence to the extent that they are whole-hearted and unambiguous.

Clear-cut, non-alliance objectives would thus be in the Canadian national interest in two senses: they would be our only possible contribution to the kind of world in which alone it is possible for a country such as ours to exist, and they would in themselves strengthen our national experiment by extending to our foreign policy the principles of tolerance, compromise and equality which we endeavour to establish at home. While to some the detailed implications of the policy basis I have suggested will appear to be merely anti-American, in fact this bogey is now an irrelevant, timorous excuse for inaction. Imperial Washington's loyalty requirements are tougher than were those of Imperial London. But the conditions of the present require, just because this is so, a vigorous response and return to a concept of survival and balance in our external relations.

* See below, chapters 16, 18 and 19

SECTION IV:

EFFECTIVENESS
IN
THE
UNDER-DEVELOPED
WORLD

If we accept McNaught's view that Canada's relative importance in the prosperous Atlantic area is decreasing and if we wish Canada to develop a more effective foreign policy, we must surely look to the despairing "third world" of Latin America, Africa and Asia where the needs are so great that our diplomatic efforts can be most constructive.

David Cox shows in chapter 15 how Canada can still play a limited yet independent role as fire extinguisher on the edges of international conflagrations by carefully exploiting our American image. Latin America, in Ian Lumsden's analysis, should not be an area of Canadian efforts. He argues in chapter 16 that the United States' strong ideological and economic commitment to counter-revolution makes it impossible for Canada to have a beneficent influence on the explosive course of events. We should, therefore, only expand our aid and trade activities with countries such as Cuba that have already achieved a real socio-economic transformation and for whom Canada can play the important role of communication link to the West.

In Southern Rhodesia an independent foreign policy might clash more with British than with American policy. Cranford Pratt and

Clyde Sanger provide a detailed programme of international action to oppose the minority white rebel regime showing how Canada has a special responsibility to resist British compromise in this grave situation.

The section concludes with two contributions on the problem of aid. Stephen Hymer and Brian Van Arkadie make a strong case in chapter 18 for the possibilities of significant new directions in Canadian aid – if only Canada can decide to follow them. Robert McKinnell adds a concrete formula for how to choose between many competing demands on the inadequate resources that we devote to the have-not world.

CANADA'S LAWRENCE OF ARABIA, LESTER PEARSON. HIS PLEA FOR ARAB WITHDRAWAL FROM THE GULF OF AQABA FELL ON DEAF EARS

David Cox

PEACE-KEEPING
IN
CANADIAN
FOREIGN
POLICY

David Cox is Assistant Professor in the Department of Political Studies at Queen's University. Mr. Cox's article appears in expanded form in Peace-keeping: International Challenge and Canadian Response.

Although the recent debates on triservice unification have drawn attention to the Canadian commitment to peace-keeping, there has been little discussion, either at a scholarly or a general public level, of the merits of these proposals and policies. Nor has there been very much attempt to follow the development of policy on this subject. Peace-keeping activities have not so far imposed unacceptable or even controversial sacrifices and they have not, apparently, seriously prejudiced other Canadian policies. In short, peace-keeping has not disturbed the foreign policy consensus. The view, propogated by both Liberal and Conservative Governments, that Canada is a middle power with excellent, if not impeccable, credentials, and that it has a duty to support peace-keeping operations, has gone virtually unchallenged.

In terms of the general objectives and motivations of its foreign policy, the Canadian Government, perhaps more than any other, has been a persistently enthusistic supporter of peace-keeping activities since the Korean War. When the Liberal Party returned to office, there was a significant increase in Canadian initiatives in this area. Pearson devoted a considerable part of his speech to the General Assembly in 1963 to the need for international police peace-keeping forces on a standby basis.[1] He urged interested members to share their experience in peace-keeping, and suggested that this could lead to a pooling of resources and the creation of a multi-national force for the UN:

> To do so would require a number of middle powers whose credentials and whose motives are above reproach to work out standby arrangements among themselves consistent with the United Nations Charter. What is needed, in fact, is an entirely new arrangement by which these nations would establish an international peace force, its contingents trained and equipped for the purpose, and operating under principles agreed in advance.[2]

To examine the policies suggested in this article, in November 1964, Canada hosted a meeting of military experts from twenty-three countries to discuss the technical aspects – political problems were specifically excluded – of peace-keeping operations. Canada participated in, and was actively involved in the creation of, the UN force in Cyprus. And, of course, in 1964 the *White Paper on Defence* indicated that defence and foreign policy planners sought to integrate peace-keeping forces into the overall structure of Canadian defence. In the *White Paper*, for example, there is specific reference in the statement of defence objectives (p. 5) to support of "Canadian foreign policy including that arising out of our participation in international organization"; there is heavy emphasis on the range of conflict situations, and the usefulness of the UN in stabilizing conflicts at the lower end of the scale; and central to the policy proposals of the *White Paper* are the plans for mobile, flexible, multi-purpose defence forces which, whatever their other uses, are eminently suited for peace-keeping operations of the Suez and Cyprus types.

It must be emphasised that the *White Paper* reaffirms the importance of the Canadian commitment to Nato, both militarily and politically. However, it also makes a clear distinction between "the North Atlantic Areas," in which Nato remains essential, and other parts in the world, especially in less-developed areas, in which "instability will probably continue into the decade ahead and call for containment measures which do not lend themselves to Great Power or Alliance action. The peacekeeping responsibilities devolving upon the United Nations can be expected to grow correspondingly."

While the vague talk of good credentials and international responsibilities has been deservedly called in question by some critics, there is more to this commitment than pharisean middle powermanship. On the whole, I believe that peace-keeping has made a modest but valuable contribution to international stability and to a distinctively Canadian foreign policy in the past ten years offering a partial alternative to a small power support for a military alliance whose objectives are increasingly obscure; and it provides a useful example of the way in which Canada may hope to move beyond the principal constraining element in its foreign policy: its commitment to, and support of, the United States and the North Atlantic alliance.

From Free World Fighter to Fire Brigade

In any analysis of Canada's peace-keeping activities, the Suez crisis and the formation of UNEF mark a turning point in Canadian policy. Yet in explaining Canada's role in the Suez crisis, Mr. Pearson, then Secretary of State for External Affairs, took care to point out that a UN force was *not* a new policy as far as Canada was concerned. He emphasized the early post-war concern of Canada with the organization of enforcement measures under Article 43 of the UN Charter, and drew attention to the Canadian policy at the beginning of the Korean war in offering an infantry brigade to be made available for UN service generally, and not simply in Korea. This comparison is misleading. It is not difficult to demonstrate that the Canadian Government in 1950 saw the Korean operation as an alliance against Communist aggression. In ministerial speeches the United Nations, Nato and the "free world" tended to be closely identified; the "Uniting for Peace" resolution was clearly intended by the United States to rally and legitimize the cooperative efforts of the non-Communist countries.

It is unnecessary to enter into the details of Canadian diplomacy at the United Nations in 1956 or of the creation of UNEF, in order to establish the quite different principle of UN peace-keeping in which Canada found itself involved. However, some observations about the character of UNEF, as expressed in the two reports of the Secretary-General of November 4th and 6th, are necessary.

189

As expressed in these reports, the nature of the force, and its legal and political bases, were very different from previous ideas of UN enforcement schemes. By the terms of the Assembly Resolution of November 5th sponsored by Canada, Columbia and Norway, Hammarskjold concluded that the great powers were excluded from participation in UNEF and this subsequently became an accepted principle of UN peace-keeping. In the interpretation of Resolution 998 (ES-1), the phrase "with the consent of the nations concerned" came to mean not only that member states contributed to the force on a voluntary basis but that the force could not be stationed on the territory of a state without the consent of that state.

The consent principle in turn indicated the passive nature of UNEF, which was not intended to influence the military or political outcome of the dispute. Its purpose was not to impose but to supervise a cease-fire. Like ONUC in its initial phases, its mission was inter-position, and its military capability was to be used only for defensive purposes. As a consequence, in one commentator's words, "UNEF has been in fact a larger and more physically impenetrable UNTSO."[3] The idea of a passive and peaceful force has been central to UN peace-keeping since 1956.

Granted these aspects of the force, it is clear that the political situations in which it might be used had changed completely the UN security role which Pearson had earlier envisaged as being useful against Communist aggression. The fire brigade was not designed to be used at all in uncompromising conflicts between rival power blocs, but instead for conflicts amongst smaller powers, in "non-bloc" areas and in situations where the great powers might find their hard-core interests so little threatened that international intervention might be preferable to unilateral interventions which could lead to unwanted great power confrontations.[4]

If it is correct, then, that in proposing UNEF in 1956 it was impossible for Mr. Pearson to foresee these principles and conditions that followed, then it is all the more important that since 1956 Canada has chosen as an act of policy to persevere in its contributions to and interest in the peace-keeping idea. The Canadian actions in Korea, 1950 were compatible, indeed stemmed from, Canada's position as a solid member of the Western Alliance. An active interest in peace-keeping after 1956 required an independence of position precisely because such activities required a detachment from the interests and conflicts of the leading powers.

Despite these important differences, the Canadian Government almost immediately demonstrated its approval of the UNEF idea. And in April 1957 Lester Pearson proposed a more permanent basis for such UN activities, commenting:

> Even if governments are unable to give the UN a fighting force ready and organized to serve it on the decision of the Security Council, they should be willing to earmark smaller forces for the more limited duty of securing a cease-fire already agreed upon by the belligerents. We might in this way be able to construct a half-way house at the crossroads of war, and utilize an intermediate technique between merely passing resolutions and actually fighting.[5]

Western or Neutral?

In the light of this analysis it is instructive to turn to the question of Canada's policy choices. To what extent has peace-keeping "redefined" Canada's position in the world? And to what extent does it mark a switch from the basic policy of alignment?

In a very general sense the redefinition, if any, has centred on the presumed development of a middle power role in lessening the potential for conflict amongst the great powers and in controlling conflicts involving the new, and relatively unstable, states which have entered the international system in the past decade. In Pearson's words:

> They [the middle powers] are and will remain the backbone of the collective effort to keep the peace as long as there is fear and suspicion between the great power blocs. They have special responsibilities in this regard which they should be proud to exercise.[6]

Here, then, is the distinction between the deadlocked forces of the great powers and the relative freedom enjoyed by the middle powers to act in an international capacity in limited and sub-limited war situations, and in circumstances where political instability requires UN support of the civil power.

But having described the middle power responsibility in peace-keeping in this way, the conflict in Canadian foreign policy is very obvious: Canada is a part of the deadlocked forces of the rival blocs, and there is perhaps an element of wishful thinking in seeking to be at once a loyal member of the Western Alliance and a neutral middle power with considerable freedom of action. (The Pearson comment illustrates this well, for Pearson talks as if Canada were remote from the "fear and suspicion" which characterizes the great power blocs.)

One may find further support for this criticism in the views of Peter Calvocoressi. Remarking on the role of the "fairly strong, moderately well provided and apparently uncommitted" middle powers in peace-keeping, he suggests that only four states – India, Brazil, Sweden and Eire – meet the requirements and continues:

> But one of the most terrifying things about the world today is that it is impossible to extend this list any further. . . . How long will the middling states, by remaining committed in the cold war, remain also debarred from helping to keep the peace except in cases where they scent an immediate danger to their own security or their sacred cows?[7]

Canada is conspicuously missing from Calvocoressi's list, and for obvious reasons in view of the conditions that he stipulates. At the same time, the dilemma that he describes is in general terms applicable to Canada's position. Yet the Canadian experience seems to suggest that there is no necessary incompatibility between keeping the peace and remaining largely committed in the cold war. So far, Canada has been remarkably successful in doing both, though nobody doubts that the balance achieved is a precarious one.

The explanation, I suspect, is a useful commentary on the ambiguities of the term "independence" in Canadian foreign policy. The fact that the great powers are excluded from peace-keeping has encouraged people, especially in Canada, it seems, to believe that here is an important international role which is performed quite independently of bloc alignments and superpower patronage. Especially as far as the US is concerned, this view is entirely misleading. Stanley Hoffman has commented:

> Appearance and reality do not always coincide: a force whose men and commanders are drawn from small states but whose equipment, means of transportation and weapons are provided by a major power has, within the international competition, a meaning quite different from that which the champions of international neutralization and "vacuum filling" would like to reserve to international force.[8]

Although the great powers are excluded from direct participation in UN peace-keeping activities, therefore, they are not inactive. In the case of the United States, the involvement is considerable. It is required for example, to provide most of the financial support. UNEF would not have been possible without the airlift or the large amount of supplies and technical knowledge which the United States provided. And it was similarly involved in the Congo, if not, perhaps, on the same scale. In these circumstances it would be unreal to expect the US to be entirely disinterested in the composition and the direction of the peace-keeping force.

It is true that, as Canada and other States develop mobile forces with adequate lift capability, dependence on the United States for logistic support will decrease. But it is unlikely that the political influence of the super-powers will decrease; on the contrary, the common desire to see the Security Council regain its dominant position in the authorization and control of peace-keeping forces suggests that they will have more influence than before. It is conceivable, therefore, that a UN peace force composed entirely of, say, Africans, and used in a purely regional situation with control largely in African hands, might soon disillusion the United States. It is equally possible that such a force would not be tolerated by other Nato members who had interests at stake in the region in which the force was to operate.

In this situation there is an obvious role for the power which is relatively free from involvement in regional politics, but which is "reliable" as far as the US is concerned. Canada fulfills both these requirements. Policy-makers tend to stress that it is not Canada's alignment so much as the absence of Canadian *interests* in such areas as the Congo or the Middle East that establish her credibility as a neutral peace-keeper. If Canada can persuade the Afro-Asians that it is a sufficiently independent member of the Western Alliance in matters not involving a direct East-West confrontation, therefore, it is possible that on the other hand it may guarantee to the United States and other western powers some measure of respectability and orthodoxy in the actions and control of UN forces and thereby assist in maintaining their interest and support.

In short, the implication is that Canada acts in part as a delegate of the Western powers (for those who like their realism in heavy doses, as a delegate of the US) in peace-keeping. This claim would be undeniable and uncontroversial if it were made about the International Control Commission in Vietnam. Although comparison of the Commissions with other peace-keeping ventures may be very misleading, I am here suggesting that there is an important element of representation in Canada's participation in UN peace-keeping activities generally which makes its pro-American, aligned position a reason for participation rather than a disqualification. In the past, the principle of representation in peace-keeping forces has tended to be obscured by the non-great power principle decreed by Secretary-General Hammarskjold. But there can be little doubt now that representation is important. In addition to the balance of regional and non-regional powers, in itself an indication of the need for a racial balance, the Soviet Union is now claiming, very understandably, that a greater proportion of Communist state contingents be included in peace-keeping forces.[9]

To say this is not to discount or dismiss the Canadian role as yet another example of subservience to the US. On the contrary, it is quite consistent to argue that the role requires, and encourages, a display of independence. It was just such a display of independence in 1956 (at least vis-à-vis Britain and France) that marked the success of Canadian diplomacy at that time. And it is arguable that Canadian disavowal of American policy in Asia may be necessary at the present time. If she cannot be a Rumania, Canada must at least be a Poland of the Western Alliance. At this point it is perhaps evident where the argument leads: it suggests that peace-keeping is a good example of one of those irritating generalities of Canadian foreign policy. Canada should affirm its basic sympathy with and support for the aims of the US and the Western alliance, while maintaining an independent attitude on a range of specific subjects which makes its commitment, and the identity of interests, less than total.

If this be the case, then peace-keeping happily reinforces another attitude which is by no means uniquely Canadian: namely, an awareness of the increasing limitations of undeviating membership in one of the blocs. Once again, the change in Canadian attitudes after Suez is worth considering.

From a Canadian point of view, Suez was noteworthy not only because of Pearson's *tour de force* at the UN, but also because it marked the partial disintegration of an alliance. Through the early 1950's Canada's inevitably subordinate position in the alliance, and especially in Nato, was made easier to accept because of the optimism which prevailed on two points. The first was the belief that the military alliance could develop into a many-sided Atlantic Community. The second was the view that, insofar as it was possible, decisions involving the alliance should be made on the basis of a prior consultation. Without such prospects the alliance from a Canadian point of view is all too easily interpreted as military and political subordination to the United States. To cite but one example, Lester Pearson said recently: "We believe in this concept of the Atlantic Alliance, but would lose interest if it degenerated into merely an old-fashioned alliance directed by three or four of its most powerful members."[10]

Suez, then, first demonstrated the limitations on the community of interest in the alliance. Nor did it augur well for the idea of consultation. Ironically, in 1956, at the very time when Suez illustrated the deep conflicts within the alliance, Lester Pearson co-authored the report of the Committee of Three on collaboration amongst Nato members. It stressed the need for consultation and integration, both in military and non-military affairs, as the only way in which the alliance could persist beyond the point where it was held together by fear.

Developments since 1956 have not made the prospects for such developments any brighter, and in the mid-60's the future of Nato itself is, of course, very uncertain. It is hardly surprising, therefore, that in the past ten years Canada should have sought other strings to its international bow. Given the basic commitment to the United States, peace-keeping in Canadian foreign policy can be understood in terms of the search for areas of flexibility, discretion, and therefore, perhaps, a kind of independence. It cannot simply be dismissed as a misguided desire to appear internationally virtuous.

Fire-fighting not Fire-prevention

While peace-keeping may hold out the prospect of a different, and valuable Canadian role in international politics, it is well to recognize that in future the commitment to peace-keeping will involve frustrations and, for the politician, perhaps, increasing domestic controversy.

Canadian diplomats are no doubt fully aware of the frustrations. Their attempts to establish standby forces, and to solve the problems of authorization and control, and financing of UN operations have already met with failure. As the Canadian commitment to peace-keeping, expressed in its military and diplomatic policies, increases, the gap between Canadian interests and the policies and preoccupations of other states will widen. The discrepancy between a defence policy geared for UN service and a United Nations which has decided to put progress on peace-keeping low on the list of priorities may well be a source of disillusionment. Already, one suspects, the awareness that in large measure Canada is powerless to influence UN actions must have given Canadian decision-makers some sober second thoughts about the emphasis which they should place on peace-keeping in their external policies.

The failure of the peace-keepers to settle the conflicts which they supervise is a related problem. Ideally, peace-keeping would be most useful if it provided a "cooling-off" period in which settlements could be achieved. In practice, however, some conflicts, notably the Arab-Israel dispute, appear to be insoluble. The withdrawal of UNEF raises in acute form the question as to whether "peaceful perpetuation" of a dispute is in itself a useful task. And if UN peacekeeping mechanisms are used merely as formal or facesaving devices, the popularity of a peace-keeping role is not likely to be enhanced.

Finally, in this brief catalogue of frustrations, a comment on the importance of a Canadian contribution to the settlement process is necessary. The assumption that the peace-keepers should take the lead in resolving the conflict seems to me a very dangerous one. If, as was suggested earlier, the absence of particular interests is a qualification for participation in peace-keeping, it seems probable that intervening in the settlement process may well prejudice one's role as a peace-keeper. In short, offering solutions to the problem at hand is a very effective way of being declared *persona non grata* in the peace-keeping force. Paul Martin's public refusal to accept the immediate withdrawal of UNEF provides a valuable lesson for those who want more dramatic initiatives in peace-keeping operations.

Given these constraints, and as the Canadian involvement in peace-keeping increases, it seems inevitable that domestic pressures will become more important. This may be to the Government's advantage when Canadian troops are performing valuable service in crisis situations, but it is at least as likely to give Ministers some awkward moments. This is already a familiar problem. In 1956 Nasser's refusal to accept the Queen's Own Rifles as a part of UNEF placed the Canadian Government in an extremely vulnerable position in Parliament. The decision of the United Arab Republic to terminate UNEF, in which Canada has had an almost proprietorial interest, will undoubtedly cause a re-evaluation of Canadian policy. It cannot take long for critics to question the value of a peace-keeping policy when it is realized that the Canadian Government is powerless to prevent ungrateful beneficiaries from throwing out the force whenever the mood takes them. And no doubt there will be occasions in the future when a Canadian contingent is declined by the host country on the grounds that Canadian policy is insufficiently neutral or disinterested.

Viewed in this domestic context, therefore, one suspects that an effort must be made to inform the public that peace-keeping is more often disheartening than glamorous and that, loyal supporter of peace-keeping though it may be, in world politics Canada is a minor power with little ability to influence major developments.

Peace-keeping, in short, should be treated as an unspectacular policy. If the commitment is serious, but in low key, Canadians are more likely to understand peace-keeping in its international context – as an instrument for controlling the spread of conflict which is now used intermittently, but which, if attitudes and interests permit, in the future may become an accepted substitute for unilateral or alliance intervention in conflict situations.

Granted these reservations, peace-keeping may still promote an "independent" foreign policy. If Canadian diplomats wish to maintain a peace-keeping role (as they evidently do,) they cannot afford to be too conservative in other foreign policy decisions. A demonstrated willingness to resist US pressure as for example in the package-deal on UN membership in 1955 or to support Afro-Asian states in specific situations, such as the Commonwealth dispute on South Africa, may make the Canadian balancing act plausible; prevarication on Vietnam or the Rhodesian problem may easily make it unconvincing.

To borrow an expression once used about neutralism in Canada, peace-keeping may leaven the disposition of those whose basic commitment is to the United States and the North Atlantic. If in so doing, it stimulates an attitude of independence, one may, perhaps conclude that in foreign policy internationalism is as good a way as any to resist continentalism.

197

Ian Lumsden

THE
"FREE WORLD"
OF
CANADA
AND
LATIN
AMERICA

Ian Lumsden is Lecturer in Political Science at York University. He contributed an article to The Communist States at the Crossroads, *and has published several articles on Latin America.*

> The United States appear to be destined by Providence to plague America with misery in the name of liberty.
>
> *Simón Bolivár, 1829*

In recent years there has been a growing concern in Canada with the critical condition of Latin America, a concern which has been stimulated by events in Cuba and Santo Domingo. In addition, the admission of Commonwealth countries in the Caribbean into the Organization of American States (OAS) has led to a renewed interest in the possibility of Canada also applying for admission. This growing awareness of Latin America, however, has not necessarily been accompanied by a clearer perception of the region's problems. Opinions about its future and the part that Canada can play in it have, in consequence, often been based upon faulty premises.

An examination of the prospects of a more positive Canadian

role in Latin America must accordingly be based upon the prior analysis of the region's problems. This would reveal some of the external restrictions that would confine a more active policy in the Hemisphere.

The Basic Dilemmas

An obvious characteristic of Latin America is that it is not an *un*developed region, but a *mis*developed one. The two concepts must not be equated. Undevelopment suggests that a region or country has yet to be developed – sometimes due to a lack of natural resources – while misdevelopment implies that it has failed to develop a social system capable of ensuring its continuous economic growth and a reasonably balanced distribution of the social product.

The misdevelopment of Latin America can be seen in the fact that although nearly every country in the region has enjoyed some period of great economic and technological development in the past, none (with the possible exception of Mexico) has enjoyed a sustained rate of rapid growth since 1945. On the contrary, any economic growth that has taken place has been marked by its irregular and sluggish nature. This has led to great disparities in the standard of living enjoyed by the region's inhabitants, irrespective of whether they live in comparatively rich Argentina, or in impoverished Bolivia, for the former contains some areas that are quite as desolate as is most of the latter.

There is little prospect of any immediate improvement in the conditions of these poverty-stricken areas since the region's annual economic growth has slowed down to a rate of only 1 per cent per capita. The United Nation's Economic Commission for Latin America (ECLA) has calculated that at the present rate it will take seventy years or more to double the region's per capita income.[1]

A completely satisfactory explanation of the cause of misdevelopment is not yet available, but Professor André Gunder Frank of Sir George Williams University, Montreal, has persuasively argued that Latin America's present misdevelopment stems from the nature of the region's historic integration into the world capitalist system.[2] Latin America, unlike some other misdeveloped regions, has never enjoyed a period of full independence. Today, it is linked by military, economic and political ties to the United States, as it once was held by one or more of these bonds to Spain, Portugal or the United Kingdom.

The barriers to the region's balanced development are both external and internal. They are to be found in the social structure of Latin America and in its related excessive dependence upon external factors for economic growth.

Latin America's social structure, as ECLA has stressed, "constitutes a serious obstacle for technical progress and consequently to economic and social development."[3] In general, it can be summarized as an inflexible class structure dominated by a quasi-aristocratic land-owning oligarchy, that is based upon export-oriented economies. The ideological values of this class both permeate the Church and the military and extend to the bureaucracy and even to the newer industrial and commercial sectors. Unlike the nineteenth-century experience in Britain and North America, no dynamic anti-aristocratic bourgeoisie has developed that is willing and able to challenge the hegemony of these rural-based oligarchies. Thus, despite their rapid growth in the twentieth century, the middle classes in Latin America are most unlikely to introduce fundamental reforms, since they are essentially conservative in "their respect for hierarchical values, (and in) their admiration for their national aristocracies."[4]

Latin America's agrarian structure provides a further explanation for the region's economic stagnation. It is characterized by the phenomena of *latifundia* (extensive estates) and *minifundia* (marginal plots) that have led to the under-utilization of the land, declining per capita food production and the continuous migration of peasants to the cities. The failure to increase agricultural production at a satisfactory rate has resulted in declining exports, expensive food imports and inability to generate domestic capital formation at a satisfactory rate. In addition, the pattern of land-ownership has contributed to the increasing impoverishment of rural Latin America, because of the continuous transfer of capital to the cities, where it is either mis-spent by the upper class on conspicuous personal consumption (frequently of imports) or invested in relatively unnecessary real estate and service industries.

The internal impediments to development examined above, are related to external factors, notably US hegemony in the Hemisphere that, "by underpinning the anachronistic power structure, constitutes a serious obstacle to development for the majority of countries in the region."[5] This should occasion no surprise in view of Latin America's previous experience with other metropolitan powers. The continent is burdened by distorted infra-structures (such as the Argentine railroads) originally built to service the import needs of European countries and by rural areas whose present desolate condition can be traced to the intemperate exploitation of their original natural resources by foreign interests. The region's development continues to be hampered by the unequal nature of its partnership with the developed countries. This is reflected in its dependence upon declining exports of unrefined raw materials and agricultural products, imports of costly capital goods and other manufactured products, worsening terms of trade coupled with mounting outflows of capital in the form of profits, interest and debt amortization, and stunted manufacturing sectors dominated by the disproportionate influence of subsidiaries of US corporations.

To stress the detrimental nature of Latin America's reliance upon external inputs for its development (or misdevelopment) is not to deny that external financing and overseas trade has brought some benefits to Latin America. It is to imply, however, that these have frequently been temporary in kind and local in effect, while their attendant disadvantages have been general in character and long-term in consequence. The ruling oligarchies and other privileged groups are the beneficiaries of the advantages while the rural *campesinos* and the urban unemployed are the victims of the disadvantages.

The above are some of the major structural obstacles and associated factors that have distorted Latin America's development in the past and hinder the prospects of its future progress. It is important to stress these factors rather than the strictly political disturbances that receive undue popular attention. The latter merely reflect the underlying social tensions that result from the mal-distribution of the social product and from the limited opportunities for upward mobility. To suggest that Latin America's political instability is the cause of its misdevelopment is to completely reverse cause and effect. Latin America cannot develop political processes that even remotely achieve democratic standards until structural changes have been made that will permit more rapid economic growth and the meaningful participation in the nation's life of a larger segment of the population. In the meantime the familiar cycle of coups and countercoups, interspersed with periods of formal liberal democratic government, will persist irrespective of whether it takes place in the relatively advanced Argentine Republic or in the Central American domains of the United Fruit Co.

201

The American Involvement

Paradoxically, the United States is seeking to re-invigorate Latin America by means that have proved to be a conspicuous failure in the past and which, as we have seen, are themselves largely responsible for the region's present condition of mis-development and economic stagnation. It has sponsored a programme, ironically entitled the Alliance for Progress, that is intended to "revolutionize" Latin America without actually transforming the prevailing social system. The programme is based on the twin premises that the Latin American middle classes are dynamic liberal democrats and that the region needs a fresh infusion of (mainly private) foreign capital in order to attain Rostow's mythical take-off stage of development. Its sponsors believe that the middle classes, working alone, are not yet sufficiently strong to force change upon the tradition-bound oligarchies or to cope with the increasing popular demands for rapid social change. The Alliance's goals, therefore, are to ensure political stability while stimulating sufficient social, industrial and agricultural reforms to permit more rapid growth. Thus public funds are supposedly channeled into various social-welfare projects as well as into the development of a modern infrastructure for the region, while private capital is directed into manufacturing and extractive industries. The expectation is that changes will take place within a liberal democratic framework; the condition is that this framework, democratic or otherwise, is to be closely bound to the United States by economic, military and political ties.

The region's economy has so far shown little sign of being able to sustain an annual growth rate of 2.5 per cent per capita – the Alliance's modest target which, in itself, is too low to cope with the region's pressing social needs. In 1966, five years after the programme's inception, the growth rate was still hovering around the familiar figure of 1 per cent. Agricultural production per capita continues to decline, and industrial production to fluctuate erratically. Thus, it is not surprising to find that unemployment has been steadily rising, and that other urban problems have been magnified by the dramatic rural migration to the cities. Agrarian reform, which is everywhere recognized to be the key problem in Latin America is, in reality, no nearer to being realized than it was a decade ago. Apart from Mexico, Bolivia and Cuba – all of whom have experienced some form of revolutionary upheavals in the past – only Venezuela has made more than a token attempt to re-distribute land, but has done so in a manner that has been described as "gruesome, a veritable shambles" by one noted expert on Latin America.[6] The political perspective, likewise, is equally dismal. The two largest South American countries, Brazil and Argentina, are covertly or overtly ruled by reactionary military dictatorships, while the Dominican Republic, ravaged in 1965 by US marines in the name of democracy, remains as chaotic as ever.

The Alliance for Progress is in fact as far away as ever from achieving its avowed goals. There is no reason to believe that its future is any brighter. Most of the responsibility for this dreary record should be directly attributed to the United States, the sponsor of the Alliance. The United States has chosen to associate itself with a middle class that is essentially conservative and which is "far more likely to oppose reforms than to promote them."[7] It is wilful self-deception to believe otherwise. The emphasis on the role of private capital is equally detrimental to the long-term interests of Latin America. Why should it achieve in the future what it has failed to do in the past? The recent record of US foreign policy in Latin America, as in other parts of the underdeveloped world, thus compels one to question its motives.

One group with a vested interest in the Alliance for Progress, not unexpectedly, embraces US investors and exporters as well as their local associates within each Latin American country. Between 1950 and 1965, new US investments in Latin America amounted to $3.8 billion, while over $11.3 billion in profits were transferred to the United States without reducing the value of the original investments which, on the contrary, rose in value from $4.5 to $10.3 billion![8] In addition, Alliance funds, most of which take the form of loans, not grants, are used to pay for US exports to Latin America. As the American historian, Robert F. Smith, has noted, "by the end of 1964 it was quite evident that the Alliance was hardly more than the dollar diplomacy of the 1930's with a new façade."[9]

Any profound changes in Latin America are viewed as endangering the US stake in the region's economic future. In this respect, the Congressional requirement that the nationalization of US investments must be followed by immediate, adequate and effective compensation on pain of retaliation continues to provide a legal rationalization for US hostility towards any regime that might attempt to tamper with its interests. A newer device is the requirement, under the terms of the 1962 Foreign Assistance Act, that aid to underdeveloped countries must be discontinued in those cases where excessive tax burdens have been placed upon American-owned subsidiaries. The fear that social and economic changes will lead a country to move out of the US sphere of influence is, in practice, compelling the United States to strengthen the existing power structure in Latin America, a policy that it intends to enforce by every means at its disposal, be it political intervention, economic pressure or direct military action.

Prospects for Change

The foregoing analysis suggests that Latin America is in an impasse from which it will not easily extricate itself. There is no indication that the region is about to make "the basic internal reforms" or "the profound changes in the structure of the external sector" that ECLA insists are the pre-conditions for any rapid long-term growth.[10] The problem is that the Alliance for Progress, despite all the rhetoric about the need for peaceful revolution, is not designed to bring about fundamental reforms. At best, it offers no more than a temporary palliative for the region's problems. At worst, it is but a new means for extending American control over the region.

It will not be easy for Latin America to break free from the United States, but it is clear that its progress depends precisely upon this eventuality taking place. This is essential if Latin America is to restructure its society in a way that is most conducive to its well-being and future development. Like Asia and Africa, Latin America must seek new domestic forms and external relations that suit its present misdeveloped condition. There is as yet little evidence to suggest that the United States will do other than obstruct this search.

The failure to tackle the region's fundamental problems will lead to mounting tensions that are bound to errupt sooner or later. A violent outcome thus seems inevitable. Those who argue that the peasants and urban masses have always been exploited without necessarily developing a revolutionary consciousness ignore the fact that rural migration and the all-pervading communications media are rapidly shattering the peasants' previous isolation. The so-called demonstration effect is, in consequence, a potentially much more disruptive factor than it is in some other regions of the world. Mass political strife and other symptoms of the cold war era have already affected the remotest corners of Africa and Asia. There is no reason for Latin America to remain immune, a fact that is confirmed each day, be it by land seizures in Peru or by riots in Mexican cities.

One must expect dissident groups to resort increasingly to violence as a means of attaining their ends. Though the shape and direction of this violence cannot be precisely foretold, some projection of the region's future may nevertheless be ventured on the basis of its recent experience. The two most obvious manifestations of violence in recent years have been guerrilla movements and military coups. In the short-term it seems unlikely that the former will make much progress. Paradoxically, they are burdened by the very success of the model upon which they are based – the Cuban Revolution. Thus, counter-revolutionary strategies have benefited more from the Cuban experience than have the guerrillas operating in the Andean ranges. On the other hand, one must expect further military coups as a means of preserving the essence of the prevailing power structure in most countries. Argentina's reactionary military regime, and not Chile's Christian Democratic government (which has yet to prove that it offers more than a mere variation on the familiar reformist theme), is likely to become the model for most Latin American countries. Military coups, however, only exacerbate political tensions in the long run, since the latter are symptomatic of the persistent failure to cope with the region's intensified socio-economic crisis.

Political instability in Latin America stems from the failure to satisfy mass expectations. A non-violent outlet to the impasse in which most countries now find themselves will consequently have to be based upon the canalization of popular energies. In the short run this will depend upon the redistribution of the national income. In this connection, two possibilities come to mind. One is the emergence of Latin American counterparts to Nasser's Egyptian regime. The Peron government in Argentina offers a partial precedent for such a development. The Dominican events in 1965 suggest, however, that the prospects for progressive military elements being able to challenge and then replace the otherwise conservative armed forces are very slender. The second possibility is that of a civilian populist movement. Populism, which has strong historical roots in Latin America, is essentially a mass movement whose appeal cuts across class lines. Accordingly, a populist movement will normally lack a coherent ideology. The unifying factor is likely to be the underlying discontent against forces associated with the status quo, be they domestic oligarchies or foreign interests. Nationalism and simple socialist slogans are typical rallying cries for populist movements. From the viewpoint of effecting change in Latin America the problem lies in preserving the unity of the movement while attempting to implement social reforms. This can be most readily achieved by ensuring that the movement develop into a full socialist organization. Indeed, a populist regime implementing progressively more socialist policies would seem to offer the type of government that is most suited to bringing about the social transformation necessary for a rapid economic growth in Latin America. But such a development would *prima facie* conflict with the present policies of the Johnson Administration that has proclaimed it will neither permit another socialist system to emerge in Latin America nor allow any political development that might even lead to such an eventuality – implying almost any popularly supported movement.

The Cuban Alternative

Tragically it seems almost inevitable that a solution to the region's problems must ultimately depend upon some form of revolutionary violence, even though its realization may be postponed for some time yet. In the meantime, the Cuban Revolution is testimony to the fact that socialism offers a more viable solution to Latin America's problems than any alternative model sponsored by the United States, in addition to providing a rationale for opposition to US intervention in the region's domestic affairs.

In certain respects the Cuban revolution is the most significant event that has taken place in Latin America since the Spaniards were ejected in the early nineteenth century. Cuba has demonstrated that a small Latin American nation within 90 miles of the United States can undergo a genuine revolution and then, short of a large-scale war, defy all American attempts to overthrow the new social order – one that implies the total renunciation of everything that the United States represents today. Consequently one may be certain that its influence in the Hemisphere has only begun to be felt.

In view of its magnitude and the controversy which surrounds it, no brief appraisal of the Revolution's achievements may be expected to either persuade its detractors or to satisfy its admirers. Nevertheless, it is worthwhile emphasizing certain features that are relevant to the present discussion.

One fact about Cuba is not open to dispute. A genuine social revolution has led to the restructuring of the island's economy and society, as well as to the transformation of the country's external relations. Before the Revolution, Cuba had many characteristics common to the rest of Latin America. That is to say it was essentially a misdeveloped country with a distorted economic structure, whose economy, based on agriculture, could best be described as an appendage of that of the US mainland. Its stagnant economy was dominated by the sugar industry, and over two-thirds of its trade was controlled by the United States. Its social structure was equally characteristic of Latin America, being distinguished by parasitic non-functional élites and unemployed lower classes.

Since 1959, most of the land has been collectivized and the whole of industry nationalized. This has permitted Cuba to modernize its agriculture and to plan its economy along more rational lines. In turn, the severance of the umbilical cord binding it to the United States has permitted it to place its external trade sector at the service of its overall development. It is doubtful if these profound changes would have proved possible if the Revolution had not been social and socialist in character and if the price of banishing the middle classes to Miami had not been paid.

The Cuban Revolution represents a remarkable milestone in the history of the Americas. The economic changes that have taken place have laid the groundwork for rapid and continuing economic growth in the future, while the equally impressive social changes affecting education, public health and numerous other social services have improved the quality of life of vast numbers of Cubans. Cuba's progress must surely be apparent to all within the not too distant future. Of course, all but the most blind must perceive and should decry the absence of political democracy in Cuba. However, in comparison to the preceding regimes and to the rest of Latin America's political systems, Cuba is in some respects a relatively democratic society, for its government effectively promotes the social and economic interests of the majority of the population, an assertion that cannot be made for the rest of Latin America where you can find neither stable political democracy, nor genuine social democracy, nor tangible evidence of much economic growth.

The analysis of Latin America's fundamental problems may now be recapitulated. The region's critical condition is the product both of an unviable social system and of its domination by the United States. Neither factor can be changed without affecting the other. The Cuban Revolution, for its part, offers proof that

207

alternative social systems are both viable and necessary if Latin America is to extricate itself from its present impasse.

What Role for Canada?

The question is whether Canada can play a positive role in helping to bring about the changes that are so desperately needed in Latin America. Certainly membership in the OAS does not seem conducive to this end, for this institution was not designed with a view to either altering the region's internal social structures or to transforming its external relations with the United States. On the contrary, membership in the OAS would help to bolster an essentially conservative organization that helps to legitimize US hegemony in the Hemisphere.

All indications suggest that Latin America cannot solve its major problems via the Alliance for Progress and that violent structural changes must be expected sooner or later. The time and precise character of these cannot be foretold. Canada can have little influence on such developments. In any case, a more positive role in the region, intended to stimulate concrete reforms, would conflict with US policy. Any consideration of a Canadian role in the Hemisphere must be based upon the prior recognition of a fact stressed by Toynbee but which Canadians are nevertheless extremely loathe to admit:

"America is today the leader of a world-wide anti-revolutionary movement in defense of vested interests."[12]

In spite of all these negative factors, recent Canadian relations with Latin America suggest that Canada may yet play a significant, but limited, role in the region's future. The striking fact about Canada's Latin American policy is that it is the only Hemisphere country, with the exception of Mexico, that still has diplomatic and active trading relations with Cuba. What can account for the maintenance of normal relations with Cuba in spite of the hostile attitude of the United States, to whom Canada is linked by so many economic and political ties? Some fairly simple explanations come to mind. Canada, unlike the United States, was never emotionally bound up with Cuba, nor tied to it by military and political links. Likewise, Canada's pre-1959 investments in Cuba were small and were not associated with such sensitive sectors as natural resources and public utilities. Moreover, since 1959 Canada has been given no serious grounds for complaint by the policies of the Revolutionary Government. In return, Canada has acted with restraint, taking neither undue advantage of its opportunity to replace the United States' trading role nor placing major restrictions upon trade with Cuba.

The relationship that has developed between Canada and Cuba is essentially a pragmatic one. Neither country feels threatened by the other, and each has something to contribute in exchange for amicable relations. Though the majority of the Canadian public probably shares the United States' hostility towards socialist regimes, it lacks the psychotic fear of losing potential markets and investments overseas that dominates the United States. The difference can be explained in part by the fact that Canada itself is still at the stage of being a net importer of capital and has relatively few investments in Latin America.

The diplomatically correct relations that have continued between Cuba and Canada since 1959 have allowed the latter country considerable freedom of manoeuvre in its future relations with Cuba, as well as with any revolutionary regimes that may emerge in Latin America. In other words, though closely identified with the United States in the eyes of the rest of the Hemisphere, Canada has not, by its own actions towards Cuba, branded itself as an intransigent counter-revolutionary country. On the contrary, their relationship has demonstrated that it is possible for capitalist countries, even those as closely tied to the United States as is Canada, to coexist with revolutionary socialist regimes in the Western Hemisphere.

This relationship has benefited Cuba by providing a badly needed outlet to Western liberalism as a counterbalance to East European authoritarianism and also by helping to meet Cuba's objective needs for certain North American products. In turn, the relationship with the Castro regime has permitted Canada to pursue an independent Caribbean policy that is consistent with its middle-power aspirations. The continued association with Cuba has encouraged those progressive forces both in Canada and the United States that are opposed to imperialist policies. Furthermore, it seems quite probable that there has been some feedback into Canada. This has led to the consolidation of Canada's independent foreign policy towards Cuba and to a greater awareness and understanding of the problems of the underdeveloped countries in general.

It would be wrong to assume, on the basis of Canada's relations with the Castro regime, that there is any possibility of Canada offering positive encouragement to revolutionary movements in the Hemisphere. There is nothing to suggest that it is willing to pursue such a policy, for it would be strongly opposed by the United States and other established interests in the Hemisphere and Canada would have nothing to gain from it.

Only two feasible alternatives seem open to Canada at present. It can either offer more aid, trade and capital to Latin America, and thus implicitly participate in the Alliance for Progress, or it can leave matters much as they are at present. Since the whole burden of the argument so far has been that external intrusion in Latin America's affairs has been the principal obstacle to the region's progress, the first alternative is obviously not the preferred one. This does not imply that Canadian aid may not temporarily alleviate some of the region's worst pains nor, of course, that it would be undesirable to offer such aid to Cuba. It is, however, a reaffirmation of the belief that such aid mainly helps to stabilize outmoded social systems that have offered no indication of their ability to solve the region's problems. Furthermore, to the extent that this aid associates Canada with the existing power structures, it impairs the prospects of Canada playing a more constructive role if and when such regimes are overthrown. Finally, it is perhaps pertinent here to refer to a remark attributed to Pepé Figueres, a former President of Costa Rica and one of Latin America's leading liberal democrats, in connection with the role of foreign investment: "Please do not offer us as a remedy the very [consequences] of which we complain."[13]

It is the contention of this chapter that Canadian external aid would be put to much better use in Africa or Asia than in Latin America* First, because in certain countries such as Tanzania and Kenya there is a closer approximation to an identity of interest between the people and their rulers than in any Latin American country barring Cuba and second because on purely humane grounds, it seems preferable to offer aid to those countries with the lowest per capita incomes. A minor consideration is that Canada is culturally much better equipped to offer aid to English- and French-speaking countries than to those with an Iberian heritage.

It is an error to believe that, in the present circumstances, increased aid would allow Canada to play a more important role in the Hemisphere. No foreseeable increase in aid or trade seems likely to alter the fact that where Canada is not identified with the United States, it is ignored by Latin America – again with the

---

* See below Robert McKinnell's discussion, chapter 19, pp. 244-52.

exception of Cuba. Surely no better evidence of this fact is needed than the dismal Latin America representation in Expo '67. Only Cuba, Venezuela, Mexico and Haiti had pavilions in Montreal, whereas presumably most countries (barring Cuba) will be represented in no less a place than San Antonio, Texas, in Hemisfair '68.

The argument for Canada remaining as detached as possible from Latin America in the immediate future is thus compelling. It is the only way in which Canada can reserve the option of playing a more positive role in the future. Accordingly, it should offer no increased economic aid to the region and, while it cannot prevent corporations from investing there, it should offer them no encouragement to do so. The role of Brazilian Light and Power Co., a prime apologist within Canada for the reactionary regime now governing Brazil, is sufficient evidence of the political consequences of Canadian foreign investments abroad. In view of Brazilian's quintupled profits since 1961, one may be forgiven for taking a rather cynical view of its president's claim that Brazil enjoyed "one of the most productive periods of government" under Castelo Branco.[14]

In conclusion, it is worth repeating that although Canada is highly unlikely to offer positive support to revolutionary *movements* in Latin America, it has shown that it is prepared to co-exist with revolutionary *governments*. In the case of Cuba, Canada has played a useful role that has served both its own interests and those of a country undergoing profound social change. Any country that can act as a link between the United States and a Latin American revolutionary regime can play an important role that may be very much needed in the future. Like France in Europe, Canada is the only country in the Americas capable of performing such a role. Nothing should be done now that would jeopardize its prospect of doing so. For these reasons Canada should continue to have limited bilateral relations with Latin America. In the meanwhile it could serve Latin America best by giving maximum support to the regional agencies of the United Nations that are still relatively free from US domination. The Canadian presence in each Latin American country could be established in a relatively independent way by sponsoring limited research in such fields as medicine and agronomy. Such a programme would lend support neither to the ruling interests in each country nor to the goals of the United States, for these are not the same as those of Canada.

Cranford Pratt
Clyde Sanger

TOWARDS
JUSTICE
IN
RHODESIA

Cranford Pratt, former Principal of University College at Dar-es-Salaam, is at present Professor of Political Science and President of the Committee on African Studies in Canada at the University of Toronto. He is the co-author of two books, A New Deal in Central Africa *and* Buganda and British Over-Rule.

Clyde Sanger is a member of the Editorial Board of the Globe and Mail. *A former African correspondent for the Manchester* Guardian, *he has also published* Central African Emergency.

Canada is not a major power; but she is wealthy, militarily competent and technically and diplomatically skilful. We should use our talents, our independence and our wealth to promote the settlement of those international disputes in which Canada has, for whatever reasons, a special status which permits to her an initiating role.

One such dispute is the Rhodesian rebellion. Our present membership on the Security Council and our commitment to the ideal of a multi-racial Commonwealth give us special and immediate responsibilities in the Southern Rhodesian issue.

An understanding of the background to the Rhodesian crisis is essential to a discussion of possible Canadian initiatives. As in other Southern African countries, the key event in the history of the country was the establishment of white minority domination in the nineteenth century. By the middle of the present century severe franchise limitations on African political activity, a 50:50 apportionment of land for the African and white populations (despite a population ratio of 18:1 in the Africans' favour) and a division of funds for education which allowed ten times more expenditure on white than on African children served to prevent the African from achieving his rightful position in society.

Despite this trend signs of progress could be seen in the early 'sixties. The last few months of the administration of Sir Edgar Whitehead (Prime Minister from 1958 to 1962) provided evidence that some whites were beginning to adapt to a more integrated and equal society – to follow in the path of states like Kenya where the whites had abandoned any hope of minority control and were adjusting to African majority rule with remarkable ease.

Early in his term of office Whitehead had established an all-party Quinton Committee (Select Committee on the Resettlement of Natives) to review the Land Apportionment Act of 1930 under which most of Rhodesia was divided into African and European areas. In 1960 this committee calculated there were more than 100,000 families subsisting in the African Reserves without land, and recommended that for economic as well as other reasons the law should be repealed. Whitehead welcomed the recommendation and promised to repeal the law. In the meantime he set up an Unreserved Land Board to consider applications from white farmers to schedule their land as "unreserved," which would allow them to sell to Africans. These applications had to be published in the official gazette to give neighbouring farmers a chance to object. In the next year and a half 670,000 acres had been declared unreserved, and applications for another 1 million acres were waiting to be considered.

A second aspect of Whitehead's liberalizing initiatives was the 1961 constitution which he negotiated with Duncan Sandys. Certainly it was an improvement over the previous constitution, but the admission of Africans onto the rolls was so narrowly de-

213

fined and so specially arranged as to produce a strange bit of nonsense. The franchise was only broadened to the extent that 15 electoral districts controlled by a "B" roll were added to the 50 constituencies already established and controlled by an "A" roll. There were income and schooling qualifications for the "A" roll that had been raised in four successive stages since 1923 (a sample 1961 qualification was 900 dollars a year income and four years' high school) and which meant that it was dominated by whites; the "B" roll, with slightly lower qualifications, was planned for African control. All the subsequent offers to broaden the franchise by Winston Field and Ian Smith (and the proposal contained in the "HMS Tiger" plan endorsed by Harold Wilson) referred only to widening the "B" roll. This would, of course, do nothing to alter the balance of power between the races.

For a few days in 1961 the African leaders thought they were indeed over the first hump; they could win the 15 districts, and perhaps 7 constituencies – just enough to prevent a white two-thirds majority which would have power to amend the constitution. But a revision of their mathematics convinced them they had not been assured of what became the most important of Mr. Wilson's "six principles" – unimpeded progress to majority rule – and they rejected the franchise arrangements and subsequently boycotted the referendum and the 1962 elections.

In campaigning for a positive vote to endorse the 1961 constitution Whitehead tried to convince both races that the new constitution was to their advantage. To the whites he stressed that it provided for "95 per cent independence"; to the Africans he concentrated on the 15 seats for which they could dominate the voting. Whitehead misinterpreted the meaning of the referendum vote in favour of the new constitution and used it as an encouragement to introduce land and education reforms. In fact the white voters had been attracted to the new constitution because of the virtual independence it offered them, not because it opened the way to a multi-racial state.

Though his measures were too timid and circumspect to win African support, they were sufficiently liberal to arouse a majority of European voters against him. As these voters controlled the legislature, Whitehead was defeated in 1962 and replaced by the Rhodesian Front headed initially by Winston Field and Ian Smith.

The government came to power because its leaders had severely opposed the limited African participation permitted under the new constitution and because they opposed the repeal of the Land Apportionment Act. The work of the Unreserved Land Board was reversed by Lord Graham who as Minister of Lands allowed only 30,000 acres to be unreserved. The new government's policy that "farming patterns should conform with the area," i.e. there should be no "black islands" in a white area, thus rejecting Whitehead's tentative liberal initiative.

This is a prime example of the way white Rhodesian had *begun* to adapt to a more integrated society. The important point is that the process was halted, or actually reversed, by the action and influence of the Rhodesian Front. There are other examples. The Constitutional Council introduced as a watch-dog against new discriminatory legislation was easily bypassed by "certificates of urgency." Hotels that had "gone multi-racial" were resegregated, like the Victoria in Bulawayo. Private schools were not allowed to continue opening to all races.

The big unresolved issue, however, was freedom from the remnants of British control. Ian Smith became Prime Minister in April 1964 after Winston Field had proved too half-hearted for the Rhodesian Front back-benchers on this issue. Smith began his major effort to win independence for a white-dominated Rhodesia before Harold Wilson came to power in Britain in 1964. Rebuffed by Douglas-Home and Sandys, he continued to press such demands on Wilson, while orchestrating a whole repertoire of supporters' demonstrations – an indaba of government chiefs, a referendum and finally a general (i.e. predominantly white) election.

British Concession and Compromise

As the confidential negotiations between Wilson and Smith dragged on, Africans within and outside Rhodesia became increasingly suspicious that Britain might agree to full independence for Rhodesia under the Smith government. Consequently their spokesmen within the Commonwealth, and particularly Presidents Nyerere of Tanzania and Kauanda of Zambia, sought from Wilson the assurance that there would be no independence for Rhodesia before majority rule in that country. The essential moderation of this African demand must be noted. They wanted Britain to pursue in Rhodesia the policies of trusteeship and training for self-government that had marked its post-war colonial policies elsewhere in Africa. Both President Nyerere and President Kaunda went out of their way to stress that they would accept a period of colonial tutelage in Rhodesia as long as it was clearly established that, when it ended, there would be majority rule.

The British government, however, did not want to sustain a long period of British tutelage. Whatever its historical and legal responsibilities for Rhodesia, the main British preoccupation by 1965 was to discharge them as cheaply and quickly as possible, without open conflict with their racial "kith and kin" in Rhodesia but with as little damage as possible to Britain's liberal good name in Africa. Wilson was therefore willing to abandon what had been a central British policy in tropical Africa at least since 1923, when the Duke of Devonshire pronounced the principle that independence in Kenya could not be conceded to a white minority regime. Instead he sought sufficient safeguards within an independence constitution for Rhodesia, which would assure unimpeded progress towards majority rule even though a white minority was still in charge on independence day.

Soon after coming to power, Prime Minister Wilson had summarized the British position in terms of these five principles:

1 The principle and intention of unimpeded progress to majority rule would have to be maintained and guaranteed.
2 Guarantees against retrogressive amendments to the Constitution.
3 Immediate improvement in the political status of the African population.
4 Progress towards ending racial discrimination.
5 The British government would need to be satisfied that any basis proposed for independence was acceptable to the people of Rhodesia as a whole.

Smith in contrast insisted that the local European minority must itself control the place at which Africans would assume political power and must therefore remain in a position to check or to reverse this process if it so desired.

By the time the Smith-Wilson negotiations had broken down in 1965, Wilson's concern to achieve a settlement at almost any cost had led him to accept a number of very far-reaching compromises.

Prime Minister Wilson had conceded so much to the European minority in Rhodesia during the last weeks of negotiation that the hard question which remains is why Smith did not then and there accept Wilson's final offer. No doubt the major part of the answer lies in the dynamics of European politics in Southern Rhodesia which propelled the Smith cabinet and a reluctant Smith towards a Unilateral Declaration of Independence (UDI). But insofar as the negotiations themselves were an important factor, the fifth principle remained a stumbling block. At the end the negotiations bogged down in discussions of how opinion of Rhodesians would be tested and in arguments about the representative characeter of a chiefs' assembly. The seemingly secondary nature of these issues is deceptive. They represented a matter of fundamental importance. If Wilson stuck to the clear meaning of the fifth principle, then African rights might well continue to be safeguarded whatever concessions he nominally accepted because Africans could be counted upon to reject a constitution which would subjugate them to the wealthy and exclusive white minority living in their midst.

Smith, failing to get Wilson to accept the subterfuge of a chiefs' indaba that would get around this fifth principle, broke off the negotiations with the British Prime Minister and unilaterally declared independence for Rhodesia on November 11, 1965.

In the mists that swirled around British-Rhodesian relations after UDI, a few landmarks stand out. Listed briefly, they are these:

In December 1965 Britain called on all countries to impose voluntary sanctions on all petroleum supplies to Rhodesia. If it had been effective it might have ended the rebellion in two or three months. It presumably gave the grounds for Mr. Wilson's claim at the Lagos Commonwealth leaders' conference in January that the end would come "in a matter of weeks, not months."

The Lagos Conference was particularly noteworthy for its reference to the use of force:

The Prime Ministers discussed the question of the use of military force in Rhodesia, and it was accepted that its use could not be precluded if this proved necessary to restore law and order.

It was also noteworthy for the growing Canadian involvement in the issue. Prime Minister Pearson who was present gave vigorous support to Britain in convincing the majority of the Commonwealth not to press for the use of force to bring down the rebel regime but rather to give Wilson the "weeks not

217

months" claimed to be all that was needed to achieve this result through the use of voluntary sanctions.

In April Britain appealed to the Security Council to sanction the use of force in international waters, to stop the oil-tanker Manuela from berthing and discharging at Beira oil known to be destined for Rhodesia. Africans and their allies objected this was hypocrisy, if forceful measures were not taken to stop the greater volume of oil that had been flowing into Rhodesia, by road-tanker across Beit Bridge or by rail via Lourenco Marques. The British argued that the Manuela interception could be swift and effective, unlike the other preventive measures demanded; and, after African amendments were defeated by abstentions, the British resolution was approved.

The Commonwealth Conference of September 1966 was a moment of major crisis. Wilson reaffirmed the British plan for a legal government in Rhodesia. Paragraph VIII of the Commonwealth Conference Communique outlined Wilson's plan: it called for the appointment of a widely representative interim government by the Governor of Rhodesia, the releasing of all political detainees and the assumption of normal political activity. The British government would then negotiate with this interim government an independence constitution which would be based on what had now grown to six principles of British policy, the sixth being that there must be safeguards assuring that no racial group would be subjected to domination by another. Britain was not ready, despite pressure from a large majority of the Commonwealth, to support the position that there could be no independence for Rhodesia before majority rule. She wanted one further chance to put proposals to Smith. However, Wilson agreed that if these final proposals to Smith were rejected, he would no longer be willing to consider any independence constitution which was not based on majority rule.

In the end Wilson refused to yield to the view of the majority of the Commonwealth that Britain should use force to restore constitutional government in Rhodesia. He did agree, however, that if Britain's proposals to Smith were rejected and if she continued to be supported by the other Commonwealth members, Britain would then propose to the United Nations that selective mandatory sanctions be imposed on Rhodesia.

Canada played a crucial role at the September 1966 Commonwealth Conference. Prime Minister Pearson did not rule out the legitimacy of an eventual use of force if all other measures were to fail to bring about a return to constitutional government in Rhodesia. Moreover, Pearson made public this crucial view when he distinguished before the House of Commons in September, 1966 between police action taken under the United Nations and the use of force as normally understood. Canada also made it clear that the only acceptable constitutional solution would be majority rule before independence, which assuredly would then lead to adult suffrage as soon as possible after independence. Finally Pearson reaffirmed his conviction that the resolution of the Rhodesia issue was vital to the very survival of the Commonwealth, because it involved the issue of racial equality which was the only basis on which the new Commonwealth could survive.

Because the Canadian delegation thus stood with the new members of the Commonwealth on these important grounds of long-term principle, it was in turn able to influence these members to give Wilson the one last chance to negotiate with Smith, to refrain at this stage from pressing for the use of force, and to accept the terms of Prime Minister Wilson's proposed appeal to the United Nations for mandatory sanctions.

Thus Canada had won over to a moderate position the new members of the Commonwealth by demonstrating that she supported the same basic long-term objectives as they did. Similarly, Canada helped to win British acquiescence in a reaffirmation of these long-term objectives as the price for support for the more immediate short-term objectives of British policy. It was a positive, proper, and entirely honorable policy for Canada to follow as long as, these immediate objectives accepted, Canada then remained faithful in her support also of the long-run objectives and exerted in their support the same diplomatic skills and initiatives which she had devoted to winning acquiescence for the immediate British policies from the rest of the Commonwealth.

The latter half of September and November 1966 saw renewed British efforts to reach an accord with the Smith regime. These efforts culminated in the meetings between Prime Minister Wilson and Mr. Smith on "HMS Tiger" in December 1966. When the terms on which they had tentatively agreed on "HMS Tiger" were rejected by Smith on his return to Salisbury, Prime Minister Wilson, true to his word, first turned to the Security Council to impose sanctions and, these secured, then announced in the House of Commons that the commitment contained in paragraph 10b of the Commonwealth Conference communique

219

would be honoured: Britain would no longer consider a constitutional settlement that conceded to Rhodesia independence before majority rule.

Later in December, Britain asked the Security Council to impose mandatory sanctions on the main Rhodesian exports, as well as on imports of oil supplies and automobile and aircraft parts. Its Foreign Secretary George Brown said voluntary sanctions had cut Rhodesian exports from $370 million in 1965 to $240 million in 1966, and these further measures should reduce exports to about $150 million. Britain opposed, and organized the defeat of, an amendment which would have added "coal and manufactured products" to the list of sanctioned exports arguing that this would hurt Zambia more than Rhodesia. Zambia's foreign Minister had spoken strongly for the amendment. This defeat left Africans angry and suspicious of Britain.

Canada's Responsibility

As the immediate economic effects of sanctions are taking far longer to develop than expected and as the political consequences are by no means clear, Canada must be prepared to restate its position. Broadly speaking, there are three possible directions which Canadian policy might be able to take without entailing a fundamental reversal of its position so far: having noted the fact that alternative policies have failed, we could recommend the use of force by Britain to bring down the Smith regime; we could combine declared opposition to the regime with a policy of non-involvement other than the support of United Nations decisions; we could take the initiative in defining policies to be publicly recommended by the Security Council to Britain and to the Commonwealth.

The first of these policies is not recommended. Although Britain has always insisted that Rhodesia is her sole responsibility, it is unrealistic to expect her on her own and at this late stage to use force to bring down the Smith regime. This first position would win Canada easy approval from African states but would not further the resolution of the crisis.

Several factors strongly urge the third rather than the second policy on Canada. The Rhodesian issue is one of those few international crises in which Canada is in a position to play a crucial and possibly unique role. We are trusted by the African members of the Commonwealth and our opinion cannot be ignored by the British. In this conflict which could so easily divide the Commonwealth on racial lines and do it the very gravest damage, we have a particular responsibility to act.

Secondly, the United Nations has now clearly declared itself on the need for a constitutional regime in Rhodesia which will lead to majority rule. It would surely be damaging to the United Nations if a regime of 220,000 Europeans was able to defy it. Our present membership on the Security Council gives us a special and immediate responsibility in this setting as well. If Canada does not take the initiative and define a meaningful and vigorous next phase in the pressures to be applied to the Smith regime, the Council may very well find that it has to choose between a tacit surrender to the Smith regime and a variety of African resolutions which call upon Britain to use force. Both these alternatives would do the United Nations harm. The first, because it would concede that a tiny white minority could defy it with success and the second, because it would involve the United Nations in passing resolutions that stood no chance of being enforced.

Furthermore we cannot honorably avoid continued involvement. We have used our influence on African leaders to convince them to try sanctions first. A major test of the sincerity of our earlier advice and of our earlier affirmations is therefore immediately at hand.

There is a refinement to the "do nothing at present" argument, which might be called the radical realist line. It accepts that no intervention save a military one will succeed in defeating the Smith regime but argues that it can only come if there were to be a breakdown of law and order in Rhodesia and a very real increase in articulate Rhodesian-African opposition towards the present regime. Therefore, it is premature to do much more than to continue to condemn this regime. Wait for the violence, wait until the African majority demonstrates that it refuses to accept white minority rule and then – "but only" then – will effective intervention be possible.

This line of argument is not so much worldly as it is desperate. It demands a long and bloody anti-colonial struggle in a highly organized police state by a still very weak and disorganized African majority before those nations, which are capable swiftly and with comparative ease of bringing about a just solution, would be willing to intervene. It is an unrealistic line of argument because it is hard to conceive that, after such a period of bitter racial violence, there could ever be in Rhodesia a racially harmonious society. Even viewed from a narrow western perspective it is short-sighted: any African regime which came to power in such circumstances would be bound to regard with hostility and contempt those Western nations who held back their support and refrained from intervening at a time when such intervention could have saved so many lives and called a halt to a period of uneven and desperate struggle.

Finally, our inactivity on the South West Africa issue makes the need for independent Canadian initiatives on the Rhodesian crisis even more compelling. Having urged caution over South West Africa, Canada should now bend her efforts to achieve the quickest possible solution in Rhodesia. This would offset the frustrated hopes of those 85 countries who in May 1967 voted for measures aimed at bringing independence within a year to South West Africa. If advance is seen on one front, these countries will more easily accept the slower pace Canada and other western states have advocated on the other.

For this reason, Canada must take the initiative in defining policies in regard to Rhodesia which she could recommend to the United Nations and to the Commonwealth. Our central commitment must be that the Smith regime be replaced by a constitutional government under which there will be unimpeded progress to majority rule and thence to independence. Within the framework of this objective every effort should be made to ensure that the legitimate rights of the white minority are protected.

Our initiatives toward this end should exhaust all means other than force before the use of force is contemplated. There must, however, be an increasing and sustained application of the whole range of alternative policies if our central commitment is to be credited. Moreover in the interests of solving the Rhodesian problem swiftly, every effort should be made to contain the crisis so that it is not merged into the much more intractable problem of Southern Africa as a whole.

From these basic propositions, these more specific policy recommendations can be derived:

1 Canada must reaffirm in forthright terms its support for the proposition that there can be no independence in Rhodesia before the introduction of majority rule. That has been our position in the past and every precedent is on our side. The entrenched clauses of the Union of South Africa act proved worthless. The elaborate powers of reservation given to the

African Affairs Board within the Central African Federation proved useless. The entrenched clauses in the Bill of Rights in the 1961 Southern Rhodesian constitution did not stop a new Preventive Detention Act being passed. The moral from all these closely relevant experiences is clear: there can be no constitutional guarantees without the reality of power to enforce them. Either Africans must be given the electoral power to ensure their own rights or Britain must continue to act as their trustee until that electoral power is extended to them. Our recognition of these truths must be reaffirmed publicly. This will make more difficult any British retreat on the principle of no independence before majority rule, and will prevent her making arrangements which, however elaborate and complex, amount to a sellout to the Smith regime.

2 Canada must also reaffirm its support for constitutional arrangements after the fall of Smith along the lines which were sketched by Britain in paragraph 8 of the September 1966 Commonwealth Conference Communique: These arrangements should provide continued British or international final authority; a British or international military presence; a widely based interim administration which would include nationalist leaders and a reasonable transition period to majority rule.

3 We must in particular make it clear that our support for these first two propositions involves Canadian opposition to the type of settlement envisaged in the agreement made between Prime Minister Wilson and Mr. Smith on "HMS Tiger." As the conservative opposition in Britain has been seeking since early 1967 to revive the Tiger agreement, it is of importance to establish publicly that the Agreement is unacceptable. (Even if Canada were to accept the theoretical possibility that independence could be granted before majority rule on the understanding that there would be "copper-bottomed guarantees" of unimpeded progress to majority rule, the Tiger proposals had no such assurances.) *

4 Canada should support the assisted emigration of whites from Rhodesia who are unwilling to remain in Rhodesia if they lose their position of privilege and domination. Canada should also support schemes to purchase their farms so that leaving

Rhodesia will not involve for them a major economic loss. Schemes such as these were important in Kenya in helping its transition to African rule.

5 Canada should take the lead in an urgent reinvigorating of a training programme for Rhodesian African administrators. An important difference between Rhodesia and the ex-colonies to the north is the complete reliance on locally recruited whites for the running of the civil service. Until 1960 the Public Service Act barred non-Europeans; in December 1962 Whitehead could claim only 120 non-Europeans in the service. At UDI it is believed that were only 84 African civil servants doing jobs above the level of menial tasks[1] – and most of these were in the field as school inspectors and agricultural supervisors. In contrast, Kenya never had more than 4,000 white civil servants; the crucial middle ranks were filled substantially with Asians, while even through the Mau Mau Emergency some of the 50,000 Africans in the public service were moving into senior posts. In Kenya when the transition to majority rule began, the process of Africanization of the civil service went relatively smoothly: the great majority of the whites were expatriates who worked out their notice for their changing masters with good spirits, assured of their "lumpers" and a passage home. The Asians had their moments of panic, but most adapted swiftly; never having been accepted as part of the colonial élite, they had not tasted the fruits of privilege.

In Rhodesia it has been totally different. The white civil servants are now, as much as the farmers, the backbone of the Smith regime. Their votes bring in the Rhodesian Front, and in their daily work they bear the weight of opposing world sanctions. It is impossible to calculate the numbers who will stay on, when majority rule becomes inevitable, but clearly there will be thousands of vacancies to be filled by Africans. Equally clearly, there should be thousands of Africans in senior and middle posts. The Commonwealth Lagos Conference saw this point: it approved the establishment of a special Commonwealth programme "to help accelerate the training of Rhodesian Africans" and called for a meeting of experts as soon as possible (that was January 1966) "to consider detailed projects of aid by Commonwealth countries". The former head of the Ghanaian civil service, A. L. Adu, who had helped reorganize the East African common services was put in charge. But this programme has moved extremely slowly, with Adu concentrating on establishing a training centre. If thousands need to be trained as administrators in a short time, surely the scheme needs maximum publicity to draw schoolteachers and others out of Rhodesia (as well as attract students already aboard); and surely they need to be spread around the Commonwealth, so that all its resources can be used. This seems to have been the intent at Lagos; but while a good deal has been heard of the Chevrier sanctions committee established there, little if anything has been heard of the companion Adu committee.

6 We should affirm our acceptance that, if all else fails, international, Commonwealth or British military intervention in Rhodesia would be preferable to permitting a racist minority regime to defy the Commonwealth and the United Nations and to establish its permanent domination over an African majority fourteen times its size. In making such an affirmation now we should announce our readiness, should the Security Council so decide, to have our forces join the forces of Britain and other nations in this international police action.

7 Before any such military intervention is undertaken there are a variety of initiatives still possible which may convince the Smith regime that it must surrender its monopoly of power. These initiatives may also satisfy African and other critics of the regime that the United Nations' efforts to achieve this end are genuine. At the least, these include Canadian support for a further intensification and augmentation of UN sanctions, Canadian lead in offering major assistance to Zambia and Malawi to permit these states further to cut their Rhodesian imports, and especially support to help complete the road and rail links between Zambia and Tanzania.

The pursuit of these policies would not involve any sacrifice of essential Canadian interests. Rather they would allow the imaginative and purposeful use of Canadian influence, resources and diplomatic skills in an international crisis which will not be justly settled if left to our great power allies. These policies are, therefore an important example of the positive international contribution which Canada can make if she is willing to pursue an independent foreign policy.

Stephen Hymer
Brian Van Arkadie

OFFERING
OPTIONS
TO
THE
"THIRD WORLD"

*Stephen Hymer is Associate Professor of Economics at Yale University.
He has taught at the University of Ghana and is at present at work on
a book about the economic growth of that country.*

*Brian Van Arkadie was formerly attached to the British Ministry of Over-
seas Development and has written several books and articles on development economics.*

The settler's town is a strongly-built town, all made of
stone and steel. It is a brightly-lit town; the streets are
covered with asphalt, and the garbage-cans swallow all the
leavings, unseen, unknown and hardly thought about. The settler's feet are never visible, except perhaps in the sea; but
there you're never close enough to see them. His feet are protected by strong shoes although the streets of his town are
clean and even, with no holes or stones. The settler's town is a
well-fed town; its belly is always full of good things. The settler's town is a town of white people, of foreigners.

The town belonging to the colonized people, or at least the
native town, the negro village, the medina, the reservation, is
a place of ill fame, peopled by men of evil repute. They are

226

born there, it matters little where or how; they die there, it matters not where nor how. It is a world without spaciousness: men live there on top of each other, and their huts are built one on top of the other. The native town is a hungry town, starved of bread, of meat, of shoes, of coal, of light. The native town is a crouching village, a town on its knees, a town wallowing in the mire. It is a town of niggers and dirty arabs. The look that the native turns on the settler's town is a look of lust, a look of envy . . . . (Fanon, *The Wretched of the Earth*, p. 32)

The year 2000 is only 33 years away. It can serve as a useful horizon for viewing the terrible problems of the underdeveloped world and the possible role for Canada.

The prospects for the world in our time are not good. It is in the context of a bleak picture that Canadians must choose and act. It is likely that at the outset of the 21st century the number of people living in poverty will be as much as double the current number. We have few illusions about what Canada will be willing to do. We suggest policies that are possible even if not probable. Independence is meaningful only in relation to the great issues the world now faces.

There is a conflict of interest between the "first" and "third" world. Canada has a choice between being a middle power in the first world or making a heroic effort to transcend this conflict. It seems it can do this by providing wider options for under-developed countries. Canada cannot by itself solve the problems of the under-developed world, but it can contribute to an environ-ment in which the under-developed countries have a chance to help themselves.

The under-developed countries do not have much scope for independent action. Even with their limited resources, they do not do as well as they might. They inherit from their past, and from their colonial experience, institutions unsuited to their pres-ent problems.

In Canada, it is will rather than ability which is lacking. We are on the threshold of a new era where our own problems of food, clothing and shelter can be solved, in the old form at least. The material base provides the opportunity for new initiatives. There is the possibility for experiment.

This is clear when we examine the question of independence for Canada in relation to the third world. For our lifetime the problems of these countries will intensify and though we try to ignore them, we can do so only by sacrificing part of ourselves. "There are no innocents and no onlookers. We all have dirty hands." (Fanon)

Even a small power, if it understands the situation, can do something to help and in some cases can even be done with little cost and great benefit to itself.

The facts about world poverty are well known.[1] They are publicized and repeated from the most respectable sources – but like the death statistics of great disasters, they are beyond comprehension. Nevertheless, it is worth repeating them, because they are to be with us for the foreseeable future, perhaps with increasing horror.

Such a recitation of the crude facts must include the information that follows:

1 At current growth rates, the gap between the poor and the wealthy nations increases steadily; in the rich countries rapid and steady technological change provides the main impetus for growth while the underdeveloped countries have the greatest difficulty in absorbing the technology that already exists. "In the rich countries average income per head is going up about $50 a year, in the poor countries by about $2.50 a year and in the very poor countries by about $1.50 per year."[2] The gap between what they do and the potential provided by modern technology grows each year.

2 Within the poor world, the more prosperous nuclei are not growing fast enough to lower the absolute number living in rural poverty. Growing pools of unemployment are the result.

3 Population growth has become such that it is becoming more difficult to meet even minimal requirements of bare existence.

4 Even if growth rates of 6 per cent per annum were achieved – well in excess of past average performance and even greater than the objectives of the UN development decade – by the end of this century the per capita income of the poor countries would still be dismally low – perhaps only $100 per capita in India and in some African countries, for example.

Economics is again the dismal science.

Typically, these facts are introduced as a prelude to charitable instincts; we parade the poor and pass the plate. That little comes of this is perhaps to be expected. On the domestic scene very few of our deep-seated social or economic problems have been solved by an appeal to predominantly charitable instincts. The amounts generated are inevitably small and their allocation is more closely tailored to the tastes of the donor than the needs of the recipient.[3]

In the development of the first world, primary reliance has been placed on the private initiative of businessmen to mobilize resources for capital formation and technological change. The government has acted to help business and to ameliorate some of the more serious dislocations resulting from industrialization, but by and large has not played an initiating role except for over-head capital. There is little reason to expect the government to do abroad what it does not do at home. It is more in line with our history that governments look at their aid programmes as handmaidens to the private business sector (their own or those abroad) rather than as the main vehicle of growth. Even if the government wished to do otherwise it has little scope because it is not government but our private corporations that possess the capital, technology and enterprise that are so badly needed abroad. If such institutions can be little influenced even at home, it is hardly surprising that they cannot be mobilized for public purposes abroad.

The total volume of world aid, after a period of rapid growth, has stagnated in recent years.[4] Since some of what we call aid is not an outright gift but merely a long term loan at interest rates which are low only in comparison with recent market rates, the net free foreign exchange made available to countries on public account is declining, the flow of interest costs and debt repayment out of the under-developed countries offsets a substantial proportion of the gross aid. A number of developing countries have therefore found themselves in severe balance of payments difficulties, in which heavy fixed obligations to service overseas holdings of public debt have a significant place.[5]

Even more serious are private account flows: the reverse flow of earnings and of capital transfer have more than outweighed new foreign investment. The foreign investment which does occur is concentrated in industries satisfying the needs of the developed world, such as the petroleum industry, rather than being directed towards engendering endogenous growth processes within the under-developed countries. The lack of donor enthusiasm to provide a long-term finance on soft terms has been combined with an overwillingness to provide short-term loans. Businessmen wishing to sell to the under-developed world receive great encouragement from the government through export credit guarantee arrangements for commercial credits and contractor finance. Often these are for precisely the projects which would be rejected in the context of an aid programme and the harassed bureaucracies of underdeveloped countries accept this form of help. This short-term commercial credit on hard terms creates fixed obligations, sometimes of alarming proportion. Overseas finance in these circumstances creates a resource transfer in the short-term but fairly soon the debt must be repaid, often before the investment yields a return. The under-developed countries then must appeal for refinancing and, through virtual international bankruptcy, lose control over their policies to the lending nations, typically through the medium of international agencies.

The *Economist's* report (August 6, 1966) on the treatment of Ghana provides a case in point. The *Economist* estimated that Ghana's public debt was over one billion dollars and over two-thirds of this total was in debt of average maturity of six years or less. Their tongue-in-cheek description of the preliminary creditor's meeting of June, 1966, runs:

> Ghana explained its plight to the representatives of 13 western countries, the general reaction was somewhat reserved. The Swiss said, predictably, that debts were debts and they hoped Swiss debts would be paid promptly. The German delegate brought up the question of German property confiscated in Ghana during the war. The Israeli delegate said he hoped Israel would be considered to qualify as one of the underdeveloped countries entitled to uninterrupted repayment. The British delegate said he hoped any stretch-out of repayments would be a "reasonably short one."

The ineffectiveness of aid not only derives from the inadequacy of the net flows and the dangers of excessive international indebtedness, but also from the character of the aid given.

Politics and development are necessarily interrelated. But the political content of aid programmes is unfortunate, for the distribution of aid is more influenced by the strategic and ideological pre-conceptions of the major donors than by any assessment of the genuine development implications of the political institutions of the recipients.[6] Since there is no underlying harmony of interest, these differences are critical. Only too often strategic considerations are interpreted in a short-term context, stressing foreign rather than domestic policies of the recipients.

This is perhaps not surprising. Aid, after all, could only have reached the level it has if something more than the charitable instincts had been aroused.

It would matter less if the amount involved were very large. "Client" states of the United States in the Far East have achieved very favourable rates of growth – Formosa and South Korea, for example. If the wealthy countries are willing to take a sizeable enough interest in a country it may well develop irrespective of the other circumstances.

However, overall no such large flow is likely and the effectiveness of the meagre flow is reduced by non-economic choices, sometimes to the point of counter-effectiveness – bolstering regimes alien to development, for example.

Not surprisingly, aid has not worked miracles. Throughout the third world political tensions and conflicts continue and are, if anything, aggravated by growth.

Tragically, however, the frustrations and tensions are not finding their outlet in creative social transformation, both in civil and regional strife with destructive consequences. Programmes of national independence, initially focused against colonial powers, become banners for struggles between groups in the underdeveloped world. These tensions and conflicts are inevitable. The appeal to increase aid to avoid revolution is both dangerous, because it avoids the reality of the poor world, and dishonest, in that it cannot succeed in any such purpose, at the aid levels which are envisaged. If the prevention of revolution is seen as one of the purposes of aid, it is only too easy to turn to other tools when aid fails to achieve the desired counter-revolutionary purpose.

Seen at the deepest level, the dilemma of aid, both in the form of capital and technical assistance, is that it bolsters the metropolitan influence in the ex-colonial world, when the most profound problems in the recipient countries involve the need to break from certain social, economic and cultural metropolitan influences, no matter how altruistic the motivation of the mother country. Development is made at home.

The answer that is sometimes offered is multilateralism – a popular view in Canada. But international agencies take on the ideological overtones and cultural assumptions of their major sponsors. This is certainly true of the World Bank, for example, with its American ambience. Even when international agencies develop views and interests which are not too tied to the foreign policy objectives of a major country, multilateralism is only satisfactory as an addition to the constellation, rather than as a consolidation and replacement for other aid sources. In the end, individual under-developed countries are better off when faced with a number of parties on the other side of the table in international financial negotiations. "When thieves fall out. . . ."

A range of choice is necessary for poor countries so that the consequences of breaking with one source of support is not necessarily disastrous.

Effectiveness of aid is also reduced by policies which use aid programmes as a tool of trade policy.[7] The now prevalent practice of tying bilateral aid to imported goods from the donor (even the US is now forced in this direction by her chronic balance of payments problem) warps the design of plans and projects, reduces the real value of the aid flow and has undesirable effects on the evolution of trade patterns by inhibiting trade within the poor world.

In criticizing aid policy there is no intention to imply maliciousness amongst aid agencies anymore than it characterized the colonial civil service. They are staffed by the most humane of public servants. However, the exigencies of the balance of payments crises in the United Kingdom, for example, have been such that it is hardly surprising that there should have been an attempt to minimize the foreign exchange costs of the aid programme.[8] Foreign aid supporters are forced to demonstrate to those public servants responsible for the balance of payments situation or for trade promotion the consistency of the aid effort with other public objectives. Only in that way do programmes survive. A necessary result, in a world with chronic shortage of foreign exchange reserves, has been increasing tying of aid to the exports of the donor countries, rather than allowing bilateral transfers to generate multilateral trade flows.

A look at the performance of major donors illustrates some of the problems of aid. Both Britain and France remain heavily committed to their traditional imperial interests.[9] This is especially true in Africa, where programmes of financial aid are combined with the maintenance of elaborate programmes of technical assistance, with the objective of making the transfer of administrations to full local control as painless, and perhaps as slow, as possible. In some countries, government is still dependent on the mother country for recurrent costs. The virtue in these programmes has been to maintain high levels of civil administration where there would otherwise have been the danger of swift deterioration. The cost has been the failure to initiate any great experiments in administrative practice with the achievement of formal independence. The result has been, only too often, the creation of élites who occupy the offices without any noticeable improvement in responsiveness to the country's problems.

Too great an exercise of independence on the part of the new African powers diminishes the flow of aid – this happened abruptly at a very early stage in the relationship between Guinea and France, for example, and has resulted from the recent break between Tanzania and Britain. Again, from the point of view of the donor, the action may not be malicious; it was not surprising, after all, that suspension of a £7 million aid offer should flow from Tanzania's decision to break diplomatic relations with Britain's Labour Government over the weak British policy towards the Rhodesian rebellion.

Generally, however, both Britain and France have managed to maintain a considerable degree of influence in previous colonies. In many parts of Africa, the most serious competitor for influence is the US. The United States' position is different:

> The United States became involved in international development aid on a major scale principally as a byproduct of the world wide responsibilities thrown upon it as a leader of the Western World after World War II. The size as well as the direction of US aid is an extraordinary blend of humanitarian sentiment and cold war strategy.[10]

While Britain and France have been moving from a situation of outright control, back to prepared positions of pervasive but less obtrusive influence, the US has been engaged in the reverse process. The US has asserted dominant and overt influence in many areas over the past decade. The extent of her involvement tends to be carried through to any necessary breadth of activity and strength of commitment.

When the United States decides to make a major commitment, the penetration can be pervasive and the effect overwhelming – capital aid, food supplies, economic, political and military advisors, educational support. Such involvement can lead to economic growth but it cannot be a satisfactory technique throughout the underdeveloped world. In the context of severe social tensions, the tendency is for the United States to identify with conservatives, and as they come under attack the possibility of American military involvement arises. The sequence is not unlike that which in the past has led to the establishment of great empires. But for several reasons, the United States is condemned to create an empire based almost exclusively on an extreme system of indirect rule. This could be most effective in conditions in which there are appropriate indigenous groups who can form effective agencies of US policy. However, too often the only material available is of sorry quality, and might be expected to perform very inadequately as promoters of development. Perhaps, given the inevitability of American influence, it would be healthier if it performed more directly. There can be little doubt that if American control were directly implemented, and American technology and ideology brought directly to work on the development problems in those regions of current American interest, the effects would be economically more satisfactory than those of the dubious governments they find themselves bolstering.

One view of the dilemmas America faces was set out by Millikan and Rostow in an article in *Foreign Affairs* in April 1958. We quote at length because their article has proved to be a good prediction of subsequent policy. Rostow has since become the major Presidential advisor on these problems. They comment that,

the building of modern economies and centralized modern governments has been driven along less by the profit motive than by the aspirations for increased national and human dignity.

The American interest in the third world is fundamentally political, as they see it. Countries in the third world are in a transitional phase in which nationalism may turn in varying proportions to three objectives: one, the consolidation of the power of the new state over old regional interests; two, external adventure; three, economic and social modernization. At the time of writing the article, they thought that these strategies were typified by Diem, Nasser and Nehru respectively.

The third objective is critical because it determines the length of the transition to modernity:

Communist policy is based squarely on an understanding of this precarious transitional process . . . Soviet diplomacy and propaganda have systematically sought to divert their attention from the tasks of modernization towards "bloody shirt" policies;

234

that is, an obsessive concern to redress real or believed past humiliation – colonialism, Israel, Kashmir, West Irian, etc.

We are confronted with a systematic effort – diplomatic, psychological, economic and political – to exploit the weaknesses, confusions and temptations of new nations in the transitional period so as to clamp communism down finally on them before steady economic growth and the political resilience of a modern state emerge.

Faced with this challenge Millikan and Rostow see:

the essential objective of American policy in the transitional areas is to use whatever influence we can bring to bear to focus the local energies, talents, and resources on the constructive tasks of modernization.

They identify three propositions:

first, that private enterprise is superior in efficiency to public enterprise, even in the underdeveloped areas; second, that substantial untapped potentialities exist in public policy both for expanding American private capital exports and for increased collaboration between public and private sources of capital; and third, that the American government could do more than it is now doing to create a more favourable climate for private investment in the underdeveloped areas.

They see, however, that too swift returns on their proposed programme must not be expected. What is needed is

a sense of history and patience . . . to see us through into the stage when most men and governments in the world come to perceive that private capitalism, domestic and foreign, has an expanding role to play in the new nations capable of reinforcing their larger political and social objectives.

At the conclusion, the writers comment:

In addition, there remains the challenging and extremely important task of finding a method and an instrument for coordinating the economic development programs, now mainly bilateral, within the free world.

A major question for Canada is to examine the degree to which it agrees with this perception of the problem and the remedies proposed.

The major fault of this position is that it grossly oversimplifies the problem of the under-developed countries and leads to a form of involvement which is good for neither the first nor the third world. It involves the under-developed world in the internal problems of the US and in the conflict between the first and second worlds. Fairly quickly the goal of opening up these countries to private capital and of protecting them from their "weakness, confusions and temptations" becomes the end in itself.

Under-developed countries must solve their problems in the context of their own history. Instead of forcing upon them the myths and conventional wisdoms of other countries, stress should be placed on giving them more room to manoeuvre. Imported development strategies did not work under paleo-colonialism, and there is not much reason to expect it to work under neo-colonialism.

For the "third world" one possibility was to manipulate cold war competition. The existence of a Soviet Bloc might be thought to provide aid and trade possibilities, that allow the poor countries more manoeuvrability in their efforts to maintain their freedom from the "free world." That this could be so in practice was indicated by the performance of the UAR over the years. The remarkable success of the Nasser regime may be in part due to the fact that its most severe confrontation with the "free world" came in its conflict with Britain and France rather than the US. The possibilities of this alternative must not be exaggerated. The Soviet Union has shown no enthusiasm for any great expansion of its role in the less developed world. If anything, it has tended towards increasing caution. Soviet aid has been limited and has been as much attached to the particular export potentialities of the Soviet economy as has the bilateral aid which emanates from the West, and in many cases, a good deal less skilfully applied. Further, the increasing détente between the Soviet and the US in the cold war must narrow the possibilities of the less developed world in respect.

China has, surprisingly enough, at times provided generous and sensible finance. Surprisingly, as her own economic situation is no better than that of the countries she has aided. However, the possible material contribution of China must obviously be extremely limited by the urgency of her own needs. The role of China is more likely to serve as an example of the possibility of development without dependence – not in the sense of Maoist revolution, but rather in a more general sense of the possibility of independent action, if backed by sufficient will and unity over a large enough area.

Thus, in a broad outline, the global context in which Canada must consider its relationship with the under-developed world is one in which:

1 colonial dependency has ended but independence has not been achieved;
2 the new forms of control may be less effective in engendering development than the benevolent paternalism of some parts of the old colonialism;
3 freedom of manoeuvre in the less developed world depends partly on the diversity of alternatives in the rich world.

A Productive Role for Canada

It is well for small countries not to exaggerate their own importance. They should also recognize that the grand design of world affairs is not exclusively the product of the great powers.

Canada cannot transform the world because of her small size and because the pursuit of policies contradictory to those of the US will involve costs of retaliation and loss of goodwill.

Further, there is nothing in the character of Canadian society which would suggest that if it became a major participant in the communication with the poor countries it would not eventually develop similar policies and attitudes as the other great powers. It has not, in the West Indies, performed notably differently from other powers. Canada, with a gross national product of $57 billion commands a greater annual flow of output than the whole of black Africa, or of India. Canada, a midget compared with the North American colossus, still has economic capabilities comparable to major regions of considerable significance. If Canada ever allocated 1 per cent of her national product to the aid programme as promised in the recent speech from the Throne (instead of one quarter of one per cent true in past years) her programme would be of similar order to that currently made by Britain; when it is also considered that there is a heavy concentration of the American programme in regions of special American interests (particularly those areas in which heavy military aid is provided), it becomes clear that it would be feasible for Canada to maintain a programme in selected regions of the developing world of financial magnitudes similar to those of the existing major donors.

Moreover, Canada has more potential for a flexible programme than governments who have maintained major programmes over

237

the long period. The British are hamstrung by existing and ongoing political obligations. Givers as well as receivers are bound by the past. Britain finds that with a programme stagnant in total size there is very little flexibility to strike out in new directions, even if there is a desire to do so. The lack of pattern of traditional commitments, or strongly defined existing interests, makes it possible to conceive of a Canadian aid policy with more flexibility and more attention to the needs of the developing world than would be expected of many other major donors.

If Canada were willing, it could have an impact beyond the immediate effect of the transfers involved. If, for example, Canada stood ready to increase the level of her commitment in cases where the recipient country had fallen foul of other donors, this would strengthen the bargaining position of the poorer countries in their dealings with the other rich countries. The fact that Canada was, for example, able to fill part of the gap following the dismantling of the West German assistance programme to Tanzania minimized the costs to Tanzania of pursuing an independent political policy. Had this alternative not been open to Tanzania, there would be a depressing effect on other African countries contemplating efforts to assert their political independence.

Such a role will not be easy, especially where major conflicts with entrenched economic interests are involved. As this paper is being written, the Congo-Kinshasa government is engaged in direct confrontation with Union Minière over the control of the Congolese copper industry. The record of the Union Minière in the Congo has been a sorry one of subversion and intrigue. In light of recent and past Congolese history, a Congolese government of any repute would wish to assume control over the decisions and gain access to the property of the Union Minière. Their ability to do so effectively, however, will depend not only on the ability of the indigenous government to withstand incursions of foreign elements into their politics but will also require them to maintain the operation of the industry in the event of the withdrawal of Belgian technical personnel and an internationally organized attempt to prevent access of Congolese copper to world markets. Unfortunately, one suspects that the Belgium government and Union Minière would be more effective in controlling the sales of Congolese exports than the British government has been in restraining Rhodesian exports.

In a case such as this, if it comes to eventual confrontation, it seems unlikely that Canada would pursue policies openly at vari-

238

ance with those of the rest of the West. Indeed, one sees no special reason to suppose that Canadians would have any desire to do so. The point is that it is Canada's own choice, not her limited resources, which restrain her independence.

Canada will only provide alternatives when the confrontation between poor and rich does not impinge on those interests which the rich share and clearly recognize.

However, short of such confrontations, Canada can also have an effect by distributing whatever effort she decides to make according to criteria quite different from those of other donors. One set of such criteria could be, for example, based upon the attempt to identify the countries more likely to achieve the maximum development impact. Such criteria would have the virtue, in the Canadian context, of an appearance of neutrality. It is doubtful, of course, whether a simple set of such criteria could be defined; there are also, for example, simple redistributive objectives which might also seem desirable (e.g., famine relief).

Provision of aid to those likely to make most effective use of it would provide for patterns of finance quite different from those of other major donors. How far would it be possible for Canada in practice to pursue such a radically neutral course?

A little thought would indicate some difficulties. Could Canada envisage the possibility of providing aid programmes to North Korea, or North Vietnam, for example? This is too extreme for most Canadians, but the dramatic diplomatic achievements of France suggest that independent courses of action are possible.

Possibly, however, the course which could most easily be followed, is for Canada to move in significantly different directions from Anglo-American policy, while avoiding overt challenge. When a developing country begins to pursue policies rendering it somewhat suspect in terms of foreign policies of the "free world," but has not yet been promoted to the list of public enemies, it might be possible for Canada to extend support without appearing too obviously outrageous.

If Canada were willing to adopt such a role, could it not be argued that her own programmes would contain the same seeds of demoralization which were identified above as the key danger of existing programmes? This is unlikely, for a number of reasons. If Canada sought out those countries who smelt rather bad in the noses of the other western governments, the chances are that the governments concerned would be precisely those who are asserting national autonomy and are least susceptible to cultural demoralization. Secondly, Canada will always enter the scene as an influence slightly different from the previous external influence. US involvement in Africa, for example, often has the beneficial effect in undermining the mystique and cultural influence of the previous colonial power, merely because alternatives are offered, in relation to education for example, which implicitly challenge the assumptions of existing institutions. To some degree Canadian influence would not present the danger of bolstering inherited colonial institutions.

Also, Canada has all the blandness of a prosperous but minor power. Along with Switzerland and Scandinavia, Canada shares the characteristics of substantial success in achieving economic well-being along with the absence of imperial ambition, either as a contemporary career, or as an historical inheritance, or even as a dream of things to come. One has only to talk of a Canadian or a Swiss empire to realize how ludicrous the idea is. It is the fate of such countries to produce neither revolutions nor empires – but as Switzerland has shown, it is possible for them to become havens both for fugitive funds and refugee politicians. It is possible for them to consider revolutions with equanimity – they are neither likely to be imported nor do they challenge any ambition. It is reasonable to suppose that Canada could mount an aid programme less attached to a set of ideological values than those nations responsible for the world's future. Therein lies the importance of unimportance.

However skilfully Canada uses her aid programme there is an upper limit on the effect that can be obtained from this instrument. We may through clever planning increase the leverage of our aid, but the pressure we can exert is still limited by the fact that it is unlikely that we will spend much more than 1 percent of GNP, if that. If we want to play a more important role, we must find less costly devices. International trade is one such instrument, since it has the advantage of benefiting both trading partners. An imaginative trade policy will enable us to help others as well as ourselves and without straining charitable instincts.

There can be little doubt that there is much room for improvement in the efficiency with which we trade with the third world; the obstacle is that it would require us to think the unthinkable. If, for example, we decided to import certain manufactured goods from under-developed countries, they would gain because of the increased market, while we would gain from lower costs. In other words, through trade we can use the production facilities of other countries to supplement our own. At the same time, they can use our specific resources to supplement theirs.

We would have to pay for these increased imports through increased exports and there's the rub. We have been so used to thinking in terms of export pessimism that this problem seems to be an overwhelming one. A little care would show that it is not.

First and most important, there is a severe shortage of food looming on the horizon. Canada could probably increase production of foodstuffs at constant prices much more quickly than under-developed countries can. The reason we will have difficulty selling as much as we can produce is that the underdeveloped countries will have difficulty paying for it. If we bought more manufactured goods, we could sell more agricultural products. Clearly, there is a need for a far more imaginative trade-creating policy by Canada than has been the case to date.

There is no need to restrict our thinking to the export of foodstuffs. The under-developed countries have an insatiable demand for machinery of all kinds. If Canadian industry used its ingenuity, it could open up large markets for sale to the third world, provided of course, we were willing to buy from it as well.

If these profitable possibilities for trade are not taken advantage of, it will not be because they do not exist, but because Canada has not had enough imagination.

The first requirement would be a willingness to imagine gradual but radical changes in our economic structure. We could give up some of our industries and import these goods from afar. We would therefore gain flexibility, diversifying our trade sources and increasing our independence by loosening certain of our present close ties. Secondly, our comparative advantage would come to depend more on our skills and technology than our natural resource base. The skills of our entrepreneurs and labour could be increased and our "capacity to transform" enhanced.

If we decided on this course of action, new institutions for promoting trade would be needed. Just lowering tariff and other barriers is not enough. One of the most important obstacles to increased trade is inadequate information on marketing opportunities. The present international distribution and commercial system is more suited to the inadequate patterns of trade of the past than to the task of creating new possibilities for the future. Construction of new trade channels requires government as well as private initiative and though it would involve many difficulties, the payoff will be correspondingly high.

In the present context, United States and Europe have not taken advantage of profitable new opportunities, partly because of their political obligations, partly because they have a vested interest in the existing structure, and partly because they are trapped by their old ideas. Canada could use the opportunities available not only to increase her own trade with the third world, but also to increase trade between other rich countries and the third world. Canada could play an active role as an economic middleman in the international economy just as she prides herself in playing a middle role in the political system. Although a small power, Canada can act as a broker between more powerful interests.

Not only could Canada trade more, she might think in terms of investing more abroad. Canadians are so used to thinking of themselves as a capital-scarce country and a recipient of foreign investment that they have not considered the possibility of reversing the role.

Canada, relative to the world as a whole, is richly endowed with capital, technology and entrepreneurship. Her long experience with foreign investors could be used to devise new forms, more beneficial to the recipient country than those available at present. Canada could perhaps create a new type of international corporation. Most firms at present are not international but, in fact, have their centre of gravity in a particular developed country. Their marketing concepts, personnel policies and technology are developed in the conditions of the advanced countries and are often ill-suited to more backward countries. These corporations have limited horizons and do not understand the production problems and factor availability in the under-developed world. They are very large, few in number and have great bargaining power vis-à-vis the weak governments of the under-developed worlds. As profit maximizing institutions, they use this power fully, often backed up by the political strength of their country. As an example of what Canada could do, consider the effect of the government-owned Italian oil company, ENI, a publicly owned corporation, which for a while challenged the oligopolistic position of the existing oil firms. It offered better terms, new forms of organization, and gave the under-developed country an enlarged set of alternatives from which to choose.

As Dudley Seers points out, small countries facing big companies are in a much stronger bargaining position when there is genuine competition.[12] If it were possible to create Canadian public and private corporations capable of independent action in the international economy and willing to upset existing structures, Canadian business might be able to play a creative role.

Canada is small, rich and fits nicely into her niche. Her policies are sober and sensible, in aid as elsewhere. One choice is to continue along established paths.

What does it mean to have an independent policy vis-à-vis the World? If we agree with the policies of the major powers, there is no reason to behave differently. If we disagree, we have some difficult decisions to make.

There is a small bird which feeds by picking food from between the teeth of the crocodile; this bird is most expert in judging when crocodiles close their mouths. (Note: One source claims that the story is apocryphal. Perhaps!)

Robert McKinnell

EXTERNAL
AID:
HOW
TO
CHOOSE

Robert McKinnell is Associate Professor in the Department of Economics and Political Science at the University of New Brunswick. He is currently a Research Associate at the Institute of Economics and Statistics at Oxford, where he is studying economic problems in countries in Southern Africa.

In an ideal world, the prosperous nations, acting from the purest of motives, would direct an ever-mounting flow of assistance to the developing countries, without attaching any conditions. The less-developed nations in turn would reveal an exemplary understanding of the development process, would exorcise corruption, eliminate waste, and ensure social and political as well as economic progress. All would proceed, peacefully and unremittingly, into a future of increasing affluence, equality and grace.

In fact, a feeling of disenchantment pervades the second half of the Development Decade, for there is not merely a growing gap between the rich and the poor, but also to a critical extent a distinction between the white, Western world and that of the "wretched of the earth" who are predominantly non-white. The collective task of the developed countries must therefore be to increase their efforts rather than diminish them.

But what role can Canada play within such a broad general strategy? I contend that through an enlightened aid programme Canada can simultaneously contribute to the amelioration of a desperate world problem, find a proper expression of a burgeoning nationalism and demonstrate a purposeful independence in her foreign policy.

The preceding chapter has shown that the potential for an independent and fruitful initiative in our external aid programme is undoubtedly there; the limitations lie only in our willingness to mount and sustain such a venture. Paul Martin has already made a verbal commitment to an expanded external aid programme:

> The government of Canada has for many years been committed to the principle of foreign aid. I (have) expressed the hope that by 1970 we would have reached the UNCTAD figure of 1 percent of the Gross National Product.[1]

The remaining important issues are these: What should be the objectives of the aid programme? What forms of aid are best? To which nations in particular should Canadian aid be directed?

It is apparent that the donor nations maintain aid programmes for a variety of reasons. Canada must surely share with others the paramount objective of promoting more rapid economic development in the less-developed countries of the world. In keeping with this aim, the distinction between grants and loans must be preserved, as only the former are truly aid. The fact that in some developing countries the annual commitment to servicing past borrowing exceeds the inflow of fresh aid makes obvious their need for grants rather than loans.

The political implications of external aid programmes require careful analysis and quite explicit recognition. A second objective then, of the external aid programme should be to serve the needs of the total foreign policy of which it is a part. In the Canadian case this is confirmed by the fact that from its inception in 1951 through to 1965 Canada had allocated more than 80 per cent of total external aid to four Commonwealth participants in the Colombo Plan. As the aid programme expands and adapts, a high diplomatic priority will tend to be placed on the Commonwealth and *La Francophonie*.

The Canadian aid programme to date may be described briefly as small-scale, mainly bilateral and directed largely to Asia. In the future, it is clearly desirable that our aid effort be increased. But quality should be esteemed above quantity.

Who Should Receive Canadian Aid?

One of the most critical questions to be asked, especially by a small donor confronted by limitless requests is: To whom should aid be given? Should it be directed to the poorest, the most neglected; the friendliest, the most democratic, the most stable; the thriftiest, the most mature, the fastest-growing? This list of qualifications could be extended, is clearly heterogeneous and invites answers that depend a good deal on subjective assessments. Nevertheless, it is possible to start with certain objective criteria and thus narrow the list of potential recipients. Thereafter, individual judgments and preferences must increasingly enter, but a systematic approach is possible, on the lines developed below.

The first principle, that of concentration on relatively few developing countries, is likely to command agreement (and is in fact already operative). Otherwise the Canadian effort will be spread too thinly, will be incapable of efficient administration and can hardly be based on a deep understanding of each recipient's economy, polity and society. But the Commonwealth and French-speaking countries comprise more than 40 less-developed nations. Clearly even greater concentration is needed.

The second criterion is size. Only massive aid donors can have an impact on the basic problems of huge countries. The Canadian effort should therefore concentrate on smaller recipients. Even if the relative size of the Canadian aid programme is doubled or tripled, it will remain too small to have much impact on the problems of a country such as India. A very crude measure of the flow of funds to the Third World is $4.00 per capita.[2] India's "share" of the total would therefore be of the order of $2,000 million. A country like Canada clearly confronts a dilemma: where the need is greatest, a distinctive Canadian role is precluded. Canada must continue to aid India, Pakistan and Nigeria, but the emphasis of her expanded programme must be put on the remaining countries of our list.

What of small countries, of less than 3 million people, say? The general proposition is that, while some aid will be extended to small countries, particularly in regional programmes, the administrative costs are disproportionately high and our effort should by and large concentrate on medium-sized countries. Once again this is not to be interpreted as a proposal that small countries be struck from the Canadian list. In the case of the Caribbean in particular, such a step would be very harmful. But I would argue that, if the aid programme is to be informed and effective, the mainstream of our effort should concern medium-sized nations.

Thirdly, the requirement that aid shall involve more than the simple transfer of funds but must lead to real economic development, together with the principle of concentration, suggests that the list be reduced to those where aid will be effective. Once again, this presupposes a knowledge of the recipient's economy that may be lacking. But certain measures might serve as indicators. If a country has grown rapidly recently, has a high marginal savings ratio, or is judged to have expert development planning, it should rank high.

Applying these criteria to a shortened list of medium-sized Commonwealth and Francophone countries, we find that Malaysia, Cambodia, Tunisia and Zambia are highly-rated, followed by Ceylon, Algeria, Ghana, and the three East African Territories. These ratings are indicated in the following Table.

There are additional non-economic principles to be considered. The Department of External Affairs would seem likely to attach importance to Commonwealth links, to former French colonies, particularly in West Africa, and to countries not glaringly corrupt, undemocratic, unjust or anti-West. These diplomatic factors may sometimes conflict with other considerations, but a further ranking in these terms provides additional insight. In the Table, those countries in which Canada maintains a diplomatic mission are starred to indicate the priority already given them. Top diplomatic priority would therefore be accorded Cameroon and Senegal, followed by the former British colonies in Asia and by Ghana, Tunisia, Kenya and Tanzania in Africa.

However, this ranking is partially inverted when we consider our criterion of 'effectiveness' in terms of that important socio-economic variable, the level of per capita income. Clearly we cannot ignore the fact that our list includes incomes that range from an estimated $392 in the case of Hong Kong to as little as $39 in Malawi.[3] While relative prosperity may reflect a capacity to grow further and hence produce the maximum long-term effect for the Canadian programme, such desperately low levels of current income indicate a potential for a striking short-run impact, possibly from quite modest programmes. Also, the present need of such 'wealthy' countries as Malaysia, Ghana, Ivory Coast, Senegal and Rhodesia is less pressing. Accordingly a further ranking is included to reflect estimated income-levels. Malawi and Upper Volta emerge as most deserving, followed by the East African countries and most of the French-speaking West African countries.

Finally, let us adduce the principle that Canada should strive for an independent, sympathetic, distinctive initiative. Other things being equal, this suggests little attention to such countries as Vietnam or Hong Kong where major donors have an overwhelming interest. Conversely, Canada should consider major programmes in the case of those countries most neglected by other donors. Morocco and Tunisia have been favoured by the attention of the USA, Kenya and Tanzania by Britain, but on a much smaller scale. Conversely, the independent stance of Guinea led to the severance of French assistance, otherwise so lavishly extended to former colonies in Africa. This criterion suggests a higher priority for programmes in Cambodia, Guinea, Uganda and Malawi.

What overall conclusions emerge from the application of these diverse criteria? Zambia, with a high economic potential, does not apparently earn additional emphasis. Conversely, Guinea scores to some extent on all criteria except the economic. Does this mean no overall priorities can be determined? One solution is to attach equal importance to all criteria, and discover which countries emerge as most important. Alternatively, if it is felt that economic factors are pre-eminent, extra weight will be attached to this ranking. In this way, alternative emphases can be placed on different criteria in turn, depending on a careful judgement of relative priorities.

From the data I have used a stable pattern emerges, with some countries generally earning a high rating, some only at times and others never at all. This picture can be seen graphically in the Table. Of the five countries receiving top priority by this reckoning, Cambodia and Ceylon are in Asia and Kenya, Tanzania and Uganda are in Africa. Of the twelve countries in the next two categories one, Malaysia, is Asian and the rest are African. The seven countries rejected by this analysis are Hong Kong, Ivory Coast, Mali, Morocco, Southern Rhodesia, Senegal and Vietnam.

In order to bring out more clearly the implications of this assessment, we can estimate the annual assistance required at the rate of $2.50 per capita – the approximate rate of promised assistance to the relatively small population of the Caribbean Commonwealth. If the current level of commitment to India, Pakistan, Nigeria (and some other recipients) is to be maintained, the allocation of such sums is not possible. Nor, in terms of efficiency is it desirable. Let us therefore consider aid on this scale to only the first nine countries on the priority list. On this basis, some $160 million would be allocated to these nine, with almost $100 million to countries in Africa.

Admittedly this exercise is only a partial approach to the problem and is capable of further refinement. But the major implications are clear. If the earlier premises and arguments are accepted, then the expanded Canadian aid effort must be distributed geographically in a radically different pattern. The level of assistance to the nations that presently receive most Canadian aid would remain static or grow rather slowly. Ad hoc decisions would be taken to deal with special situations in individual countries or with the needs of particular nations. But the main brunt of the programme would be directed to selected Commonwealth and Francophone nations meeting the prescribed criteria. Latin America would remain marginal in the Canadian perspective, the allocation to the Caribbean would be of great consequence in that area but would absorb a rather small part of the total, the programme in Africa would expand beyond recognition provided technical and administrative problems could be solved, and the programme in Asia would undergo a drastic shift of emphasis.

Concluding Summary

Canada's international relations with the less-developed, non-Western nations of the world are a critical part of current and prospective foreign policy. I have argued that the external aid programme should be an increasingly important facet of the whole, since it could reflect the present Canadian mood, is appropriate to specific Canadian qualities and circumstances, but above all because it can contribute significantly to the progress of some developing lands. But a mediocre effort will not serve; the external aid programme must be well-conceived, of significant size, and expertly implemented.

The economic development of those who receive Canadian aid must be the overriding objective. Other goals need not be ignored but should be secondary. Domestic commercial needs should receive very low priority: diplomatic considerations must be expected to influence the selection of aid partners, but delib-

TABLE 24 *Medium-sized Asian and African Countries Ranked as Candidates for Canadian Aid*

Asian / African	Potential Effectiveness of Aid (** most potential, * good potential, ● less potential)	Income Level (□ very low, ● low, * medium, ** relatively high)	Attention from Other Donors (□ neglected, ● average, * relatively more)	Political Importance (C Commonwealth, F Francophonie)	Diplomatic Importance (M Canadian Mission, O no Canadian Mission)	Proposed Canadian Aid at $2.50 per capita (in $ millions)
HIGHEST PRIORITY						
Cambodia	**	*	□		M	15
Ceylon	*	*	□	C	O	28
Kenya	*	●	●	C	O	24
Tanzania	*	●	●	C	O	26
Uganda	*	●	●	C	M	19
						$112 million
NEXT PRIORITY						
Malawi	●	□	●	C	O	10
Malaysia	**	**	●	C	M	20
Tunisia	**	*	*	F	M	11
Zambia	**	*	●	C	O	9
						$50 million
MEDIUM PRIORITY						
Ghana	*	**	●	C	M	19
Guinea	●	●	●	F	O	9
Malagasy Rep.	●	●	●	F	O	16
Upper Volta	●	□	●	F	O	12
						$56 million

Asian / African	Potential Effectiveness of Aid	Income Level	Attention from Other Donors	Political Importance	Diplomatic Importance	Proposed Canadian Aid at $2.50 per capita
	** most potential * good potential ● less potential	□ very low ● low * medium ** relatively high	□ neglected ● average * relatively more	C Commonwealth F Francophonie	M Canadian Mission O no Canadian Mission	in $ millions
LOW PRIORITY						
Algeria	*	*	*	F	O	30
Cameroon	●	*	●	F	M	13
Chad	●	●	●	F	O	8
Niger	●	●	●	F	O	8
						$59 million
REJECTED						
Hongkong	●	**	*	C	M	
Ivory Coast	●	**	●	F	O	
Mali	●		●	F	O	
Morocco	●	*	●	F	O	
S. Rhodesia	●	**	●	C	O	
Senegal	●	**	●	F	M	
Vietnam	●	*	*	F	O	

NOTES:

1./ In 1966-67 Canadian aid in grants and loans amounted to $307 million, of which $218 million went to India, and $54 million to Pakistan.

2./ Countries listed in alphabetical order within each grouping.

3./ Potential Effectiveness of Aid measured in terms of recent rapid growth and the national savings ratio. Where information is not available, aid is presumed to be ineffective.

251

erate political and social manipulation is deemed impractical at present. However, the non-economic implications of development assistance must be anticipated and accounted for. The key to an effective effort is detailed knowledge and competence.

The size of the external aid programme is important but it is its quality that should become an obsession. Bilateral aid must continue to dominate if suitable Canadian purposes are to be served, but multilateral efforts will deserve attention too. At present, unless a very small amount of assistance is to be forthcoming, aid must remain basically tied. The ideal of untied aid may be kept in mind, but the present task is to ensure that the penalty imposed by tying is a minimum. That is to say, the capabilities of the Canadian economy in relation to development needs must be properly assessed and exploited.

The additional sums coming available in an expanded aid programme should be allocated mainly to a small number of medium-sized countries or regions, where it is judged the economic impact will be greatest. Diplomatic priorities will influence the further reduction of the list of prospective candidates (The priorities in a world attack on underdevelopment would not be the same). A first approach to the problem suggests continuing interest in the Caribbean and in large traditional recipients of aid, but with the emphasis steadily shifting to different Asian countries, rather few in number, and, above all, to selected countries in all regions of Africa where a Canadian initiative will achieve a significant economic impact and also serve accepted political and diplomatic ends.

Any assessment of the proper role of external aid in an independent Canadian foreign policy is subjective, imperfect, changeable. Similarly, the principles, forms, and direction of an aid programme will continue to be debated.

However, it is clear that external aid is an important aspect of our relations with the Third World and it has been argued here and earlier that this deserves a high priority in overall foreign policy. The goal should be an independent, distinctively Canadian initiative, but above all one dedicated to improving, as significantly as possible, the fortunes of those whom Fanon has dubbed *les damnés de la terre*.

Stephen Clarkson

THE
CHOICE
TO
BE
MADE

It would be presumptuous to attempt to summarize the sophisticated and often conflicting arguments put forward by the twenty-five authors of these nineteen chapters. Yet it would be unfortunate if these unresolved disagreements left the impression that the problems of Canadian foreign policy are too complex for any clear conclusions to be made.

In most cases disagreements over foreign policy appear to revolve round matters of fact. Von Riekhoff believes that our membership in Nato increases our political influence, while McNaught rejects the link between the Atlantic alliance and Canada's international effectiveness. Yet only part of the dispute is really concerned with "hard facts." The major points at issue are questions of evaluation and interpretation. We can establish as facts what amounts of money and manpower we devote to our Nato commitments, but this does not *prove* von Riekhoff right in his contention that our contribution of guns and troops increases Canada's power in West Europe or Washington. Nor does it *prove* McNaught's contrary thesis that the influence we may have is not worth the cost which would better be devoted to peacekeeping through an international police force. In both cases the authors are really invoking the support of conflicting assumptions to which they make tacit appeal: that political influence through collective action is desirable in von Riekhoff's view (insignificant in McNaught's), that the communist threat is serious (or unreal), that the Atlantic area is more (or less) important to Canada than the under-developed world, and so on. The authors of all the chapters bring to their discussions a group of assumptions and beliefs that they do not have the space to develop fully.

The Two Alternatives

Once we recognize this, we can see that the key to the often confusing debate on what Canadian foreign policy should be can be found in the underlying clash between two opposing foreign policy theories. Each theory contains a complete, if implicit, explanation of the world situation and of Canada's role in it, including a view of the American relationship and a statement of objectives for Canadian diplomacy. Let's follow current fashion and call the contending theories "quiet" and "independent." By the "quiet" foreign policy approach I mean the official policy as expressed in statements, the government's practice as seen over the last five years and the image projected by our diplomats in their execution of this policy. Although what has been referred to throughout this book as an "independent" foreign policy has not been systematically articulated as a coherent doctrine, I shall present briefly what appear to me to be the major positions of each theory in order to crystallize their differences and so make possible a choice between these opposing approaches to Canada's foreign policy.

The International Situation

QUIET APPROACH	INDEPENDENT APPROACH
As in the late 1940's and 1950's, the world is still polarized along ideological lines between the forces of Communism and the West. Despite the splits in the Marxist-Leninist bloc, the defence of the free world is still the major priority. Revolution is a continuing threat to world stability, especially in the under-developed continents of Asia, Africa, and Latin America. This makes it all the more important to contain Communism in Vietnam and Cuba lest the whole "third world" fall to the Reds like a row of dominoes. The United States is the only power able to pursue a containment policy on a world-wide basis. Its allies must support this effort.	The stabilization of Soviet and European communism has reduced the former Communist military threat to the West, turning the Cold War into a cold peace. The major world problem is no longer the East-West ideological confrontation but the North-South economic division of the world into rich and poor. Revolution is less a Red menace than an aspect of achieving the urgently needed socio-economic transformations in the under-developed world; in any case it is no direct threat to our society. Naïve American impulses to save the world from Communism are misguided, out of date, and a menace to world peace. The breakdown of the monolithic unity of both the Communist and Western blocs gives middle powers like Canada greater margins for independent manoeuvre.

QUIET APPROACH

As a Western, democratic and industrial country, Canada's national interests are essentially similar to those of our continental neighbour and friend, the USA, which is still the arsenal and defender of the free world. Worrying about national unity is of far less importance than pulling our weight in the Atlantic Alliance. Collective security is the only defence against new Hitlers or Stalins; we must not forget the lessons of 1939 and 1948.

INDEPENDENT APPROACH

A less ideologically but more socially concerned view of the world shows that Canada's national interests coincide more with general progress than with the maintenance of the USA's super-power status. Our external economic and political interest in trade with Communist countries diverges from American restrictions against "trading with the enemy." Canada's internal political divisions and our national identity crisis create another urgent national task for our policy: reinforce Canada's sense of bicultural personality.

Independence

QUIET APPROACH

Foreign policy independence is an illusion in the present-day world unless it is defined as head-in-the-sand isolation. We might just as well try to cut Canada off from North America and float out into the Atlantic. Independence must also mean a narrow and harmful anti-Americanism.

INDEPENDENT APPROACH

Far from being illusory, independence – being able to control one's own socio-economic environment – is an essential condition for the healthy development of the nation-state. Independence means neither isolation nor anti-Americanism, unless making up our own minds on the merits of individual foreign policies is considered un-American.

Interdependence

QUIET APPROACH

Relations of interdependence are the situations within which middle powers must normally operate. Alliances and supranational organizations provide Canada with the best way to exercise influence and be useful in day-to-day international affairs. Ties of interdependence also guarantee weaker powers against arbitrary action by the strong, both by binding the super-powers to listen and by giving the small a forum within which to unite their forces.

INDEPENDENT APPROACH

Obligations freely undertaken in cooperation with other countries are perfectly legitimate if they improve both the national and the world situation, e.g. IMF or GATT. Interdependence can create new opportunities that can be exploited to further the national interest commercially and increase our influence diplomatically. Fulfilling our many international commitments is the staple of our diplomatic activity and the means of building our influence. But we must be ready to use this credit when initiatives are needed. Too much interdependence can become glorified dependence.

255

QUIET APPROACH

INDEPENDENT APPROACH

In the light of this analysis of the international situation and our national interests, we should strive to defend the status quo, nurturing our influence in Washington and helping maintain the solidarity of the Western alliance as the expression of our commitment to internationalism and the defence of democracy. Our order of priorities should be the American relationship first, then the Atlantic Alliance, finally the developing countries. All our actions should keep in mind the central importance of collective action as the appropriate activity of a middle power.

Given the more relaxed international environment and our internal need for a more distinctive foreign activity, Canadian objectives should outgrow our anti-communism to embrace the aims of international equality and socio-economic modernization. This may entail more economic sacrifice and more tolerance of revolutionary change, but an enlightened nationalism requires re-evaluating our aims in terms of the most pressing needs of the whole world and will refuse to hide behind any alliance apron strings. Accordingly the "third world" should now come first in our priorities as the affairs of the Atlantic community can more easily take care of themselves. Our American relationship should not prejudice these international priorities.

Over-all Foreign Policy Strategy

QUIET APPROACH

INDEPENDENT APPROACH

Our general strategy should be affiliation, or close alignment and cooperation with our super-power neighbour to achieve maximum diplomatic power by our influence on the Western bloc leader. We can only enjoy this influence by accepting the American foreign policy framework and restraining our urge to criticize the Americans. This then gives us access to the inner corridors of US power.

Canada is too unimportant in Washington's world view for us to have significant direct influence on American foreign policy. Our strategy should be to act directly in a given situation after making an independent evaluation of the problem. Except for continental matters of direct Canadian-American concern, influence on Washington would normally be a secondary objective. Even then our power to affect Washington's policy will depend on our international effectiveness, not our allegedly "special" relationship.

Tactics to Implement the Strategy

QUIET APPROACH

"Quiet diplomacy" describes the foreign policy method most appropriate to implement an affiliation strategy. It puts especial emphasis on confidential, friendly contacts with our allies, primarily the Americans, so that any differences that may arise are ironed out before they can reach crisis proportions and come out in the open. American views should be anticipated and taken into consideration as part of our own policy-making. Publicity is to be avoided as are public declarations of criticism by our leaders. Rather, our role should be to seek common ground between those in disagreement.

INDEPENDENT APPROACH

Communications between our diplomats and those of other countries are by definition quiet. Carrying on our routine diplomatic business will therefore be unobtrusive. But there is no reason to make quietness a cardinal feature of our foreign policy, for this is to renounce in advance one of the most effective of a small power's bargaining tools, the use of exposure and public pressure to strengthen our position against a big power. If we have something to say and want to be heard, we must speak up. In dealing with the State Department that has dozens of importunate allies to cope with, not to mention its enemies, the demure may earn some gratitude from harried American diplomats. It does not follow that the "smooth" diplomat will get more response than his "raucous" rival.

Foreign Policy Style

QUIET APPROACH

Our international style for quiet diplomacy should be that of the discreet professionals who operate outside the glare of the TV lights and the prying eye of the press in close harmony with the diplomats of our allies, unobtrusively husbanding our stock of goodwill and influence. This would maintain our credit as a responsible friend in Washington, preserve our special access to inside information and so maximize our ability to affect American policy-making when we do disagree privately with it.

INDEPENDENT APPROACH

A hush-puppy style may be proper for our diplomats but is not the manner that our political leaders should adopt if they want to reinforce the Canadian identity. Without having to bang their shoes on the United Nations podium they could adopt a more assertive stance that makes clear Canada's existence as a bicultural nation with a unique set of policies. It is unrealistic not to be concerned with the "public relations" aspect of our foreign policy, since the way we present ourselves in the world – our international image – has a direct bearing on our international effectiveness. To this extent it is true that the posture of independence is a vital part of the policy.

257

QUIET APPROACH

As it is this relationship which gives Canada special influence through our geographical, political, and psychological proximity, nurturing the American relationship should have highest priority. We should not question the ultimate goals of the United States that has, after all, world-wide responsibilites for the defence of the free world. In addition we must realize that Canada cannot survive economically without the goodwill of the Americans upon whom we depend for our high standard of living. It would be "counter-productive" to try to influence American policies by publicly opposing them. This would only reinforce the extremist elements advocating the policies we opposed.

INDEPENDENT APPROACH

Our relations with the USA are "special" because of the disparity of our power and the degree to which we depend on American trade and capital inflows. We should for this reason devote careful attention to our relations, especially if we are planning international moves of which they do not approve. The huge military and political power of the USA should make us particularly critical of American policies however well-intentioned the Average American may be. Our well-being is not a product of bounteous concessions made by the US but of economic development considered to be to both countries' advantage. Our relationship should be governed by this awareness of mutual benefit. There is no evidence that independent actions strengthen extremism in the USA. If we really wish to influence American public opinion, we have to make it clear what policy we advocate. There is no better way than actually pursuing it.

Retaliation

QUIET APPROACH

We are so dependent on the American economy that we cannot afford to do anything that might annoy them such as taking some foreign policy intiative that displeases Congress or the Administration. The price of independence would be a 25 per cent drop in our standard of living, according to Mr. Pearson. We are, after all, the little pig that must be eternally vigilant lest the big pig roll over, in Mr. Plumptre's phrase. We cannot increase this risk

INDEPENDENT APPROACH

The possibility of retaliation is present in all international relationships. It is true that we are more vulnerable to American than the US is to Canadian retaliation, but we must not forget that retaliation is a reaction of last resort showing that all milder negotiation has failed. By being willing to use the whole armory of diplomatic weapons – bilateral and multilateral, informal and public – we could reduce the dangers of retaliation conjured up by the all-or-nothing approach of Quiet Diplomacy. We must realize that as

QUIET APPROACH

by provoking it to roll deliberately. In such areas as the Defence Production Sharing Agreements we gain enormously from being able to bid on American defence contracts. The share of the US market we have won pays for our own purchases of American war material at prices cheaper than we could produce it ourselves. We cannot afford the luxury of independence, whatever our conscience might say, since independent actions might jeopardize these arrangements.

INDEPENDENT APPROACH

the little power, we have important advantages. We can concentrate our whole attention on defending our interests in the continental relationship which, from the American point of view is but one of dozens of issues of greater importance. We have important hostages in Canada, the very subsidiaries that are the instruments of US political and economic pressure. We can also use the threat of mobilizing public opinion to strengthen our hand against possible intimidation and economic blackmail. Our goodwill and our favourable image in the US as a long-standing friend is a further asset we should not ignore.

Internal Impact of Foreign Policy

QUIET APPROACH

The internal implications of our diplomacy are negligible and should remain so. Foreign policy should be practised to achieve specific external goals and not to boost the national ego. If Canadians have an identity problem, they should cure it themselves, not resort to artificial stimulation. Similarly we should not let our concern for internal problems of biculturalism distort our foreign policy. External affairs and internal politics should be kept in their proper places. Quebec should not drag foreign policy into her federal arguments with Ottawa.

INDEPENDENT APPROACH

It is impossible to dissociate external from internal policies if only because external relations are carried out by all branches of government – Finance, Commerce, Defence, and Citizenship are involved and even the provinces, quite apart from External Affairs. Foreign policy must in any case be seen as only one aspect of the government's total network of policies. We cannot afford *not* to exploit the nation-building potential of our foreign policies, since the way others perceive us – dynamic and bicultural, or ineffectual and divided – can strengthen, or undermine, our own national identity. Similarly, if we accept French-Canadian desires for cultural equality and Quebec's demands for greater self-control, our foreign policy should reflect and reinforce Canada's new binational politics.

259

The "quiet" approach to our foreign policy is not an extremist absurdity, however unlike most nations' foreign policy doctrines it may appear. It is the rationale of Canadian diplomacy. The overriding concern for kid glove relations with our American neighbours was articulated in 1965 by the Merchant-Heeney Report with all the hallmarks of official policy. The feeling of economic dependence is not an Opposition charge but a situation acknowledged by the Prime Minister himself.[1] The surprisingly unsophisticated cold warrior analysis complete with Domino Theory of Asian Communism is heard time after time from our diplomats, both senior officers and newly inducted recruits. In our discussions with these foreign service officers during our ULSR seminars, we found them cut off from the Canadian public whose views they take to be adequately expressed by *Globe and Mail* editorials or questions posed in the House of Commons. More disconcerting is the professionals' scorn for the amateur which colours their attitude towards the value of the public's opinion. Far from being a straw man set up for easy refutation, Quiet Diplomacy is enshrined as the conventional wisdom of our federal political establishment.

Independence Yes, Quiet Diplomacy No

However accepted this doctrine may be, I would submit that it is no longer suitable for Canadian foreign policy in the late 'sixties. It is inappropriate first of all for the reasons stated in the "independent" replies to the "quiet" positions summarized above: its view of the world is ten years out of date; its understanding of Canada's international needs and capabilities is hopelessly circumscribed.

"Quiet" foreign policy is also unacceptable in a mass democracy. If to be effective, our quiet foreign policy must be carried on in complete secrecy so that even its successes should not be known lest they compromise further success, as Peyton Lyon argues, how is the voter ever to know whether the policy is justified? Is he simply to accept the protestations of diligence and sincerity by the Minister of External Affairs or the Prime Minister and the assurances of our diplomats, all claiming to plead impartially in their own cause? Until all the files are open, Peyton Lyon writes, we cannot know for sure. But even then how would proof be certain? To be sure that the quiet approach had been the more effective it would be necessary to show what results the independent approach would have produced in exactly the same circumstances – an obviously impossible condition. We cannot wait fifty years for the files to be open, even if they did promise final proof. Quiet diplomacy has been practised long enough for the onus to be on its defenders to demonstrate their case. The record does not lend them very strong support. Such a diplomatic success as Pearson's constructive role in the 1956 Suez crisis is an example of independent initiative, well conceived at an appropriate time, as both Hanly and Cox Point out.

Nor is it good enough for the Merchant-Heeney Report to admonish Canadians to

> have confidence that the practice of quiet diplomacy is not only neighbourly and convenient to the United States but that it is in fact more effective than the alternative of raising a row and being unpleasant in public.

One can readily agree that it is more "convenient" for the United States that Canada be quiet, but it is less convincing that Canadian foreign policy will be more "effective" as a result. The only alternative envisaged by this defence of quietness is "raising a row and being unpleasant in public." Either accept American policy or protest, we are told; don't consider acting independently. This paints a disconcertingly small picture of the possible role Canada can play. Surely Canada can aspire to a more significant international activity than just having some influence in Washington, as if we were one more state in the Union with two Senators and a dozen Representatives all clamouring bilingually in Congress for patronage and action on Vietnam!

When the defenders of quiet diplomacy expound on our influence in Washington, their argument raises more doubts. To start with they are hard put to provide empirical evidence of Canada's power to make Washington act in the way we want. They go on to insist that this putative special influence in Washington is the basis for Canada's power in other countries who take us seriously because they assume we have a unique path to American waiting chambers. But they then warn that we should not actually try to use this influence for this would undermine this special position and so our international status. Strange logic, a sophisticated rationalization for inaction. Influence is like credit: it has to be used to exist. The quiet diplomatists manage to underrate Canada's real power to act by exaggerating our potential influence.

The alternative to quiet diplomacy is not "raising a row"; it is developing an independent foreign policy. Independence means above all striving for maximum effectiveness. Those times when

261

Canada has been most clearly effective she has acted directly – achieving negotiations in Korea or the exclusion of South Africa from the Commonwealth. This means neither that she acted alone nor against a big power. Kicking Uncle Sam in the shins or twisting the Lion's tail has no necessary part in any of Canada's more independent actions. Canadians are not even aware that our enlightened aid programme towards Tanzania was pushed forward despite Dar-es-Salaam's rupture of relations with Britain. Such acts are satisfactory because they are effective. They are effective because the Canadian initiative itself contributed directly to achieve the particular goal. They achieved this goal because in these situations the Canadian government acted flexibly, not out of deference or automatic loyalty to another power. To act flexibly means to make up one's own mind – to be independent.

To make independence the standard for our foreign policy is not to opt out of the many undramatic areas of collective diplomacy in which Canada makes a continuing major contribution at a supranational level. Nor does independence imply anti-Americanism, however much the bogey of "making a row" is raised. Deciding policies on their own merits may well lead to disagreement with American policy – in Vietnam for Steele, over China for Hanly, in Latin America in Lumsden's view. Still there is no reason to inflate such policy disagreements to disastrous proportions unless the defendants of quiet diplomacy really believe the Americans to be the most vindictive politicians on earth. According to Stairs' study we have followed a line directly counter to American policy on a problem of the highest sensitivity, Cuba, and still not suffered retaliation. The point is that if we diverge it is not for the sake of a quarrel but to practise what we feel to be the correct policy, after due consideration of the Americans' reasons. It is hard to believe that a more assertive Canadian foreign policy would be countered in Washington by a concerted anti-Canadian policy. The more truculent General de Gaulle has become, the gentler has been the Americans' treatment of France. With so much direct investment in Canada, it is unlikely that the Americans, in Baldwin's phrase, would want to get rid of a blemish on the finger by amputating the arm.

Independence also requires realism in our conception of the American relationship. Our interactions with the USA are so intense and multitudinous at all levels of political, economic, cultural and personal contact that we should make a fundamental distinction between our foreign policies on one hand and our

American policies on the other. While pursuing what we consider to be the best policy abroad, it is in our interest to place the strongest emphasis on the maintenance of good neighbourly relations with the USA. In all matters of mutual concern, whether financial investment, tariff policy, resource development or cultural interchange, the policies of both countries toward each other must continue to be formulated in close consultation. We clearly have an essential unity of self-interests with the Americans in our continental partnership. But partnership requires equality, and equality implies independence.

That the obsession with the Americans should not stifle our foreign activity is the first message of the independent approach; that our fascination with American power should not blind us to the extent of our own influence on American policy is the second. Canada has a comparatively strong bargaining position it can use *if it wants to* in dealing with the United States. The continentalists point out the many relations of dependence exposing Canada to American pressure and retaliation. But it is elementary political science to recognize that dependence is a two-way street. Every aspect of our relationship – our resources (our highly coveted supplies of fresh water very much included), the American branch plants, our debts, our trade deficit, our goodwill as a reliable ally – can be used by a determined leadership *if necessary* to achieve its objectives. "If necessary," for most bargaining weapons are more effective as a threat than in use – as the continentalists' terror of US retaliation shows.

An independent foreign policy is an ethically just policy. Peyton Lyon attacks the critics of quiet diplomacy for being "ostentatiously on the side of virtue, regardless of practical consequences." One can heartily agree that a "tub-thumping moralistic approach" is distasteful and that a disregard for practical consequences is irresponsible. Yet an argument for independence is not *moralistic* for raising *moral* problems. As Hanly argues, an independent approach is necessarily more ethical for it requires an autonomous calculation for every policy of the probable consequences both for Canada and for those our policy will affect. It is the defenders of quiet diplomacy who are open to the charge of moralism if they cling dogmatically to a moral judgment of American policy made twenty years ago.

An independent foreign policy also presupposes responsibility. As only a free man is considered responsible for his actions, only a nation which makes its own decisions can be considered in charge of its destiny and can expect its citizenry to believe in its integrity. And like the youth who can only develop maturely if he liberates himself from parental controls, the nation-state can only achieve full expression if it is master in its own house, able to act in the community of nations as a fully responsible entity.

The Problem of Reform

If independence is more desirable as an overall guideline for our foreign policy, why is quietness still the guiding light of Canadian diplomacy? Not from American pressure as has been demonstrated in Section I. Nor for lack of international scope, particularly in the under-developed world, as the authors of Section III and IV make clear. The conclusion must be that the problem is here at home. Yet we can hardly blame public opinion. The opinion polls, for all their inaccuracies, indicate that the general public's views have been consistently more nationalist on foreign policy issues like Vietnam, the Dominican Republic and China than the Government.[2] All the major parties have, at the very least, strong wings in favour of a more independent diplomacy. Predominant editorial opinion, church statements, students groups, and academic protests complete the general picture of a public opinion that increasingly rejects quietness.

While the University League for Social Reform is particularly oriented towards making reform proposals, it would be superficial to conclude with facile exhortations to the leadership to change its policy. The conditions are so favourable for an independent foreign policy that the persistence of a quiet approach indicates more fundamental problems are involved. If we are to make some proposals for reform we must assess the underlying reasons for this anomalous state of affairs. These are threefold and interconnected: a decision-making structure that isolates the Government from public participation and control, an élitist ideology for the civil service that legitimizes this insulation, and a leadership that perpetuates this situation.

As Griffiths shows in his discussion of our political institutions, chapter 9, the foreign policy making process is almost completely sealed off from the normal give and take between public and government. Even Members of Parliament have no significant access to this "closed circuit." In a recent article surveying the problems of the Department of External Affairs, the Under-Secretary of State for External Affairs, Marcel Cadieux, deals quite extensively with his relationship with the Minister. Yet, with the exception of consulting university specialists, he makes no mention of the contribution that members of the public, Parliamentarians included, can make to the formation of the nation's foreign policy. "Without public understanding," he concedes, "we can hardly hope to develop Canada's role in world affairs."[3] He doesn't seem to feel that the public has any greater part to play than to stand and wait, deferentially yet comprehendingly in the spectators' boxes.

It is institutional security from criticism which makes Quiet Diplomacy the natural ideology of the diplomatic caste. It gives a theoretical justification for the handling of all business by routine bureaucratic channels. If foreign policy is the private domain of the administrator, he need not take seriously clamour, interest group opinion or, God forbid, Parliamentary interference. Public discussion of foreign policy problems is fine and even desirable, our diplomats will hasten to profess, so long as it does not disturb their professional activity.

The crucial link in this combination of institutional isolation and bureaucratic élitism is its endorsement by the leadership. Paradoxically the Liberal leaders bring an unprecedented background of experience to their handling of foreign affairs. Yet Mr. Pearson, the Nobel Prize winner, has turned the "unobtrusive oil can" tactics which led to his own international successes in the mid 'fifties into a dogma which frustrates the continuation of this early record. Mr. Martin, for all his concern for his public image, is unable to convey to the nation a convincing and unambiguous understanding of what Canada can achieve internationally and has not been able to transmit the growing public concern for foreign policy questions into revised governmental policies. Nor has he shown any sign of opening the major issues of foreign policy, such as the decision to renew the Norad agreement, to public debate in parliament. Institutions, ideology and leadership: we have here a troika of conditions that require basic reforms and changes. Yet remedies cannot be solely of relevance to our foreign policy. We face a general problem of Canadian democracy – the responsiveness of governmental policy and the civil service to public scrutiny and control. Reforms needed in this area of public policy are needed in other branches as well.

All bureaucracy's conservative, but the conservatism of diplomatic bureaucracy is in a class by itself. The ethos of diplomacy is an ethos of suspicion – suspicion tempered by scepticism, snow tempered by ice. The foreign service officer is a nay-sayer in statecraft, the abominable no-man of diplomacy. His mission in life is to preserve the status quo from those who propose to alter it.[4]

As James Eayrs points out, the problem of foreign policy change is the problem of subjecting bureaucratic inertia to some reasonable form of public control.

Let the Public In

The first step is to open the process of policy-forming so that the expression of expert, informed and articulate opinions can have a major impact on foreign making. Yet in this age of McLuhan, our channels for public participation in politics are still using a Walter Bagehot technology. Gallup polls give irregular insights into public views on simplified issues, but their findings are ignored unless politically exploitable. A partial solution is to put the measuring of attitudes on a regular and scientific basis, possibly by a research institute that would, by continuous sampling, make "what public opinion wants" no longer a subject for guesswork. More important, structural change such as the activation of the parliamentary committee on foreign affairs, as suggested by Griffiths, could institutionalize the public scrutiny of foreign policy in a way compatible with the parliamentary system. To be meaningful the committee would need a full-time research staff and would have to be able to require testimony from expert and interested groups as well as diplomats. While such a watchdog committee could not actually make policy, the defence committee hearings on tri-service unification have proved that basic public issues can be brought out into the open for thorough airing. The hearings would also provide our diplomats with a link to articulate opinion; they would start to see themselves as public servants rather than tight-lipped agents.

Another by-product would be important, if intangible. Coverage of the committee hearings by mass media would help give the public a sense of being involved in this hitherto exclusive area of policy. Other ways should be initiated to increase the public's interest in foreign policy.

If our foreign activity is to have the strength of public participation, the public must be sufficiently informed. Never has the man-in-the-street been so exposed by instant communications to international events, so bombarded with journalistic commentary

266

and academic debate. Never has he had such a high level of education to absorb this information. But the data on Canadian foreign policy with which the public could come to policy conclusions is not made available. The change that is needed here is less quantitative than qualitative. To make public opinion aware of Canada's foreign policy problems, mass media and newspaper reports must relate their analysis of foreign affairs to Canadian external activity.

Civil Masters or Civil Servants?

To change from a quiet to a more independent approach to our foreign policy will require a transformation of the values of the practitioners, the diplomats in the Department of External Affairs. So long as the personnel of External Affairs maintain a secretive, distrustful attitude towards the public, an independent foreign policy is doubly stymied. An informed, alert public opinion cannot be developed if extensive, relevant information is not made regularly and easily available. As long as External maintains its Mandarin mystique explicitly tied to Quiet Diplomacy and anti-communism, the civil servants would be likely to block the implementation of an alternative foreign policy, even if the Government should desire it.

To change our diplomats from civil masters to civil servants will require a change in their ideology. A partial measure is to modify the environment they enter when they are recruited into the service so that the values they absorb conform to the desire of the public and the views of the leadership. In France, for example, recruits to all branches of the upper civil service receive three full years of practical and theoretical training at the National Administration School where they absorb the dynamic, nationalist values of the French state and so start their career as activist, not conservative civil servants. The excellence and dynamism of the French civil service is one of the principal reasons for the impact of de Gaulle's foreign policy in Europe. Rather than have our new diplomats absorb willy-nilly the smug, conservative attitudes of the established bureaucracy, an introductory training programme – needed in any case to improve technical and linguistic competence – could give them an awareness of the role that the political leadership wants Canada to play and a consciousness of the challenge of achieving these goals in a democratic framework.

To prevent the diplomats from becoming cut off from public

267

and informed opinion they need continual "professional retraining" just as any doctor or engineer. Sabbatical leaves for research and senior staff officer courses are needed if our international crisis managers are to keep up intellectually with the rate of change of the crises they are entrusted to manage.

Leadership from the Top

No change in our diplomats' value system and no structural reform will be very productive without a third innovation: dynamic leadership. The muddling through of the quiet approach will continue until Canada's leaders realize that determination and a clear articulation of political objectives are needed to turn potentiality into reality. Canada is wealthy, strong and developed. It does not need the mountain-moving voluntarism of Mao Tse-Tung. It simply needs a leadership that can make it clear to the public – if not in a little *Red Book* at least in a *White Paper* – what role Canada can play and how its objectives are to be achieved. This would give a sense of direction to the unusual talents in our diplomatic service and harness the force of public opinion behind this effort.

Partnership with Quebec

It is finally necessary to remove the uncertainty overshadowing the future of confederation. Although Quebec nationalism has made a major contribution to the development of a more independent Canadian activity, particularly in starting an aid programme to the French-speaking African states, the open diplomatic warfare between Ottawa and Quebec that broke out in conjunction with de Gaulle's visit to Quebec is rapidly becoming self-destructive.

It is time to come to some firm decision whether or not Quebec can satisfy its international aspirations as a special province in the federation acting both through Ottawa and autonomously in its areas of provincial jurisdiction. This is essentially an issue for Quebeckers to decide, though their compatriots can reasonably urge that the debate be fair and full before any irrevocable step is taken. It is for the French-Canadian intellectuals to spell out the costs and benefits of special status in the federation versus complete separation. Their English-speaking colleagues can point out, however, why they would like Quebec to stay in the effort to develop a new foreign policy. Not only does Quebec's wealth add strength to Canada's foreign power. More important, Quebec's culture and technology makes it possible for the total Canadian international effort in the under-developed world to have a unique impact. But the only finally convincing argument is the demonstration that Ottawa can mount a foreign policy that would be more independent and more effective than the foreign role that Quebec could play by itself, as a single state. Quiet diplomacy has failed to provide this proof.

It is our belief that an independent foreign policy could give this proof to French and English Canadians alike by, first, rejecting its lingering anti-communism and downgrading the cold war alliances while, second, redirecting its resources and redefining its priorities to a determined support for the political, economic and social needs of the developing countries – both through its multilateral diplomacy in international organizations and by directly making Canada a "great power in foreign aid."[5]

The Public Should Choose

We need more open diplomats, we need more public participation in policy-making. But most of all we need to choose: to choose between the quiet, continental foreign policy we have followed in the main over the past decade and an independent foreign policy.

At a time when the Government is showing some quiet doubts about wisdom of its foreign policy approach, the expression of articulate opinion on this matter can have a significant effect. You, the reader, can write to your Member of Parliament. More simply you can answer and return the appended questionnaire that is designed to elicit your views on the policy questions raised in these pages. The answer received before June 1, 1968 will be tabulated and made public after being sent to the Prime Minister and the Minister of External Affairs. By returning this questionnaire, you can indicate to our leadership or to potential leaders waiting for the sign how you want the choice between quiet diplomacy and an independent foreign policy to be made.

NOTES

Notes to Chapter 1 (pp. 5-16)

1 Douglas V. LePan, "The Outlook for the Relationship," *The United States and Canada*, ed. John S. Dickey, Englewood Cliffs, N.J., Prentice-Hall, 1964, pp. 152-69.

2 John W. Holmes, "The Relationship in Alliance and World Affairs," *The United States and Canada*, p. 95.

3 Bruce Hutchison, "The Long Border," *Neighbours Taken for Granted*, ed. Livingston Merchant, New York, Frederick A. Praeger, 1966, p. 32.

4 Inis L. Claude, Jr., *Power and International Relations*, New York: Random House, 1962, p. 214; Chadwick F. Alger, "Comparison of Intranational and International Politics," *American Political Science Review*, LVII, June, 1963, p. 408.

5 Walter L. Gordon, *A Choice for Canada: Independence or Colonial Status*, Toronto, McClelland and Stewart, 1966, p. 122.

6 Francis O. Wilcox, Foreword to *Neighbours Taken for Granted*, p. vii.

7 Melvin Conant, *The Long Polar Watch*, New York, Harper & Bros., 1962, p. 8. Italics mine.

8 Livingston Merchant and A. D. P. Heeney, *"Canada and the United States – Principles for Partnership,"* Department of State Bulletin, Aug. 2, 1965, p. 199.

9 Paul Hellyer and Lucien Cardin, *White Paper on Defence*, March, 1964, p. 10.

10 *Ibid.*, p. 12.

11 Jacob Viner, "The Outlook for the Relationship," *The United States and Canada*, p. 151.

12 Livingston Merchant and A. D. P. Heeney, *loc. cit.*, pp. 195-196.

13 See for example, C. S. Burchill, " 'Canada's Long Term Strategic Situation' – Three Critical Views," *International Journal*, XVIII, Winter, 1962-63, p. 79.

14 J. David Singer and Melvin Small, "The Composition and Status Ordering of the International System: 1815-1940," *World Politics*, XVIII, Jan., 1966, 236-82.

15 James Eayrs, "Military Policy and Middle Power: The Canadian Experience," *Canada's Role as a Middle Power*, ed. J. King Gordon, Toronto, Canadian Institute of International Affairs, 1966, p. 84.

16 For two quite different ways of answering this question see Walter Gordon, *op. cit.*, and Harry G. Johnson, "Problems of Canadian Nationalism," *International Journal*, XVI, Summer, 1961, 238-49.

17 On this point see Peyton V. Lyon, "Problems of Canadian Independence," *International Journal*, XVI, Summer, 1961, 252.

18 *Op. cit.*, p. 77.

19 This is a loose paraphrasing of a comment by Viner, *op. cit.*, p. 148.

20 On this point see Albert O. Hirschman, *National Power and the Structure of Foreign Trade*, Berkeley and Los Angeles, University of California Press, 1945.

21 Cf. Johnson, *op. cit.*, p. 241.

22 Livingston Merchant and A. D. P. Heeney, *loc. cit.*, p. 193.

23 George Ball, "Interdependence – The Basis of U.S.-Canada Relations," *Department of State Bulletin*, May 18, 1964, p. 770.

24 Inis L. Claude, Jr., *Swords into Ploughshares*, 3rd ed., New York, Random House, 1964, pp. 213, 14.

25 Thomas C. Schelling, *The Strategy of Conflict*, Cambridge, Mass., Harvard University Press, 1960, pp. 29-30.

26 See for example, Walter Gordon, *op. cit.*, p. 93.

27 *Ibid.*, pp. xviii-xix.

28 *Ibid.*, p. xviii.

29 *Ibid.*, p. 124.

30 See for example, Adolfe A. Berle, Jr., *Power without Property*, New York, Harcourt, Brace, 1959; Grant McConnell, *Private Power and American Democracy*, New York, Alfred A. Knopf, 1966; and Michael D. Reagan, *The Management Economy*, New York, Oxford University Press, 1963.

31 Johnson, *op. cit.*, pp. 244-45.

Notes to Chapter 2 (pp. 17-28)

1 Recent attitude studies have shown that in Canada and the United States "Christians are more war-like in their attitudes than non-Christians, and that the most dogmatic Christians are more war-like than the less dogmatic Christians, or than the less church-going Christians," N. Z. Alcock, "What We Have Learned Through Peace Research," *The United Church Observer*, Vol. 27, No. 18. pp. 18-19. Also "Militarism in our Culture Today," W. Eckhardt, Annual Meeting of the American Psychological Association, 1965.

2 See my "A Psychoanalysis of Nationalist Sentiment" in *Nationalism in Canada*, ed. P. Russell, Toronto: McGraw-Hill, 1966, for further discussion.

3 For a detailed discussion, see Chester Ronning's "Canada and the United Nations," in *Canada's Role as a Middle Power*, ed. J. King Gordon, Toronto, Canadian Institute of International Affairs, 1966.

4 The logic of counter-insurgency policy has been analysed by J. McDermott in "Vietnam is No Mistake," *The Nation*, Vol. 204, No. 7, p. 205. The counter-productivity of counter-insurgency strategy has been demonstrated by I. L. Horowitz in "Military Elite," *Elites of Latin America*, ed. Seymor M. Lipset, Oxford: Oxford University Press, 1967.

5 Cf. Z. K. Brzezinski, "Revolution and Ideological Conflict," *Revolution and Response*, ed. C. Hanly, Toronto: McClelland and Stewart, 1966, pp. 3-13.

Notes to Chapter 3 (pp. 29-41)

1 For a fuller discussion of Canadian influence in Washington, see my book, *The Policy Question*, Toronto, McClelland and Stewart, 1963, pp. 51-66.
2 These limitations on official, public criticism of the United States do not apply, of course to private Canadians; occasionally, indeed, their strongly expressed misgivings can strengthen the hand of Canadian representatives in Washington. Nor do I suggest that the Canadian Government should keep silent if it ever believes that the United States is engaged in a clearly immoral enterprise.
3 "Was This Trip Necessary?" *Globe and Mail*, April 4, 1967.
4 Canada's response to the Middle East crisis of 1967 was less quiet, and less successful. The government's eagerness to show that it was giving a lead within the United Nations, and its public stand on the moral and legal aspects of the dispute, convinced the Arabs that Canada had ceased to be impartial. This prompted Cairo's demand that the Canadians serving with the UNEF be the first to be withdrawn, and may have reduced permanently Canada's respectability as a peace-keeper.
5 "Pin-stripe Boys are Pro-US," *Ottawa Journal*, April 3, 1967.
6 His colleague, Mr. Walter Gordon, has expressed publicly the gravest misgivings about American policies in the Far East, and these views may be shared privately by some other members of the cabinet.

Notes to Chapter 5 (pp. 57-68)

Footnotes:

1 "Herter Rebuffed Still Asks Canada Cut Cuban Trade," *Globe and Mail,* December 12, 1960, p. 1.
2 Quoted by Robert Spencer in his "Cuba and the OAS," *Canadian Annual Review for 1962*, p. 81.
3 *Ibid.*, p. 82.
4 Canadian Press Washington Dispatch, *Globe and Mail*, January 16, 1961.
5 Quoted by Ralph Allen in his "A Calm Report from inside Cuba," *Maclean's Magazine*, Vol. 75, No. 23, November 17, 1962, p. 83
6 *House of Commons Debates*, November 22, 1960, p. 68.
7 *Ibid.*, December 12, 1960, p. 700.
8 See, for example, Royal Bank of Canada, *Report of the Proceedings of the Ninety-Second Annual General Meeting of Shareholders*, Montreal, January 12, 1961, p. 19, and the *Report* of the following year, January 11, 1962, p. 17.
9 Leon Gordenker, *The United Nations and the Peaceful Unification of Korea*, The Hague, Nijhoff, 1959, p. 31.
10 Quoted by Robert A. Spencer, *Canada in World Affairs. From U.N. to NATO, 1946-1949*, Toronto, Oxford University Press, 1959, p. 106.
11 Gordenker, p. 73.
12 Quoted by St. Laurent in *House of Commons Debates*, March 10, 1948, p. 2075.
13 Gordenker, p. 78.
14 *Ibid.*, p. 81.

1 For an exposition of this rationale by Mr. Martin, see *External Affairs*, Vol. XVII, No. 7, July, 1965. See also the text of Mr. Pearson's speech to the Canadian Society of New York delivered on March 5, 1965.

2 Mr. Pearson made this point in a statement issued on August 14, 1965.

3 A concise account of early American intervention in Vietnam may be found in *Peace in Vietnam*, a report prepared last year for the American Friends Service Committee. For indispensable surveys of more recent developments, see Schurmann, Scott and Zelnick, *The Politics of Escalation in Vietnam*, New York, Beacon Press, 1966, and Theodore Draper in *The New York Review of Books*, May 4, 1967.

4 For a full discussion of the legal issue, see *Vietnam and International Law*, Flanders, N.J., 1967. Among other things, this volume contains the text of the State Department's memorandum, "The legality of the U.S. participation in the defense of Vietnam" and the full text of the brief by American lawyers which was previously published in summary form in the *New York Times*, January 15, 1967. The argument propounded at the first session of the Russell-Sartre War Crimes Tribunal, which is rather hard to come by in this country, may be found in Hanoi's *Vietnam Courier*, May 29, 1967. Also noteworthy is Max Gordon's "Communication" in the *New Republic*, July 22, 1967.

5 This adjective is U Thant's. For testimonials concerning the use of anti-personnel bombs against civilian targets in North Vietnam, see articles by David Dellinger in *Liberation*, December, 1966; April, and May-June, 1967; Carol Brightman in *Viet Report*, April/May, 1967 and Lee Lockwood in *The New York Review of Books*, August 3, 1967. Dr. Tolentino showed Torontonians ghastly photographic evidence at convocation Hall March 11, 1967. The development of anti-personnel weapons is described by Donald Duncan in *Ramparts*, May, 1967. For a precise and thoroughly documented account of chemical warfare in Vietnam, see Carol Brightman *Viet Report*, June/July, 1966.

6 For contrary discussions of this remarkable event, see William Bauer, "The Conflict in the Far East," *The Communist States and the West,* ed. Adam Bromke and Philip Uren, New York, Praeger, 1967 and my "Ottawa/Saigon/New York Complicity," *Our Generation*, Vol. IV, No. 2, September, 1966. The unilateral French declaration recognizing the sovereignty of Vietnam quoted by Mr. Bauer in his article on page 157 but not specifically identified appears to be the declaration made on July 21 after the signing of the Geneva Agreement and not an earlier statement as Mr. Bauer implies by his wording. Consideration of the precise timing of this utterance is of course essential to any fair assessment of South Vietnam's legal obligations with respect to the Geneva Agreement.

7 *The Montreal Star*, May 9 and 10, 1967. It should be noted that the accuracy of both these allegations was hastily – and without full investigation – denied by Mr. Pearson.

8 *House of Commons Debates* for March 4, 1965, p. 11971.

9 Canadian Institute of International Affairs, *Monthly Report*, February, 1966.

10 See Schurmann *et al*, p. 119.

11 Schurmann *et al*, p. 67, n. 6.

12 *New York Times*, November 17, 1965.

13 See Schurmann *et al*, p. 104.

14 *External Affairs*, Vol. XVIII, No. 8, August 1966.

15 This is my translation of the French text which appeared in *Le Devoir*, on January 27, 1967. It was originally published as an authoritative editorial statement in the North Vietnamese Daily *Nhan Dan*.

16 The most comprehensive analysis of this whole problem has been done by Curtin Crawford in a three part study published in *Viet Report*, August/September and October, 1966; April/May, 1967.

.17 This *Report* of January 14, 1966 should be read in the light of a further statement made by Senator Mansfield some six months later. He then stated (and the Department of Defense confirmed) that in February of 1965 there were about 400 North Vietnamese troops in South Vietnam (*Washington Daily News*, June 23, 1966).

18 *I. F. Stone's Weekly*, September 12, 1966, quoting a *Saigon Post* interview with General Ky.

19 *House of Commons Debates* for August 5, 1965, p. 6418. The bombardment was still going on two years later.

20 This statement of Mr. Pearson's was included in a letter of March, 1967 written in reply to 360 University of Toronto professors.

21 The success of Mr. Ronning's second mission appears to have been torpedoed by deliberate and premature American reaction to his visit. (See Schurmann *et al*, p. 138).

22 It is possible that Mr. Pearson and Mr. Martin have decided to collaborate with the American Administration from a belief that our national safety would inevitably lie in supporting the United States (right or wrong) should the Vietnam war develop into a much wider conflict. If considerations of this type are the tacit assumptions of our policymakers, then it is of the utmost importance that they be declared and openly discussed.

Notes to Chapter 9 (pp. 110-18)

1 It would be an error to assume that those engaged in Canadian foreign policy making are uniformly satisfied with the existing state of affairs. Some would doubtless welcome more active public participation. We should be aware of a source of support here for change in the Canadian foreign policy process.

2 Lester B. Pearson, *Democracy in World Politics*, Toronto, 1955, p. 68.

3 See, for example, R. H. S. Crossman, "Machine Politics," *Encounter*, Vol. XX, No. 4, April, 1963.

Notes to Chapter 10 (pp. 119-30)

1 *Globe and Mail*, Jan. 10, 1966, p. 1.

2 See below chapter 17 by Cranford Pratt and Clyde Sanger.

3 Speech to I.R. Club of University of Montreal, March 12, 1966.

4 This is precisely what Wolfers calls for in his *Anglo-American Tradition in Foreign Affairs*, New Haven, Yale University Press, 1956.

5 *House of Commons Debates*, April 26, 1961, p. 4020.

6 *House of Commons Debates*, April 26, 1961, p. 4022.

7 *Ibid.*, p. 4037.

8 H. A. Kissinger, *The Necessity for Choice*, New York, Harper, 1961, pp. 180-191.

9 *House of Commons Debates*, April 4, 1966.

10 *House of Commons Debates*, April 26, 1961, p. 4021.

11 See the *Toronto Star*'s Centenary Special, February 13, 1967, p. 7.

Notes to Chapter 11 (pp. 135-45)

1 Hon. Paul Hellyer, *White Paper on Defence*, Ottawa, 1964, pp. 5-6.

2 Hon. G. R. Pearkes, *Canadian Defence Policy*, Ottawa, 1960, p. 7.

3 Toronto *Globe and Mail*, March 16, 1967.

4 *House of Commons Debates*, December 20, 1966, p. 1357.

5 *Globe and Mail*, February 17, 1967.

6 House of Commons, *Standing Committee on National Defence*, February 10, 1967, p. 758.

7 House of Commons, *Special Committee on Defence*, December 17-18, 1963, Third Report to the House, p. 805.

8 *Globe and Mail*, March 16, 1967.

9 *Standing Committee on National Defence*, May 12, 1966, p. 14.

10 House of Commons, *Standing Committee on External Affairs*, April 4, 1966 (Mr. Martin). See also Mr. Martin's speech at Toronto when he said that Canada would remain in Nato and Norad (*Globe and Mail*, August 28, 1967).

11 *Standing Committee on National Defence*, May 12, 1966, p. 14.

12 *Ibid.*, p. 16.

13 *Ibid.*, pp. 14-15.

14 *Ibid.*, June 28, 1966, p. 409.

15 *Ibid.*, May 12, 1966, pp. 19-21.

16 *Ibid.*, p. 19. Cf. WO2 J. L. Wilson, "Mobcom Briefing," *Canadian Forces Sentinel*, III, February, 1967, pp. 3-4.

17 *Globe and Mail*, March 16, 1967.

18 It should be noted, too, that if Canadian troops are stationed outside Europe, their hostage value is ended. The key question then becomes the circumstances that warrant their commitment onto the continent. Mr. Hellyer raised this point in the *Standing Committee on National Defence*, February 8, 1967, p. 535.

19 See General Moncel's delightful comments in *ibid.*, February 20, 1967, pp. 1338-39.

20 *Ibid.*, February 7, 1967, p. 464.

21 *Ibid.*, February 17, 1967, p. 1285.

22 *Ibid.*, February 10, 1967, p. 767.

Notes to Chapter 12 (pp. 146-59)

1 *House of Commons Debates*, June 3, 1965, p. 1948.

2 Leonard Beaton and John Maddox, *The Spread of Nuclear Weapons*, New York, Praeger and London, Institute for Strategic Studies, 1962, p. 60-61.

3 *Postwar Negotiations for Arms Control*, Washington, D.C., 1961, p. 121.

Notes to Chapter 13 (pp. 160-72)

1 *New York Times*, March 18, 1952. For a further account of Canada's role in the improvement of consultation in Nato, see Lord Ismay, *Nato: The First Five Years*, Utrecht, Bosch, 1955, p. 41.

2 James Eayrs, "Military Policy and Middle Power: The Canadian Experience," in J. King Gordon, ed., *Canada's Role as a Middle Power* Toronto, Canadian Institute of International Affairs, 1966, p. 69.

3 The total amount of material assistance given by Canada under Nato's mutual aid programme since 1949 approximates 2 billion dollars. This aid falls under two main categories: the Nato air pilot training programme on Canadian territory and the transfer of goods, such as equipment, vehicles, infantry and artillery weapons – enough to supply 3 European divisions – out of existing Canadian stocks; and items such as F-86 Sabres with spare parts, radio and radar sets and minesweepers from current production.

4 Nato should not be regarded as having a monopoly on regular consultation in the Atlantic region. Other institutions, such as OECD, already fulfill this task on subjects of a more specific nature. Multilateral consultation of a more general form might continue even after the dissolution of the alliance. However, it is questionable whether in the absence of an institutional framework and of definite common commitments consultation would be equally effective.

5 *House of Commons Debates*, February 17, 1966, p. 1420.

Notes to Chapter 15 (pp. 187-97)

1 UN Statements and Speeches, No. 63/19, "Eighteenth Session: An Assembly of Opportunity."

2 L. B. Pearson, "A New Kind of Peace Force," *Maclean's*, May 2, 1964, pp. 9-11.

3 H. G. Nicholas, "United Nations Peace Forces and the Changing Globe," *International Organization*, Vol. XVII, No. 2, Spring, 1963, p. 326 and Stanley Hoffman, "Erewhon or Lilliput? A Critical View of the Problem," *Ibid.*, p. 408, "if the consent principle were not present, the force could no longer be regarded as a fireman. Depending on the point of view, it is either the policeman in action against a delinquent or a pyromaniac."

4 I. L. Claude, Jr., *Power and International Relation*, Random House, 1962, pp. 283-284, for a brief description of the role of UN peacekeeping in the contemporary international system. He comments (p. 284): "The greatest potential contribution of the United Nations in our time to the management of international power relationships lies not in implementing collective security or instituting world government, but in helping to improve and stabilize the workings of the balance of power system which is, for better or for worse, the operative mechanism of contemporary international politics."

5 L. B. Pearson, "Force for the UN", *Foreign Affairs*, Vol. 35, No. 3, April, 1957.

6 Statements and Speeches, No. 64/12, p. 13.

7 Peter Calvocoressi, *World Order and the New States*, London, Chatto and Windus, 1962, pp. 109-110.

8 Hoffman, *op. cit.*, p. 411.

9 See, for example, the Soviet statement to the Special Committee on Peace-keeping Operations, 22 April 1965, UN Document A/AC. 121/SR.2, p. 6.

10 Lester Pearson, "Good Neighbourhood", *Foreign Affairs*, Vol. 43, No. 2, January, 1965, p. 258.

Notes to Chapter 16 (pp. 198-211)

1 United Nations, *Towards a Dynamic Development Policy for Latin America*, New York, 1963, p. 23.

2 André Gunder Frank, *Capitalism and Underdevelopment in Latin America*, New York, Monthly Review Press, 1967.

3 United Nations, *op. cit.*, p. 4.

4 Claudio Veliz, "Obstacles to Reform in Latin America," *The World Today*, Vol. 19, No. 1, January 1963, p. 24.

5 Celso Furtado, "US Hegemony and the Future of Latin America," *The World Today*, Vol. 22, No. 9, Sept. 1966, p. 385.

6 S. G. Hanson, *Inter-American Economic Affairs*, Vol. 18, No. 4, Spring 1965, p. 75.

7 John Bartlow Martin, former US ambassador to the Dominican Republic. Quoted in *New York Review of Books*, Vol. 8, No. 3, Feb. 23, 1967, p. 33.

8 Harry Magdoff, "Economic Aspects of Imperialism," *Monthly Review*, Vol. 18, No. 6, November 1966, p. 39.

9 Robert F. Smith, "Whatever Happened to Baby Alianza?" *New Politics*, Vol. 4, No. 1, Spring 1965, p. 93.

10 United Nations, *Economic Survey of Latin America 1964*, New York, 1966, p. 17.

11 See John Kenneth Galbraith, *The Underdeveloped Country*, Toronto, 1965, p. 29. These élites are economically non-functional because their income is dependent upon political influence rather than economic function. Galbraith agrees that economic development in Latin America depends upon depriving these élites of their present power. "The choice may well be between earlier and later revolutionary change." p. 41.

12 Arnold Toynbee, *America and the World Revolution*, 1961, quoted in David Horowitz, *The Free World Colossus: a Critique of American Foreign Policy in the Cold War*, New York, 1965, p. 15.

13 John Gerassi, *The Great Fear in Latin America*, New York, Collier Books, 1965, p. 208.

14 *Toronto Daily Star*, May 24, 1967.

Notes to Chapter 17 (pp. 212-25)

1 The guarantees against retrogressive legislation which are mentioned in the "Tiger Agreement" are these:

   (a) The settlement between Britain and the rebel regime would be embodied in a treaty of guarantee which would be registered with the United Nations.

(b) There would be 17 elected Africans out of 67 in a Lower House and 8 elected Africans out of 26 in an Upper House. No constitutional amendment of the entrenched clauses of the constitution would be possible save with a 75 per cent vote of both Houses.

These provisions in no sense ensure that there would be unimpeded progress to majority rule. The first of them is very nearly worthless. If Britain was unwilling to put down an act of rebellion in a colony over which she acknowledged a full legal responsibility, there can be no confidence that Britain would be able at a later date to intervene to enforce a treaty against a legally independent Rhodesia. The "blocking quarter" of African members is also a severely inadequate safeguard. Only one African member would need to be bought or bamboozled for the white majority plus the chiefs in the Upper House (who are in the government's direct employ) to be able to secure the 75 per cent vote which would override African opposition. Moreover, the franchise qualifications are defined in terms of education and income. No guarantees are proposed in the Tiger agreement to assure that the government would not manipulate its African educational programme and the economic advancement of Africans to limit the number of Africans qualifying for the vote. It is significant there are only two African secondary schools which take students up to university level, five years after the Judges Report recommended opening Grade 13 places for Africans in three other non-African schools; significant, also that in 1966 the Smith regime announced a halving of the planned increase of funds for African secondary schools.

2 Kenneth Young claims there are 1,600 Africans in "established" posts, though the two figures needn't be contradictory, (*Rhodesia and Independence*, London, Eyre and Spottiswoode, 1967.)

Notes to Chapter 18 (pp. 226-43)

1 The basic data are found in the annual world economic surveys published by the United Nations. They are eloquently presented in Chapter II of the British *White Paper on Overseas Development: The Work of the New Ministry*, London, 1965, and in the article by George Woods, president of the World Bank, "The Development Decade in Balance," in the January 1966 issue of *Foreign Affairs*. These data have been repeated by nearly every major statesman in the world.

2 Escott Reid, *The Future of the World Bank*, IBRD, Washington, D.C., Sept. 1965, p. 12.

3 Dudley Seers, now Director General of Planning, U.K. Ministry of Overseas Development, analyzed current measures of international redistribution as follows: "The machinery is primitive in the sense that it depends largely on the whims of the rich instead of being objectively determined and predictable. Internationally, we are still in the age of charity, with all that this implies, in particular the power by the donor over the receiver." "International Aid: The Next Steps," *The Journal of Modern African Studies* 1964, pp. 471-489.

4 "The crisis in foreign aid" is documented in many sources. See for example Escott Reid's article by that title in the August 1966 issue of *The World Today*, the monthly review of the Royal Institute of International Affairs, London.

Detailed statistics showing the leveling off of aid and the failure of private capital movements to rise can be found, amongst other places, in W. G. Friedman, G. Kalmanoff and R. F. Meagher, *International Financial Aid*, New York, Columbia University Press, 1966, pp. 12 and 13 and in the 1966 Review by Willard L. Thorp, Chairman of the Development Assistance Committee, *Development Assistance Efforts and Policies* OECD, Sept., 1966.

5 An important study by the World Bank staff, *Economic Growth and External Debt*, by D. Avramovic et al., The Johns Hopkins Press, Balto., 1964 highlighted an alarming situation. Their analysis demonstrated that much of the increase in aid in recent years had been flowing straight back in repayments on old loans. They found that debt servicing was growing faster than debt indicating the paradoxical fact that "while lending today is overwhelmingly for development purposes in which returns flow over a long period, the maturities have constricted".

They deduce from an analysis of existing debt and debt service "the effective average weighted rate of interest amounted to 4%" and "the average life of outstanding and disbursed loans would be slightly more than 8 years". (p. 107)

They estimate that "debt service obligations of the 74 developing countries . . . are no less than \$4 billion and could have well reached 5 billion per annum."

6 I. M. D. Little and J. M. Clifford, *International Aid*, note that "the use of finance in diplomacy has a long history." They briefly trace some of these uses from the Italian Princes in the Renaissance through the modern nation States of Europe in the 19th Century. See also Herbert Feis, *The Diplomacy of the Dollar 1919-1932*, New York, W. W. Norton, 1966.

7 Harry Johnson, in his study prepared for the Brookings Institute provides an excellent analysis of the inefficiencies involved in aid giving. Using data prepared by J. Pincus in "The Cost of Foreign Aid", *Review of Economics and Statistics*, he shows that the actual cost of foreign aid is much less than the nominal value. Pincus estimates that in the year examined total aid falls from \$7.7 billion to 4.7 billion, i.e., from .83% of G.N.P. of aid giving countries to .52% when adjustments are made for overvaluation resulting from tying and other practices.

8 The *White Paper on Overseas Development* (op. cit.) set out an accurate and moving account of the magnitude of the problem and included an enlightened statement of British intentions in the aid field. Unfortunately, policy has had to adapt itself to the exigencies of the day. The Ministry of Overseas Development began under the agressive cabinet leadership of Mrs. Barbara Castle and has slowly lost status and momentum through the successive tenancies of Mr. Greenwood and then Mr. Bottomley, until it was recently demoted from cabinet status.

9 "Both Britain and France have for decades been used to, and have developed a machinery for, development aid to dependent territories as an inevitable corollary of imperial power and responsibility."

Friedman, Kalmanoff and Meagher, op. cit. p. 45. This source provides a valuable description of aid policies of major donors (except Canada).

10 Ibid, p. 42.
11 M. F. Millikan and W. W. Rostow, "Foreign Aid: Next Phase", *Foreign Affairs*, April, 1958.
12 See Dudley Seers, "Big Companies and Small Countries: A Practical Proposal," Kyklos, 1966.

Notes to Chapter 19 (pp. 244-52)

1 The Hon. Paul Martin replying to questions in the Canadian House of Commons on October 21st, 1966.
2 Cf., W. G. Friedman, G. Kalmanoff, and R. F. Meagher, *International Financial Aid*, New York, Columbia University Press, 1966, for much useful information on this and related matters.
3 Agency for International Development, *Selected Economic Data for the Less Developed Countries*, June, 1966.

Notes to the Conclusion (pp. 253-69)

1 Interview published in *Maclean's*, July, 1967, p. 52.
2 Unpublished paper presented to the ULSR by Roman March, Carleton University.
3 Marcel Cadieux, "La Tâche du Sous-Secrétaire d'Etat aux Affaires extérieures," *International Journal*, Vol. 22, No. 3, Summer 1967, p. 527.
4 James Eayrs, *Fate and Will in Foreign Policy*, Toronto, Canadian Broadcasting Corporation, 1967, p. 50.
5 A phrase coined by Escott Reid in a speech to the Kiwanis Club, Toronto, September 27, 1967, when he argued that Canadian aid should be expanded from $300 million to $1 billion in five years.

INDEX

284

QUESTIONNAIRE

*The questionnaire
has been reprinted in the text
of this book as a useful checklist
of problem-areas
in Canada's foreign policy.*

agree	uncertain	disagree	

EVALUATIONS

1. **Listed below are a number of statements about Canada's foreign policy. Please indicate whether you agree with, are not sure about or disagree with each one.**

☐ ☐ ☐ a. The present major world problem is not the poverty of the "Third World" but the Communist revolutionary and military menace.

☐ ☐ ☐ b. Canada is too vulnerable to American economic retaliation to be able to afford an independent foreign policy.

☐ ☐ ☐ c. The chief national interest that our foreign policy should promote is internal unity rather than collective security.

☐ ☐ ☐ d. The best strategy for Canada to adopt is sticking to its alliances and supporting its friends, not planning new lines of international activity.

☐ ☐ ☐ e. An independent Canadian foreign policy does not entail anti-Americanism.

☐ ☐ ☐ f. Canada will have more influence in Washington if it uses Quiet Diplomacy than if it supplements its diplomatic activity with public pressure.

☐ ☐ ☐ g. Canada's world influence depends more on the effectiveness of its international policies than on its reputed special access to American council chambers.

2. **Check whether you agree with, are not sure about or disagree with the following objectives for Canadian foreign policy:**

☐ ☐ ☐ a. Defence of the free world against Communism.

☐ ☐ ☐ b. Western military disengagement from Asia.

☐ ☐ ☐ c. Unification of Western and Eastern Europe through reunification of Germany.

☐ ☐ ☐ d. Support for national-liberation movements seeking revolutionary change in the third world.

☐ ☐ ☐ e. Stand behind American policies in Asia and Latin America.

3. **Do you think the following Canadian diplomatic initiatives would provoke American economic retaliations?**

☐ ☐ ☐ a. Withdrawing from Nato and Norad.

☐ ☐ ☐ b. Declaring non-alignment in the cold war.

☐ ☐ ☐ c. Maintaining commercial and diplomatic relations with Cuba.

☐ ☐ ☐ d. Recognizing Communist China.

☐ ☐ ☐ e. Refusing to export military material to the US.

☐ ☐ ☐ f. Aiding communist under-developed countries.

288

agree	uncertain	disagree	

4. Do you agree that a "bicultural foreign policy" implies:

☐ ☐ ☐   a. special relations between Canada and France.

☐ ☐ ☐   b. special relations between Quebec and France.

☐ ☐ ☐   c. increased voice for Quebec in Ottawa's diplomatic decision-making.

☐ ☐ ☐   d. fully bilingual Department of External Affairs.

☐ ☐ ☐   e. special consideration for aid to French-speaking under-developed countries.

☐ ☐ ☐   f. none of these, because "bicultural foreign policy" is a meaningless phrase.

5. Do you feel Quebec could play any or all of the following roles within the framework of Ottawa's foreign policy?

☐ ☐ ☐   a. Sign treaties concerning matters of her constitutional competence, like education.

☐ ☐ ☐   b. Belong to international organizations like UNESO and ILO.

☐ ☐ ☐   c. Operate a foreign aid programme of its own.

☐ ☐ ☐   d. Administer Canada's aid programme to the French-speaking Afro-Asian countries.

☐ ☐ ☐   e. None of these because foreign policy is Ottawa's prerogative.

POLICIES: Check whether you agree with, are not sure about or disagree with the following policies for Canada.

6. The newly unified triservice should be used to:

☐ ☐ ☐   a. maintain our commitments in the Atlantic and American alliances.

☐ ☐ ☐   b. switch Canada's defence effort to more international roles like peace-keeping.

☐ ☐ ☐   c. start an international police force under UN jurisdiction.

☐ ☐ ☐   **7. Canada should stay in Nato.**

☐ ☐ ☐   **8. Canada should withdraw from continental defence agreements such as Norad.**

☐ ☐ ☐   **9. Canada should actively oppose the American war in Vietnam.**

☐ ☐ ☐   **10. Canada should not cut off the sale of war material to the US.**

☐ ☐ ☐   **11. Canada should recognize the People's Republic of China.**

☐ ☐ ☐ 12. **Canada should become more involved in Latin American relations.**

☐ ☐ ☐ 13. **Canada should strengthen its relations with China.**

14. **The countries Canada selects for its aid programmes should be:**

☐ ☐ ☐ a. the worse-off rather than the better-off under-developed countries.

☐ ☐ ☐ b. the more neglected, rather than those who receive considerable aid from others.

☐ ☐ ☐ c. those with less economic growth potential, not those with great potential.

☐ ☐ ☐ d. any countries including communist countries meeting these economic criteria.

☐ ☐ ☐ e. any countries, except communist countries, meeting these criteria.

☐ ☐ ☐ 15. **Canada should become a "great aid power" by greatly increasing its aid for the developing countries, for instance by trebling its aid budget in five years.**

☐ ☐ ☐ 16. **A major increase in aid should be financed by:**

☐   a. increased personal taxes on income and luxuries.

☐   d. increase corporation taxes.

☐   c. diverting funds from the defence budget to aid.

☐   b. importing more products from the developing countries.

☐   e. other (please specify) _____

☐ ☐ ☐ 17. **Canada should restrict its aid to countries of the following group or groups:**

☐ Commonwealth ☐ French-speaking ☐ Latin America ☐ Africa ☐ Asia

☐ ☐ ☐ 18. **What influence do you think expressions of public opinion such as editorials, letters to Members of Parliament, public opinion polls, radio discussions or TV shows have on the conduct of Canada's foreign policy?** (check one of the following)

☐ very great ☐ great ☐ moderate ☐ small ☐ none